WITHDRAWN
AUGUSTANA COLLEGE
LIBRARY

Essays of a Citizen
From National Security State to Democracy

Marcus G. Raskin
Essays of a Citizen
From National Security State to Democracy

M.E. Sharpe, Inc.
Armonk, New York
London, England

To Sam Francis for his artistic vision in a troubled world.

Copyright © 1991 by M. E. Sharpe, Inc.

All rights reserved. No part of this book may be reproduced in any
form without written permission from the publisher, M. E. Sharpe, Inc.,
80 Business Park Drive, Armonk, New York 10504.

Available in the United Kingdom and Europe from M. E. Sharpe,
Publishers, 3 Henrietta Street, London WC2E 8LU.

Library of Congress Cataloging-in-Publication Data

Raskin, Marcus G.
    Essays of a citizen: from national security state to democracy / Marcus G. Raskin.
      p. cm.
    Includes index.
    ISBN 0-87332-764-0
    1. United States—Foreign relations—1945– 2. United States—National security.
I. Title.
E840.R35 1991
327.73—dc20   90-9074
                                                            Augustana College Library
                                                               Rock Island, Illinois   CIP

Printed in the United States of America

MV 10 9 8 7 6 5 4 3 2 1

Contents

Acknowledgments	vii
Introduction	ix
1. Democracy versus the National Security State	3
2. The Kennedy Hawks Assume Power from the Eisenhower Vultures	45
3. Ideological Premises of the United States' Cold War Policies	73
4. A National Security Manager Tries to Explain	101
5. From National Security State to Democracy	119
6. American Idealism, War Crimes, and a Law of Personal Accountability	139
7. Integrity and the State: Sartre, Solzhenitsyn, and Sakharov	167
8. Ideology and the Arms Race	185
9. Dealing with Gorbachev	195
10. Post–Cold War Options: The New Order?	211
11. Draft Treaty for a Comprehensive Program for Common Security and General Disarmament	227
12. Fulfilling the Ideals of the French Revolution	293
Afterword	307
Index	311

Acknowledgments

Every book, no matter how time-consuming and personal it may be to the author, is also a time-consuming process in other people's lives. I owe special thanks to my gifted colleague and skeptical assistant, Sasha Natapoff, who insisted that I group a number of my essays into separate books so there would be thematic coherence to each book. I await her own book. I thank Joan Drake, whose competence, insight, and concern for detail as well as for the big picture are important to her colleagues at the Institute for Policy Studies. Katharina Hering, a talented exchange graduate student, gave me important aid in the final stages of manuscript preparation. Nedra Hardeman typed parts of the final manuscript under difficult circumstances.

While books are often thought of by authors as divisive and intrusive in their private lives, I must break that mold here by thanking my wife, Lynn, for seeing this book and other such projects as an important way of living our lives together. My extraordinary and exciting children, Eden, Noah, Jamin, and Erika, and grandchildren Maggie, Zach, and Emily all contributed to the book as did my daughter-in-law Sarah and my son-in-law Keith, who knows about the modern technological world.

Special thanks to Richard Barnet, Bob Borosage, John Cavanagh, Diana deVegh, Sue Goodwin, Chester Hartman, Saul Landau, Isabel Letelier, Roger Wilkins, and the staff, fellows, and trustees of the Institute for Policy Studies, a place where thought, practice, and passion come together in the public scholarship of social reconstruction. And to my fine editor, Michael Weber, who really cares about books, ideas, and authors.

Introduction

This is a period of national self-congratulation and extreme forgetfulness in the United States. Throughout the world "democracy" is praised, and communism as a social system and vision lies in tatters. Mikhail Gorbachev has been led and is being pushed to reexamine root and branch communist ideology and the political ground of the Soviet Union. Unfortunately, the example of his exercise in political psychoanalysis has not inspired Americans to undertake a similar course. Rather, our exhausted leaders, bereft of ideas or a vision for the future, are unwilling to examine the policy courses of the last generation that kept the United States in cold and hot war since 1941. We are reassured that the grand policies of the Cold War are the only way to confront the Soviet Union and the Third World. Our leadership class congratulates itself on having been steadfast and admirable in pursuing those policies.

The Cold War period has not been a free ride for the United States. Indeed, it has been costly, aimless, and continuously dangerous. Our military and spying apparatus is unparalleled, but our society is decaying. The three attempts in the post–Cold War period to bring about a measure of economic equity—namely, the Fair Deal, the New Frontier, and the Great Society—were ground up in war and cold war. Long before these presidential initiatives that took social claims of equality seriously, essayist Dwight MacDonald sensed in 1943 that the United States would enter a long period of social drift:

> Political thinking has abandoned not only the old optimism of progress, but also the very notion of any consistent attempt to direct the evolution of society in a desirable direction. Submission to the brute force of events, choice between evils rather than positive programs, a skepticism about basic values and ultimate ends, a refusal to look too far ahead. This is the mood.[1]

Reactionaries have wanted to escape this mood with an ideology whose conclusions harken to another time and that by intention or result is meant to exclude the mass of humanity from history. Of course, the fundamental spirit beneath the tumultuous changes now occurring in the world is the desire for participation, justice, and being seen; that is, of being part of the world, where one's needs and feelings in relation to those of others matter. But to make this sensibility real there must be remembrance, not only of horror stories and genocide such as the Gulag and the concentration camps, but of mistakes, misjudgments, and miscalculations that add up to moral and political disaster. It is of course easier to forget and to "put behind us" what we don't "need to know." It is hard enough to remember past reality in the best of circumstances, for it can only yield partial truth with much misunderstanding and myth.

Not long ago James Abourezk, a distinguished former senator from South Dakota, held a dinner party to honor an authentic man of letters, Gore Vidal. George McGovern was present at the party, and several of us standing in the corner spoke about the current foibles of American politics. Vidal joined the group and in a deadpan way said to McGovern: "George, I've forgotten. Were you president for one or two terms?" Of course, we all thought that Vidal had taken leave of his senses. And Vidal went on: "The one thing about your presidency that disturbed me was that you withdrew my nomination to the Supreme Court." At this point those listening could not fathom what Vidal was up to. McGovern looked excruciatingly uncomfortable. Finally, Vidal, a chronicler of American life, broke the pained silence, "George. Tell everyone you were president. No one remembers anyway." Everyone laughed and then McGovern told us that in a poll taken six months after his defeat by Richard Nixon, the overwhelming majority of those asked said that they had voted for McGovern for president.

Perhaps because they assume no one remembers, pragmatists believe in looking forward and thinking about immediate outcomes. In practice, there is a flaw in this belief. It is not likely that as a nation we will be able to know which path to follow unless we know something about the struggles that defined the immediate past. Through such an examination we might be able to transform our dysfunctional state structure and to guard against those elements of triumphalism in our national character that pushed us into the Indochina War. That war was fought at a cost and toll that are still too high to compute accurately. To find a decent path to the future a people need a vision, "the vision thing" as George Bush called it. And as the Germans did under Hitler, they will follow a perverted one unless they fashion for themselves a vision of the future that calls upon their best instincts and purposes.

By eschewing flag waving I do not want to be understood as saying that the United States does not have a leadership role. The American role in the post–Cold War period can be a special one, that of moving humanity to a world civilization. A prerequisite for that is changing many of its own—and helping to change other nations'—assumptions about force, coercion, and power.

In the post–Cold War period, the U.S. world leadership role must be catalytic, not commanding. It is only entitled to the catalytic role if the actual circumstances of the Cold War period are examined and if we are prepared to have our own glasnost. We must reexamine the insane arms race—an exercise in potlatchism that exhausted our resources and put guns before people, creating a fixation on nuclear weapons, military hardware, and the game of genocide. We can turn away from ideas of "limited" and covert wars that killed millions and enforced our political incapacity to mobilize support for policies that would have long ago ended the arms race and generated a system of rational world security. We must reexamine the inability of our leaders to take seriously the justified fears of those who said that there would be little chance of social recovery from a national security state if we became dependent on Cold War props such as the need of an enemy to explain our internal difficulties.

Some would say we lack leadership. But leadership is not the answer in the United States. The answer is an active citizenry that brings into history the formerly silenced and colonized and that stimulates people "to think for themselves" for the purpose of carrying out a common good. As I have suggested elsewhere, democracy can not be achieved at the expense of the weak. In fact the role of the citizen is to get others to discover their humanity.

> Under this definition of citizenship no one is to be left out. When any person is left out of being a citizen, or a person accepts colonized status, the common good recedes that much further from our grasp, for we are denied what that person knows, or his or her potential for knowing and feeling.... Citizenship spans the public and private realm, of a person's life. It allows the person to comprehend in concrete terms the way each aspect of life is related and interdependent.[2]

Before he died, the eminent social critic, Paul Goodman, dedicated his book *New Reformation* to me. In his dedication he made reference to my being an old-fashioned citizen. At the time, I did not much like his dedication. Now, twenty years later, I am flattered by it, and that is why I have called this book *Essays of a Citizen*. Citizenship means engagement; it is not just an exercise in following rules, accepting obligations and risks, and participating as voters in legitimating a system even though one's side may lose the election.

Citizenship is influenced by other questions of modern political life, questions I have taken up in other works, such as: by what authority does one person tell another what to do? By what authority does a person state that something is true or factual in the sense that future judgment can be based on such "truths"? Obviously, these are questions of profound importance for modern democracy. They are manifested concretely in how humankind will escape the hell of the war and arms system while setting in motion a law and peace framework that includes binding diplomatic relations above and beneath any particular nation-state. That framework will be severely limited unless we understand the framing characteristics we seek to escape, and unless we are able to build on those elements of decency and economic and social justice that were marginalized during the Cold War period but (along with other tendencies) are exploding in Eastern Europe with a force that no leadership can deny.

The fact is that many institutions of American life are in need of social reconstruction. Whether we analyze the Watergate crisis or the Iran-Contra affair or the government's steadfast determination to prepare for nuclear war and wars in the heavens, amazing activities that have used the labor, intelligence, and spirit of hundreds of thousands of us; whether we focus on the subsidy of proxy wars, unilateral executive wars, or the alarming increase in the immiserization of the poor and working classes; we see that we are desperately in need of a discourse linked to reconstruction that will allow each person to be part of a network of participation that reaches a series of demonstrably good ends, not only for one's self or nation but for struggling humanity. We are called upon to give up the hubris that undid ancient Athens. Pride in one's nation must stop short of believing that it represents the high water mark of civilization and that we in the "West" have nothing else to do but keep the status quo intact.

Deciding how we as a nation are to conduct ourselves, and what the character of a new covenant or social contract will be among ourselves as citizens and then with the rest of the world, is our next task. To know what to do, to know how to replace the war system, is not simple.

The idea and practice of a global security and disarmament framework means the replacement of the war system. To think about such matters is in a great American tradition from Jane Addams, William Jennings Bryan, and Woodrow Wilson, to Franklin Roosevelt. It is a vision that commanded the attention of modern thinkers from Immanuel Kant to John Dewey. This is a task that remains with us, and it is not too much to expect that scholars, writers, students, and major institutions—the labor unions, universities, and churches—will join in it, realizing that political realism demands such work.

It is an example of the hegemonic ideological blanket of the Cold War period that our universities as well as the overwhelming number of intellectuals and government officials, in order to prove that they were not "soft" and to keep their connections to power, avoided work on any proposals that sought alternatives to the war system. The members of this mandarin elite saw themselves as linked as if by providence to the national security state. But somewhere along the way they forgot to ask whether their purposes had any value, and if so, for whom. I invite the reader of these essays to ask that question of me, thus continuing the moral discourse necessary for social reconstruction.

Literary essays are read for delight. Since these are *political* essays, they are meant to be useful, leading to reasoned collective or individual action. If these essays have that effect, the effort of writing them and of living some of them will have been worth it.

Notes

1. Dwight MacDonald, *Memoirs of a Revolutionist* (New York: Farrar, Straus, and Cudahy, 1957), p. 111.
2. Marcus G. Raskin, *The Common Good* (London: Routledge and Kegan Paul, 1986), p. 297.

Essays of a Citizen
From National Security State to Democracy

1

Democracy versus the National Security State

After the war in Indochina and the revelations of Watergate, a number of conferences were held to discuss the related matters of law, the presidency, and national security. One such meeting was held at Duke University in 1976 where various professors and judges congregated to discuss what was considered by some to be a crisis in the American system of governing.

I was asked to participate and give my views on what I believed was a new political form that had been evolving since World War I but did not congeal until the World War II period. The following essay is based on that lecture. For a time I worked in the belly of that new political form as a member of the special staff of the National Security Council (NSC) under President Kennedy. I had been an antagonist of the NSC's policies from my first day on the job. It was not until later that I grasped what must have been obvious to others: seldom can policies contradict the institutions in which they are formed. It is only in times of crisis, when institutions have begun to calcify or when there is fear of utter collapse, that leaders are able to transform institutions. In all circumstances, leadership and governing are an imprecise and difficult task. A leader may have specific intentions, but the consequences of policies may be utterly different from what was intended. External events invariably lead leaders to results they may not have been anticipating.

Thus, faced with the emergence of the Nazis, Franklin Roosevelt was reactive to Hitler's bellicosity. It caused Roosevelt and his advisers to change their prescription and diagnosis for American society. The focus of government shifted from internal stagnation and economic depression to war preparation. Just as President Roosevelt had announced that Dr. New Deal was to give way to Dr. Win the War, by the end of World War II, it was clear that the American patient was to be moved by its leaders to a new prison hospital called the national security state. The American patient, the citizenry after 1948, was committed to an asylum with hardly a whimper, for it was told by the guards, who saw themselves as guardians, that in this way the inmates could be secure and well fed. The guardians told the inmates that beyond the frontier of the asylum were enemies who wanted to be well fed and have access to the inmates' resources, which the enemies had the temerity to claim were partially theirs. President Lyndon Johnson said to the troops in Vietnam, "There are 200 million of us and 4 billion of them. They want to take what we have and we won't give it to them."

The 1960s was a strange time for me and my colleagues at the Institute for Policy Studies. We wanted to be neither a part of an asylum nor licensed dissenters who spoke only in the terms and vocabulary of the courtiers of the state; but neither did we intend to be silent. We had learned that our garbage was regularly searched, that our phones were tapped, that there were over a dozen FBI men assigned to the institute, and that fifty informants at one time or another had come to the institute. As is true in 1990 the institute brought together various elements of society: liberals, radicals, movement people, members of Congress and their staffs; some rich and many poor; students and professors—all met for discussion at the institute with its fellows, myself included. In the sixties we sought to lead the argument against the Vietnam War and bring about a measure of civil rights justice. We forged links that were maintained across ideological lines. Even after I had been indicted for draft resistance in January 1968, several members of the government came to me for advice on the president's budget.

Linkages in American politics are very important. Those who know how to make those linkages are successful, and those who take seriously the importance of making those linkages are successful but vulnerable.

Leaders who seek to bring diverse communities and groups into a coalition for progressive change are in an especially vulnerable position. The violence of American politics should never be underestimated. Perhaps it was only accidental that when Martin Luther King, Jr., Malcolm X, or the Kennedys sought to bring together diverse constituencies, their lives were jeopardized. King sought to gather the civil rights movement, the working class poor, and the antiwar movement into a coalition. Malcolm X at the end of his life also sought a movement of blacks and whites. President Kennedy sought to turn American foreign policy away from the national security state, and Robert Kennedy sought to bring together the white working class and blacks struggling for equality, groups that supposedly were at odds with each other.

The populist right also had its problems. George Wallace made inroads in the white working class and then sought an alliance with parts of the military symbolized by General Curtis LeMay, who was his vice presidential candidate in 1968. (LeMay had been the head of the Strategic Air Command.) Wallace was shot in 1972 campaigning in Maryland. During the demonstrations of 1968 in Washington and at the Democratic convention in Chicago, the police and National Guard worked to cordon off different areas of the city, not only to protect property but to be sure that common cause was not made between groups representing the black poor and white student demonstrators.

Violence aside in the body politic, as a general matter it was excruciatingly hard for those with bureaucratic power not to use that power as if they saw the nation teeming with unruly conspirators and heretics. It was one of the peculiarities of the Cold War period that conventional historians refused to see conspiracies in anything that the leadership or bureaucracy did. On the other hand, the bureaucracy and those with political power invariably saw conspiracies against them in which citizens supposedly tried to intimidate the government. One director of the FBI, J. Edgar Hoover, kept extensive files on any individual or group that voiced doubt about him or the FBI. But the FBI did not stop at file gathering. Its array of tools often included intimidation, goading, and entrapment to ensure consensus.

During the Cold War, most nation-states used a variety of instruments to attain internal consensus, from police intimidation to propaganda to "partnerships" by consensus with major social institutions. The national security state became the political form of "choice" both in the noncommunist world and in the Soviet bloc, with each nation adjusting this form to its specific culture and economic ideology. □□

It is not possible to understand the national security state and the reasons that give rise to the need for dismantling it without mentioning the profound and wrenching events of the last fifty years. The national security state emerges from war, from fear of revolution and change, from the economic instability of capitalism, and from nuclear weapons and military technology.[1] It has been the actualizing mechanism of ruling elites to implement their imperial schemes and misplaced ideals.[2] In practical terms, its emergence is linked to the rise of a bureaucracy that administered things and people in interchangeable fashion without concern for ends or assumptions.[3] This state formation matured during a period in which the office of the president became supremely powerful as a broker and legitimating instrument of national security activity.[4]

This paper argues in somewhat tendentious and breathless form that the state system that has emerged in the United States is a constitutional deformation that menaces the freedom and well-being of its citizenry, and that poses a danger to world civilization. What is hanging in the balance in the last years of this century is whether the people, scholars, lawyers and judges, and members of the government, can so organize their understanding and their political actions as to avert fascism or Bonapartism, a debilitating arms race that could end in the kind of horror from which there will be no redemption, and a decaying economic system that impoverishes Americans as well as people elsewhere.[5] It is this cluster of questions that public scholars and statesmen need to address and act upon during the remainder of this century. It is the assumption of this paper that there is a contradictory and healthy cultural movement in this direction that seeks democratization and participation in questions of politics and economics.[6] Such participation is sought, not as an end in itself—although that would be a good end—but because more prudent and even ethical judgments would be made through popular participation and discussion.[7]

The National Security State as the Ballast for American Supremacy in the World

In 1945 the United States emerged from the Second World War as the most powerful nation in the world. Its allies were dependent on the United States for the kind of economic aid that was needed to restore the prewar social and economic structures of Europe,[8] and the vanquished were, of course, totally dependent on the largesse of the United States.[9] The colonial areas of the world looked to the United States for aid in their national independence struggles against France, Great Britain, and the Netherlands.[10] American scientists, with help from European scientists, scaled the heights to become "the destroyer of worlds," as J. Robert Oppenheimer put it, with the atomic bomb.[11] Roosevelt and Churchill had decided in 1944 that the weapon was to be kept secret from the Soviet Union to assure immediate and complete supremacy at the close of the war.[12] It was no wonder that American leaders felt a certain omnipotence and arrogance during the immediate postwar period. American leadership had gained enormously in prestige and material power from the Second World War,[13] and Americans were honored and respected by communists and colonized people alike. Indeed, during the Second World War the American Communist Party dissolved itself to become an "association" because, according to Earl Browder, the American capitalists were different from the European brand.[14] And revolutionaries like Ho Chi Minh modeled their Declaration of Independence after the American eighteenth-century document.[15]

Yet at the close of the Second World War there remained profound doubts concerning the viability of the capitalist system, doubts that had their roots in the depression, doubts that the accomplishments of the New Deal had not entirely eradicated. It was true that even big businessmen had begrudgingly accepted the New Deal as a political success.[16] After all, it had succeeded in papering over class and racial conflict by way of the political coalitions of the Democratic party aided by the FDR charisma. For the first time in American history there was a strong belief among American leaders that class conflict could be muted, managed, and perhaps transcended. But this assumption was a daring one and one that was not wholly believed. On the eve of the Second World War the United States had not recovered from its economic depression. The various measures that had been tried by Franklin Roosevelt and his advisers, such as creating public works programs, curbing the excesses of the stock market, and guaranteeing farm loans to farmers, proved insufficient to meet the challenge of an economy that was called on to respond to "pump priming" and the contradictory programs of the New Deal.[17] In 1938–39 the unemployment rate of the United States was 18 percent and there did not seem to be a means of rationalizing the needs of the people with the short- and long-term interests of capitalism. From 1931 to 1940 the jobless rate never fell below 14 percent—and in four years it averaged more than 20 percent.[18] It was generally assumed by government economists that after pent-up demand had been met, the United States in a postwar situation would again be faced with serious unemployment. It should be noted that in 1941, the last year of a quasi-mobilization economy, unemployment hovered at 10 percent.[19]

It is no wonder, then, that at the close of the Second World War there remained profound doubt about the viability of the capitalist system. As A.A. Berle has said, "[I]n terms of power, without regard to asset positions, not only do 500 corporations control two-thirds of the non-farm economy but within each of that 500 a still smaller group has the ultimate decision-making power. This is, I think, the highest concentration of economic power in recorded history."[20] There had been an active antibusiness ideology during the depression. Business concentration and the growing cynicism about consumer "goods" has recently caused the reemergence of this old hostility against the big corporations, which has been analyzed by Irving Kristol:

> The old hostility is based on what we familiarly call "populism." This is a sentiment basic to any democracy—indispensable to its establishment but also, ironically, inimical to its survival. Populism is the constant fear and suspicion that power and/or authority, whether in government or out, is being used to frustrate "the will of the people." It is a spirit that intimidates authority and provides the popular energy to curb and resist it.[21]

Kristol recognizes that populism easily degenerates into paranoia in the minds of most Americans: "[M]ost Americans are now quick to believe that 'big business' conspires secretly but most effectively to manipulate the economic and political system—an enterprise which, in prosaic fact, corporate executives are too distracted and too unimaginative even to contemplate."[22]

While the antibusiness ideology of the depression did not reach the proportion of successful demands for systemic change, it was strong enough that at the end of the Second World War it acted as a spur to business leaders to find ways of stabilizing capitalism. It was only a scant few years since the bread lines of the depression. Broken-spirited people had been demoralized by the contradiction that the corporate economic system proposed to the kind of individualism that asserted that each person "could make it on his own." This corporate order (never contemplated by the Constitution) had accumulated masses of capital and equipment to control the productive processes of the society so that the means of livelihood were controlled by an oligarchic few, out of the reach of the worker or farmer. Strike turbulence in all major industries in the 1945–48 period fueled the corporate governmental need for careful handling of the labor situation.[23] During the war most unions had accepted a no-strike pledge in exchange for certain minor management prerogatives in the plants.[24] These arrangements were dissolved at the end of the war as management sought to take back all control over life in the factory. Truman threatened to take over the coal mines and railroads, while draftees in the armed forces rioted to return to civilian life.[25]

Thus American national life seemed to be returning to economic and social chaos in the immediate postwar period. On the international scene, the British informed the United States that Greece and Turkey were now American imperial responsibilities. In March 1947 the United States intervened in both places and established its sphere of influence.[26] Such "opportunities" and problems gave rise to a different kind of governing structure: one that would enable the United States to exercise world hegemony while ensuring internal social and economic stability. The American leadership attempted to reorganize the government. It would appear to be democratic and it would appear to steer an economic and political course between socialism and fascism, the two major ideologies of the twentieth century. I have referred to this system as the national security state. It was guided by a small group of men who, through ties of interest and social class, reacted to the world in essentially the same way.

A centerpiece of the governmental reorganization was the adoption of the National Security Act of 1947 and the creation of a National Security Council which was to integrate "domestic, foreign and military policies relating to the national security so as to enable the military services and the other departments and agencies of the Government to cooperate more effectively in matters involving national security."[27] Three major structural purposes were intended to be served by this legislation. One was the development and creation of an intelligence capability known as the Central Intelligence Agency (CIA). It legitimated secrecy and intelligence as a necessary form of government. Another was the reorganization of the independent armed services under the secretary of defense, with a Joint Chiefs of Staff system. This system grew out of the need to "rationalize global responsibilities" in a common planning system. The third was to ensure that the domestic economy would make available resources and material for defense and national security purposes. It should be noted that while a "National Security Council" was created, no definition of national security was formulated in the act or in ensuing acts that ostensibly dealt with national security. The concept remained one that was to be defined through positive action and, tautologically, by those who had exercised power in the military, financial, and bureaucratic elites. The National Security Act allowed the various agencies to broaden and interpret their own mandate. The consequences of vesting the national security apparatus with such unchecked discretion were soon apparent. According to Arthur Macy Cox, a former member of the CIA, the CIA entered into covert collection and covert operations from its incipient stages, hiring a former Nazi general, Gerhard Gehlen, to develop an intelligence network on the Soviets.[28] This act had immediate international significance. "There can be little doubt that the Soviets, fearing the Germans more than any other people, were greatly influenced in their assessment of U.S. intentions by the fact that the United States selected Gehlen for this role."[29] Needless to say, governmental reorganizations have their ideological import.

Cooling Labor Unrest

Reinhold Niebuhr, an intellectually influential exponent of the national security state and the Cold War, argued that within the United States a partnership had been achieved between capital and labor, and this partnership could be maintained if organized labor were given a role in the national security system.[30] Such was the impetus behind the passage of the Employment Act of 1946,[31] a piece of legislation that was viewed by its supporters as an instrument for taming capitalism and giving the workers a stake in its maintenance. The incongruities of the act are apparent. Aimed at creating conditions "under which there will be afforded useful employment opportunities, including self-employment, for those able, willing and seeking to work, and to promote maximum employment, production, and purchasing power,"[32] the act reflected the commitment on the part of the federal government to give attention to "maximum employment" and to fit this need into the overall economic picture. But this picture also included policies directed toward protecting the high profits of the largest corporations, fostering a climate for the enterprising, and building a hedge against inflation. In a word, the Employment Act was to be consistent with the needs of an economic system that required unemployment.

The defense contract system guaranteed workers a role of sorts in the national security system. In the fifteen-year period from 1959 to 1974, 75 percent of federal government purchases of goods and services was for military purposes.[33] Since it was assumed that Congress would not spend on public services, military expenditures were used as the economic tool to hedge against catastrophic depression. They have always been seen in this context by policy planners and government economists. However, the major reason for low unemployment figures during the postwar period through 1974 is directly related to war and war preparations. As Keynes said, a capitalist economy could be helped through "pyramid building, earthquakes and even wars."[34] The pyramid builders of the defense industry were to be found in aviation and electronics, although other giants were involved. According to the staff economist of the Joint Economic Committee. "[I]n 1972, the 100 largest defense contractors received 24 billion dollars in contract awards, amounting to 72.1 percent of the total awarded. The top 10 contractors received nearly half (47.8 percent) of the value awarded to the top 100 and 31 per cent of all awards."[35] It should be noted that defense acquisition no longer picks up the unemployment slack. Indeed, in Western countries there is now a correlation between high military expenditures and high unemployment.[36] This is related to the fact that defense technology requires fewer workers.

While the Employment Act of 1946 at least gave the illusion of worker participation in the economic well-being of the United States, the Taft-Hartley Act[37] placed quite explicit limits on the power of organized labor. The wave of strikes between 1945 and 1947 had aroused fears of the growing strength of unions. In reaction to this showing of union power, the Taft-Hartley Act implemented a right to refrain from organization and concerted activities, made it clear that employers may express their opinions about unionism, outlawed the closed shop and subjected the union shop to certain limitations, and proscribed a number of union unfair labor practices, including secondary boycotts and jurisdictional strikes.[38] In short, the Taft-Hartley Act served as the instrument "to block union organization, to weaken unions and to interfere with free collective bargaining."[39] The law also kept communists from holding leadership positions in unions.

Nevertheless the position of the American worker substantially improved over the Cold War period from his or her position during the depression.[40] The overall size of the economic pie was ever-increasing, but the American dream, made tangible by this economic growth, masked the question of who would slice the shares. An important, indeed crucial, actor in selling the American dream was the president.

The Presidency as the Rationalizing Instrument for Governing

Since the New Deal, economic and political decision making has shifted to the Executive. At first it was thought by hopeful liberals and fearful conservatives that the presidency was the instrument for bringing about social reform, in the face of a Congress that did not care to disturb constitutional *stare decisis* and that favored the power of local oligarchic groups and special interests. Of course, another analysis of the presidency exists: it saved capitalism through the appearance of changing class relations and through enormous political efforts at rationalizing the long-term interests of the largest corporate elements of the society with organized labor and government.[41] Whichever point of view is taken, James Burnham's conclusion is correct: "Before and after 1933; before and after Franklin Roosevelt and the New Deal—these mark the crossing of the political line."[42] The presidency became the rationalizing instrument for the most powerful groupings in the society. By the beginning of Roosevelt's third term, it was clear that the corporations, and then the military, needed the presidency as a fundamental instrument either to extend their power or to assure that they would receive as much as they formerly received in benefits from the society. In other words, the office of the presidency was the victim of a deepening crisis in the political and economic structure in the course of which leaders of corporate, police, and military institutions sought action to "save" their class or interest.

If he is given certain legislative tools, it appears that a president can act unchecked by the theoretical restraints that were written into our Constitution and our political system. The president can act out of whim or in furtherance of a carefully laid out set of plans devised by "an inner circle of political outsiders . . . composed of members and agents of the corporate rich and of the high military in an uneasy alliance with selected professional party politicians seated primarily in the Congress, whose interests and associations are spread over a variety of local societies."[43] Congress has given the president those legislative tools and the task of being point man to save the "system" and to rationalize the various conflicting interests of ruling groups.[44]

It should be noted that first for economic reasons, and later for imperial ones, the United States has organized itself according to national emergency rules since 1933. There are some 470 provisions of the federal law that delegate to the president, and therefore his agents, extraordinary powers during states of emergency. This congressional delegation, coupled with so-called inherent powers of the president, gives him carte blanche to act as he sees fit:

> Under the powers delegated by these statutes, the President may seize properties, mobilize production, seize commodities, institute martial law, seize control of all transportation and communications, regulate private capital, restrict travel, and—in a host of particular and peculiar ways—control the activities of all American citizens.[45]

Before Nixon, Americans believed that a president is someone above politics with no dependence on special interests. "He parades as the anointed custodian of the eternal values, the true spirit of the people who have been victimized by selfish warring cliques or threatened by alien and subversive mischief-makers."[46] Where, however, a president charges too much for his services, or where he attempts to undercut the bureaucracy which has its own links to large economic interests or to fashion his own group of oligarchs to replace those groupings that have dominant social voices, such a pretender may find himself in dire trouble. Thus, the power of a modern president rests on several elements. One is his willingness to rationalize class relations in the society. This must not be done by tampering with those who hold great agglomerations of property. If he is liberal-minded, he will put forward schemes of economic growth that supposedly render "unnecessary" any redistribution plans. Additionally, until 1975, he was not to undermine the military and national security apparatus grouping. Finally, he is to pay obeisance to constitutional forms such as Congress without threatening their existence.[47] He is to recognize their legitimizing function and find a means of coopting it into the national security apparatus or the lockstep of the great corporations. A president who acts accordingly can be assured of the support of established power.

It should be noted, however, that such a president may not have the support of the people or of the various issue-oriented groups that have developed over the last fifteen years.[48] Two recent presidents, Johnson and Nixon, mistook electoral support for real support in the sense of depth of commitment to them or their programs. Even though each won an election with over 60 percent of the recorded vote, neither had a broad mass base that believed in him or recognized a coherent and nonantagonistic set of goals. Both men finally had to depend on particular ruling cliques that vanished when they became too "hot." Nixon, for example, who admired de Gaulle, had hoped in his second term to rule by decree as did de Gaulle, but he was too arrogant.[49] He told the ruling establishment once too often that it had lost the will to rule and that he intended to replace it with his own group. But his friends were too weak to help him. Johnson, the neopopulist, reflected the missionary contradictions and antagonisms of American life within himself and his own policies. He wanted to put a carpet on everyone's floor in America, turn Indochina into little Johnson City, overcome a measure of racism by bringing blacks into the American consensus, tame a new capitalist class from the Southwest, and make educational opportunity the instrument to forge a middle class. He thought all of these groups could mediate their differences and be united by American imperialism.[50] But Johnson failed at stabilizing class relations, which he hoped to ameliorate by folding them into either a war or a harmonious society of individualists and opportunists. Cities went up in flames, the universities revolted, a terrifying war was fought for an imperial bureaucratic purpose, and Johnson found himself governing with Walt Rostow and the Joint Chiefs of Staff as his sole supporters.

Effect of the National Security State in Undermining the Rule of Law

During the Cold War period, the president and his immediate entourage became the brokers for the illegitimate power wielded by the CIA, the FBI, and the various gangs within them. They also sought to use these groups for their own purposes. The powerful seek maximum flexibility for their objectives. Ad hoc committees threaded the line between legitimacy, illegality, and crime.[51] Much of the time of a president and his advisers was spent curbing or ratifying the excesses of lower-level bureaucrats emboldened by the imperial stance and the shroud of secrecy.[52] Thus, for example, after the CIA's failure at the Bay of Pigs, the president, the attorney general, and McGeorge Bundy undertook to control the national security bureaucracy through Maxwell Taylor and presidentially appointed committees. This "reform" more deeply implicated the presidency in paramilitary and criminal affairs.

It should be noted that the entire framework of "maximum flexibility" for leaderships and the national security bureaucracy is meant to encompass both domestic and foreign activity. The control techniques that war and Cold War presidents sanctioned against the poor and the "subversives" at home, and that had been transported abroad during the Cold War, were used as well against the middle classes, the bureaucracies, and finally the leaders of the major political parties.

The FBI, as well as other police agencies of the federal government, proceeded to enforce the Procrustean bed of antileft conformist ideology inside and outside the government. President Truman's Executive Order 9835, issued in March of 1947, required loyalty oaths of government officials.[53] Many who held positions in institutions such as labor unions, universities, and the media were purged. By 1949 they found themselves eliminated from policy debates on the character of American society, treated as objects of contempt or benign tolerance. (As we shall see, the nature of the debate that came to take on new and surprising forms in the 1960s was not contemplated by the national security state and its apparatus.) The effect of the Truman loyalty probes and those later undertaken by Senator Joseph McCarthy and J. Edgar Hoover was to enforce a view of the world based on hatred of "communism," and to prepare an automatic defense of corporate capitalism as the reason for American prosperity and the justification of American military adventures and alliances, both covert and overt. To this end the national security state was dedicated.

In *Powers of Government*, Bernard Schwartz outlines three fundamental elements of the rule of law: "1) The absence of arbitrary power; 2) The subjugation of the State and its officers to the ordinary law; and 3) The recognition of basic principles superior to the State itself."[54] The assumption of Schwartz and others is that the rule of law is crucial to the existence of representative democracy. Even for the radical revolutionary Thomas Paine, the law was king: "Let a crown be placed thereon, by which the world may know that, so far as we approve of monarchy, that in America *the law is king*."[55]

Arbitrary Power

We shall see that the national security state and the rule of law are mortal enemies. In the first place, by its nature and the mission that it has set for itself, the national security state apparatus needs arbitrary power. Such power has its own code, which is meant to govern or justify the behavior of the initiated—after the fact. It operates to protect the state apparatus from the citizenry. And in its defensive form it is hidden under instant and specious doctrines such as executive privilege.[56] This apparatus seeks to cede to the discretion of officials the power of the nation's citizens to manage their future or participate with others in that management. Government officials attempt to control the kinds of politics and citizen activities that they do not favor. They see no distinctions among geographic boundaries and are apt to operate in essentially the same way against Americans and non-Americans. Thus, the attempt of the CIA to assassinate Patrice Lumumba in the Congo is directly analogous to the FBI's attempt to destroy politically Martin Luther King, Jr. in the United States. President Nixon's sanctioning of the decisions of the 40 Committee to intervene and attempt to prevent the election of Allende through bribe offers and other means is strikingly similar to the methods CREEP used in Nixon's reelection campaign or to methods used against the United States Socialist Workers Party.[57]

The police agencies have attempted to serve as a brake on the political process. The COINTELPRO programs of the FBI have employed an astonishing variety of means to disrupt the activities of groups that sought to exercise their participatory rights. Programs like Operation Hoodwink were meant, for example, to incite organized crimes against the Communist party, to entrap war objectors into undertaking bombings, as in the case of the Camden, New Jersey, draft board affair, and to break up human and social relations by sending forged documents and threatening letters to victims of federal and local police enterprises.[58]

Break-ins, burglaries, wiretaps, and buggings on the citizenry have been a central aspect of the work of the FBI as they have undertaken to humiliate, ridicule, and harass civil rights workers, antiwar groups, radicals, conservatives, and any grouping that did not share the assumptions or the influence of those "in charge."[59] And the CIA has taken pride in training local police in bugging, photo surveillance, and surreptitious entry.[60] These incidents are reminiscent of the struggles in Italy under Mussolini in the 1920s. Indeed, it may be said that the virus of totalitarianism has spread from one nation to another in the twentieth century with no exception granted to the United States either by God or its leaders.

> An important fact [in the case of Mussolini's Italy] is that the fascist squadrons had at their disposal . . . not only the subsidies of their financial backers but the material and moral support of the repressive forces of the state: police, carabinieri, and army. The police recruited for the squadrons, urging outlaws to enroll in them and promising them all sorts of benefits and immunity. The police loaned their cars to squadron members, and rejected applications for arms permits by workers and peasants while extending the permits granted to fascists. The guardians of "law and order" had their orders to remain idle when the fascists attacked the "reds" and to intervene only if the latter resisted. Often the police collaborated with the fascists in preparing attacks on labor organizations.[61]

This description of fascist strategy in Italy in 1921 is striking in its resemblance to the approach followed by the CIA, Kissinger, Nixon, and McCone in their successful attempt at bringing down the Marxist government of Allende in Chile:

> a) Collect intelligence on coup-minded officers; b) Create a coup climate by propaganda, disinformation, and terrorist activities intended to provoke the left to give a pretext for a coup (Cable 611, Hq. to Sta., 10/7/70); c) Inform those coup-minded officers that the U.S. government would give them full support in a coup short of direct U.S. military intervention.[62]

The line between criminal gangs and the police is crossed often in the national security state. The purposes may appear obscure to the average law-abiding citizen, but the process of tyranny can be felt by the body politic which finds reason and justice suspended for power and domination.

One FBI provocateur resigned when he was asked to arrange the bombing of a bridge in such a way that the person who placed the booby-trapped bomb would be killed. This was in Seattle where it was revealed that FBI infiltrators had been engaged in a campaign of arson, terrorism, and bombing of university and civil buildings, and where the FBI arranged a robbery, entrapping a young black man who was paid $75 for the job and killed in a police ambush.[63]

And the *San Diego Union*, on January 10, 1976, reported that the Secret Army Organization which fire-bombed cars, burglarized the homes of antiwar protestors, and ransacked offices, was "a centrally designed and externally financed infrastructure designed for terror and sabotage." According to the *San Diego Union*, the acts took place in 1971 and 1972 and were "sanctioned by the nation's most powerful and highly respected law enforcement agency, the Federal Bureau of Investigation."[64] (This allegation has been denied by the FBI.)[65]

The attempt by holders of arbitrary power to inhibit people from exercising their participatory rights is invariably accompanied by forms of personal harassment against people who have no interest in the exercise of their rights. Their interest is limited to carrying on ordinary functions of life. Here the arbitrary power of the national security apparatus operates less obviously, in a more automatic and, to the victim, less obtrusive way. We see the building up of files on a person that are used for a variety of purposes such as to engage in blackmail or to control possibilities of future employment for the object-victim. This course of bureaucratic behavior is especially popular in a period where bureaucracies grow larger, computers more sophisticated, and leaderships more insecure. It is punctuated with the predictable danger in which vying leadership elites use police and other records as weapons to destroy their opponents or settle old scores. Such activities are common practice in the bureaucracy of the national and "internal" security apparatus.[66] And there is nothing in public law that sets limits for the FBI or, indeed, suggests that authority exists for carrying on its comprehensive surveillance activities in the area of "subversive activities."[67]

Officers above the Law

In the Dual State, specifically rejected by American law, "[l]egal concepts are not applicable to the political sphere, which is regulated by arbitrary measures, in which the dominant officials exercise unfettered discretionary prerogatives."[68] The national security state is the American version of the Dual State. Within the national security agencies we may discern several levels of paralegal and illegal activities.

At one level the national security apparatus operates according to a paralegal structure that has its own administrative and self-justifying system. It is "private," having its own standards. Thus, the now famous 40 Committee is an example of an attempt to draw the various police, military, and criminal forces at the command of the leadership into a private and self-justifying administrative system. "Beginning in 1955, the responsibility for authorizing CIA covert action operations lay with the Special Group, a subcommittee of the National Security Council (NSC) composed of the President's Assistant for National Security Affairs, the Director of Central Intelligence, the Deputy Secretary of Defense and the Undersecretary of State for Political Affairs."[69] This group has been expanded to include the chairman of the Joint Chiefs of Staff. This part of the national security apparatus operates according to its own rules and regulations, taking little or no account of public law and asserting its own definition of national security and national interest—a definition that is invariably ruling-class-oriented. We may refer to it as "lightly covered" because it may or may not surface from time to time, as in the case of the 40 Committee. When it does surface, it seeks to justify its actions by embracing principles of positive law and of the Dual State.

On another level, the national security state carries on activities that are flatly illegal. At this level, criminal behavior becomes an important operational instrument. National Security Defense Memorandum 40 of 1970 points out that the intelligence apparatus must be ready for all contingencies and must have responses basically researched and in being.[70] In other words, preparing for criminality and involving or nurturing criminal behavior must be a part of the costs of the national security state since it is never clear when such will prove useful. This includes forgery and counterfeiting, assassination, the employment of known criminals, and so on.

> CIA must necessarily be responsible for planning. Occasionally suggestions for action will come from outside sources but, to depend entirely on such requirements would be an evasion of the Agency's responsibili-

ties. Also, the average person, both in government and outside, is *thinking along normal lines* and to develop clandestine cold war activities properly, persons knowing both the capabilities and limitations of clandestine action must be studying and devising how such actions can be undertaken effectively.[71]

This kind of thinking goes beyond the paralegal procedure. It gives rise to plans and actions of a frightful nature. An unlimited choice of means has been extended to agents or hired contract officers. Thus, the sober William Colby planned and carried out the Phoenix program, which resulted in the killing of some twenty thousand Vietnamese. They were killed because they were ostensibly part of the "Viet Cong's infrastructure."[72]

Another example of the policy criminal is the imaginative General Lansdale. He was put in charge of the Mongoose program to overthrow Castro through covert means. He recommended exploiting the potential of the underworld in Cuban cities to harass and bleed the community control apparatus. Added to this plan was another suggestion (among thirty-one other planning tasks) to utilize biological and chemical warfare against the Cuban sugar crop workers.[73] (It should be noted in passing that such activities are proscribed by international law and would be so treated under the Personal Accountability Bill introduced by thirty-eight members of Congress.)[74]

The Special Group minutes on June 19, 1963, suggests the manner in which the Executive undertook war and warlike activities on its own initiative, pulling itself and the government into unaccountable policy crimes. At a meeting in which McNamara, General Kee, Harriman, McCone, Desmond Fitzgerald of the CIA, and McGeorge Bundy were present, a sabotage program was set out by the CIA to the members of the Special Group. It was to be directed at "four major segments of the Cuban economy": (a) electric power; (b) petroleum refineries and storage facilities; (c) railroad and highway transportation; and (d) production and manufacturing. Raids were to be conducted from outside Cuba, using Cuban agents under CIA control. Missions would be staged from a United States key.[75]

Here are officers of the government who have statutorily defined responsibilities in the constitutional order, acting in their hidden role as officers of the Dual State. They cannot be reached or controlled through constitutional or legal means. At the first meeting of the National Security Council in December 1947, "covert operations" were authorized, giving the go-ahead to criminal action.[76] It would take us too far afield to analyze the social class bias of the views held by this and other "executive committees" which assume a consensus by the members of the government for the carrying out of actions against the underprivileged and powerless persons of the earth. What are we to make of an ambassador, Korry, who said that once Allende the marxist was elected president, the United States would "do all within our power to condemn Chile and the Chileans to utmost deprivation and poverty...."?[77] Or of President Nixon and Secretary of State Kissinger who, having been emboldened by various multinational corporations such as IT&T and Pepsico, pursued another attempt to bring down Allende, an attempt that was operated through the White House and even kept secret from the 40 Committee?[78] According to Kissinger, this plan involved a group that was unknown to others for "reasons of security" and charged with the responsibility of working with the Chilean military in bringing about a coup against Allende.[79] They succeeded. Suffice it to say, and I will return to this point, the consensus that existed fifteen years ago among elites does not today exist among them. And more to the point, this consensus is no longer shared by the American public as a whole.

The cultural hegemony in which all classes internalized the world view of the ruling elite has been broken—as it had to be in a democracy. It is no wonder that this hegemony is broken, for the rule of law is challenged directly by the very operators of the state. Thus, as an example, former Vice President Nelson Rockefeller paid an average of 10 percent tax on his total income, approximately equal to the amount paid by the average worker who earns $8,000 a year.[80] Simultaneously, as chairman of the commission to investigate the CIA, Rockefeller attempted to legitimize the paralegal activity of the national security apparatus by turning crime into law. And in his guise as statesman, Rockefeller was representative of those oligarchs who believe in weak legislatures, favoring government by authorities who are responsible to no elected officials or legislatures but merely to the most powerful economic and military elements of the society.[81]

According to Justice Brandeis, "[a]t the foundation of our civil liberties lies the principle which denies to government officials an exceptional position before the law and which accepts the same rules of conduct that are commands to the citizen."[82] Accordingly, everyone is subject to the ordinary law and amenable to the rules of the courts. Ostensibly, this would be the one means of guarding against the Dual State. But the role of the courts is exceedingly limited with regard to the national security apparatus, thus permitting the expansion of its paralegal and illegal activities. We know when examining the decisions of the courts that the judiciary has handled precious few cases involving the CIA or the National Security Agency (NSA). The courts are frightened of the Dual State, hoping that the problem will go away if no attention is paid to it. Furthermore, where such cases have been presented to the courts, judges have been reluctant or unable for institutional reasons, to rule against the secret agencies or to inquire as to their activities.[83]

Why does the doctrine of *Marbury v. Madison* stop at the gates of Langley, Virginia? One reason is that secret agencies specialize in lying. Indeed, they are so structured by mission and organization as to give credence to the view that as much as they are the children of Allen Dulles and J. Edgar Hoover, they are also the descendants of Epimenides. A stock in trade of the CIA has been plausible deniability. This "doctrine" is meant to protect operatives "from the consequences of disclosures" and "to mask decisions of the President and his senior staff members."[84] The masking process is "designed to allow the President and other senior officials to deny knowledge of an operation should it be disclosed."[85] In other words, plausible deniability is a doctrine that encouraged the invention of false information or lies that will be acceptable to other government agencies, the courts, and the public, as well as to competing or uninformed groups within the secret agencies themselves. Related to the doctrine of plausible denial is the "need to know" principle. The operational effect of "need to know" is, as Richard Barnet has said, need not to know.[86] In other words, the FBI and the CIA operate on the basis that various groups within their own agencies, including higher officials, have little idea of what others in the same chain of command are doing.

But democracy and its operative principle, the rule of law, require a ground on which to stand, and that ground is, as former President Ford said when he was installed as president, truth.[87] In this regard the government has a higher duty to tell the truth than the citizen because it is the government that embodies the tradition and values of the body politic as a whole. Where the government lies or is so structured as to permit only lies and self-deception, it is clear that the governing process and the organization of power has become some other form than that originally intended or generally understood by the citizenry as the original constitutional form. The doctrines of "plausible denial" and "need to know" present problems of particular significance for the judiciary as enforcer of the rule of law, because with the development of the national security state, the duty of truth telling has been substantially waived. Indeed, it is taken for granted that lies and masks are the official's tools for self and group protection.

One example of the kind of falsification that is routine within the national security apparatus is the *Gatto* incident. The U.S.S. *Gatto*, against orders, drifted within one mile of the Soviet coast. A Soviet sub rammed the *Gatto* somewhere between the Bering Strait and the White Sea. The *Gatto* was ready to fire a nuclear missile at the Russian sub, but the *Gatto* escaped without needing to do so. The officers of the ship were requested to file two sets of reports. One set was to consist of six copies describing the real incident as it actually occurred, the other set to be twenty-five copies falsifying the incident. The Pentagon admitted filing the falsified reports, but said that it filed the true report with the 40 Committee. However, when interviewed, officials could not locate or remember any reports about the *Gatto*.[88] There have been at least four mid-ocean collisions between United States Navy and Soviet nuclear-powered and nuclear-weapon-carrying submarines since the mid-1960s. These were ostensibly intelligence operations that could have easily resulted in nuclear disaster.[89]

Since "unacceptable" acts—that is, actions that are constitutionally, legally, or morally questionable—are denied by the agency as a matter of course, there has been no way for courts to test the veracity of statements of the secret agencies. For example, how are we to know when the FBI engaged in a particular course of conduct such as wiretapping, burglary, or entrapment? We now learn that the FBI kept at least two separate sets of books. One set that is available to the courts reflects the FBI's "acceptable" or "legitimate" purposes. The other set appears to have been less pretty, and was unknown except to the initiated.[90] To the extent it is written, this set apparently shows the actual operations of the FBI and special groups, their special missions, and special purposes undertaken for themselves and for special friends. But this is not the record that the courts receive. *Marbury* is defeated by national security practice.

Basic Principles Superior to the State

According to Schwartz the third element of the rule of law is a recognition that there are principles that are superior to the state itself. This is an important safeguard against legislatures that pass laws that may be criminal. It is also a justification for the citizenry to act in a civilly disobedient manner against laws or governmental acts that shock the conscience of the society. The history of the twentieth century is replete with paralegal orders for bombings, concentration camps, assassinations, and break-ins.[91] A citizen does not affirm or assent to every proclamation, every law, every secret rule of a secret policy agency, whether it operates within the United States or abroad, nor does the citizen affirm every executive order that appears to operate under the color of the law. What we may discern instead is limited assent, a quality that must be continuously won from its citizenry by a government. It does so by doing justice and by recognizing human and natural rights as qualities of being that indeed define personhood.

Those generally shared notions of human rights seem to be engaged in a race against the inclinations of the national security state swollen with nuclear weapons. There exists a seeming willingness on the part of the bureaucracy, the military, and science to build and use weapons of mass destruction on hundreds of millions of people because they, as a group, or their leaders, do not see the world in similar ways as a rival set of leaders. This situation poses a question that cannot be dodged.[92] What right does a state have to commit suicide for the people? This issue raised in its baldest form has yet to be considered either by the people, the Congress, or the courts.

It may be asked whether the rule of law can begin to deal with any of these issues. What help can citizens expect to have if they raise the question of whether the state can commit suicide for the body politic by its policy of mindless armament or its use of nuclear weapons to destroy whole classes of people?

The courts have attempted to recognize constitutional rights of the citizenry as they relate to equality of opportunity. They have also attempted to give proper credence to the civil rights of people, thereby recognizing "personhood" and those rights that attach to a person qua person as well as those that attach to a person qua citizen. This objective has not been shared by the police apparatus. Thus, the FBI, throughout the period of the civil rights struggles of the 1960s, had the unfortunate habit of allowing the local police to beat and jail civil rights demonstrators. And the FBI as well as the CIA infiltrated black nationalist groups in the ghetto for the specific purpose of ridiculing and discrediting their organizing attempts.[93] There was no recognition by the police agencies that the struggles of the civil rights movement were for natural and human rights. This is not surprising. To guarantee such rights would mean that their own activities would have to come under strict scrutiny and finally be dismantled in favor of local neighborhood and community police. It should be noted that, based on a study of the Media Papers, stolen from the files of the FBI in Media, Pennsylvania, 40 percent of the FBI's time is spent in harassing and keeping tabs on political groups that sought some measure of recognition of their personhood.[94] It is hardly surprising that the national security apparatus, built as it is upon principles of unaccountability, secrecy, ultra-allegiance to the state, and willingness to lie to the courts and legislatures, is unconcerned with human or natural rights.[95] (One may recall Ambassador Popper's attempt to criticize the Chilean junta for disregarding human rights and torturing prisoners. Kissinger instructed Popper to stop giving the junta political science lessons.)[96] Yet within the American Constitution there is the seed of a radical understanding of the rights of the people. Under the Ninth Amendment the rights of the people cannot be disparaged, i.e., they cannot be disparaged by the government, the secret apparatus of the government, the gangs that operate within the secret apparatus, or the president in an effort to commit mass suicide. How is this process to be interrupted? It is only in a continuous dialogue from the "grass roots" that imperialism can be interrupted. Less than forty years ago the antiimperialist Ludlow resolution,[97] which almost became federal law, stated that wars could not be declared without a referendum of the people.

Imperialism as a Self-Justifying Instrument of Domestic Policy in the National Security State

America's historic involvement with imperialism is a complex one and is beyond the scope of this paper. It is clear that the imperial desire has played an important and continuous role throughout American history, ebbing and flowing with the appetites of different leadership groups. Nevertheless, it was not until the Second World War that imperialism was seen by an entire ruling elite as a means of permanently resolving internal problems of the United States while exporting its cultural values around the world. At the turn of the century, Brooks Adams saw imperialism as the only way to deal with internal American contradictions. Less than two generations later, a leadership elite saw American imperialism as a destiny "thrust" upon it that could save the United States and the world on their terms. It was the United States' turn to take the baton from the United Kingdom as the purveyor of the West's values and traditions. If world empire was the means to protect these values, so be it. So spoke Walter Lippmann to a more parochial-minded Charles Beard, and Reinhold Niebuhr to his former pacifist allies such as A.J. Muste.[98]

To some extent this attitude was an ideological change for many Americans. As Selig Adler, the historian, has said, "the isolationist impulse has been woven into the warp and woof of an American epic."[99] Dean Rusk once said in a moment of candor that the American people were "carried kicking and screaming by its leadership into world responsibility."[100] Like Adler, he believed that Americans were by nature isolationist, although there is little in their history that suggests this conclusion. On the other hand, there has been a middle-western antipathy to imperialism reflected in populism and La Follette progressivism.[101] To counter this American antipathy toward imperialism, the leadership cloaked its actions in the language of beneficent internationalism and explained how the American isolationists brought on World War II with their negative attitudes. The internationalism of Dean Acheson, Richard Bissell, and Will Clayton had a distinctly material cast to it. Thus, for example, 90 percent of the funds given by the United States to Marshall Plan nations was spent in the United States. And as undersecretary of state, Clayton, a millionaire cotton broker, saved the southern cotton industry at a precarious time.[102]

Nevertheless, an aura of excitement was created around the imperial enterprise in bureaucracy. Officials believed in the importance of their work, for they thought that they were continuing a crusade. In personal terms, middle-class achievers saw imperial activities as the new frontier for their energies and ambitions. In poor countries, Western methods of organizing people were embraced by local bureaucrats and elites trained by the Americans. Latin American and Asian nations organized their armed forces and internal security systems along lines laid out by the members of the national security apparatus. For close to twenty years it was assumed that the disagreements in public policy were not over ends, but merely means. Liberal ideologists like Arthur Schlesinger, Jr., referred to the "vital center," intending to legitimate the narrowness of debate. The task of liberals was to screen out views that did not fit into the corporate liberal consensus, the ground upon which the national security apparatus was constructed.[103]

The national security bureaucracies and policy leadership invented self-justifying "facts," premises, theories, and hypotheses. It is well to mention some of these statements so that we are aware of the shallowness of thought that guided the actions of officials. Such rag-tag ideas were the ideological wrapping to mask narrow class interests, ungrounded "idealistic" purposes, and one-dimensional theories of human behavior. It was hoped that if the slogans were said enough times the passive audience would salivate to them like Pavlov's dogs, without critical concern. Here are some of the ideas and official "insights": from 1967 onward the Department of Defense argued that it would not end the war in Vietnam because of the terrible bloodbath that would ensue. Another fiction was that the United States had no choice but to fight limited wars in Southeast Asia, Africa, or wherever, so that it would not be required to fight a world war to make its point.[104]

These homilies, which have so guided official thinking and have cost the lives and property of millions of people, are now unmasked and shown to be false. As Hannah Arendt has said:

> Unable to defeat, with a "1000-to-1 superiority in fire power," . . . a small nation in six years of overt warfare, unable to take care of its domestic problems and halt the swift decline of its large cities, having wasted its resources to the point where inflation and currency devaluation threaten its international trade as well as its standard of life at home, the country is in danger of losing much more than its claim to world leadership. And even if one anticipates the judgment of future historians who might see this development in the context of twentieth-century history, when the defeated nations in two world wars managed to come out on top in competition with the victors (chiefly because they were compelled by the victors to rid themselves for a relatively long period of the incredible wastefulness of armaments and military expenses), it remains hard to reconcile oneself to so much effort wasted on demonstrating the impotence of bigness. . . .[105]

By 1974 the Humpty-Dumpty fantasy world could not long be sustained. As a coup against the coup was generated against Nixon, and as United States forces left Indochina bewildered, pleased, and beaten, the era of false consciousness ended. It is not likely that the citizenry will again accept the clichés and self-deceptions of the corporate and bureaucratic institutions of the society.

This is particularly true in the cities where the tax structure and the habits of mind of the oligarchs and national security managers have imposed great burdens.[106] The public life of the cities and their possibilities as organic livable units have been badly damaged by the national security state's voracious capital requirements, its need of labor talent, and its habit of turning the attention of the people to abstract and glorious adventures that escape the humdrum. The imperial enterprise has enabled people to identify with the unauthentic. The dull work of making places that children could play in, or buildings that people could live and work in, was never able to match the overthrow of Arbenz or the romance of making nuclear weapons. The social energy of the nation went to the moon shots, wars and their preparation, or paving highways to escape the cities. The nation manifested its choices in the development of imperial architecture as in Albany, New York, or Washington, D.C.

The contradiction between the city and the national security state will grow greater over the next decade, as it becomes clear to all that to retain the imperial conceit, the alliances, the bureaucratic apparatus, the global corporations, and so on, greater and greater sacrifices will be required of the people in the cities—especially working and middle class.[107]

Leaving aside the misplaced Niebuhrian fervor or the subtle racist and elitist bias of United States leadership, a conservative pragmatist might well begin to question the entire imperial anticommunist enterprise from the enterprise's own assumptions and goals. Imagine that you were a follower of the conservatism of Robert Taft, Jr. What might you now say? In the space of twenty-five years, the following events have occurred:

1. China became communist even though the United States committed billions in material, employed Marines on the side of the Kuomintang cause, and attempted to subvert the Communists and isolate them. Twenty-five years later Chinese leadership was recognized by the United States on its own terms. American leaders journeyed to

China for a blessing from the heroes of the Long March and were treated to anti-Soviet lectures.

2. Forty years ago the Korean War, in which the United States committed 475,000 troops at one time, was fought to a standstill, without victory. The United States lost 47,000 soldiers in that police action which ended up sorely testing civilian control over the military.[108] Needless to say, the flames of McCarthyism were fanned by the war. A decade later, with one American president, Lyndon Johnson, saying that the United States had no interests in Indochina, the United States spent $160 billion, lost 60,000 men, and wounded 250,000 others,[109] while internal contradictions in the American economy were made more obvious.[110]

3. The United States corporations, much in the manner originally suggested by Donald Nelson in the mid-1940s,[111] sought markets for merchandise in the Soviet Union, believing that trade is the sine qua non for taming the Soviets and maintaining capitalism. Multinationals cursed Senator Jackson for his amendment to the Trade Act, saying that it had cost American companies $2 billion in trade with the Soviets.[112] In Portugal, meanwhile, American national security managers were faced with a choice of supporting either communism or socialism. Ninety miles from home the State Department and various groups within the foreign policy elite sought ways to open relations with the Cubans even as the Cubans insisted that the United States give independence to Puerto Rico, and impoverished Trinidad supported Puerto Rican independence without a whisper of United States criticism.[113]

4. In Western Europe Henry Kissinger had fought a rear-guard battle with the center parties, the Christian Democrats, and members of the capitalist class who wanted to include the Communist party in the governing coalitions of France and Italy. There was evidence of multinational corporations helping the communist parties of Western Europe on the theory that it would benefit trade, while the CIA sent $6 million to influence the elections.[114] Italians pointed to the arrangement of FIAT with the Soviet Union, producing the *Togliatti* car in no less than a joint operating arrangement.

Against the background of events, would not the prudent imperialist, the anticommunist and liberal-minded oligarch, have cause to wonder at least for a moment at what he has wrought? Were the $2 trillion spent on military aid and weaponry successful in preserving world hegemony? Is American society more "secure"? Have the Soviets acted less judiciously because the United States establishment fought in Indochina and spends $300 billion yearly on its defense? What we do notice is that the United States has isolated itself from the opinions of most nations. The United Nations General Assembly resolutions have found the United States often voting with virtually no other nation on matters of decolonization, trade, anti-apartheid, and so on, and yet, the United States cannot break free from the United Nations. The question that is then raised by the citizenry in neighborhood bars, church groups, and local business clubs is a very practical one. What has been the value of the imperial adventure to them, and to their community? The distribution of the tax burden is such that it is the poor and the middle classes that pay for the empire, not those oligarchs who benefit most from it. As Quincy Wright has said in his monumental *Study of War*, imperialism is not beneficial to a nation as a whole:

> Imperialism, therefore, tends to attach an exaggerated importance to nationals engaged in political or economic activity abroad, regarding them as the pioneers of empire. "Imperial welfare" is, therefore, interpreted as requiring the protection not only of the various groups and interests in the home territory but, to an even greater extent, the protection of all or certain interests abroad. These "interests" are interpreted, however, not in the purely economic sense in which the individuals immediately involved may interpret them but rather in the sense of instruments for expanding the state's imperial domain, influence, and power....
>
> Because of the costs of military and military armament, empires have seldom proved economically profitable for the population of the home country. The average plane of living of the Swiss and Scandinavian peoples without colonies has been as high or higher than that of the British and French people with great empires. It is possible that empires have served to maintain certain interests of the privileged classes and to provide a safety valve for the energies of a type of personality who might become leaders of revolutions in the home territory....[115]

Thus, while imperialism may temporarily expand the opportunities for capitalism, its long-run effect is to bring about the same tendencies toward state socialism and militarism toward which nationalism inclines us.

There is an added horror that surrounds us. The world continues to suffer the consequences of Churchill's and Roosevelt's "foresight," that "in all the circumstances our policy should be to keep the matter [the atomic bomb] so far as we can control it in American and British hands and leave the French and Russians to do what they can."[116] The national security state itself is predicated on atomic weaponry. Elsewhere in this essay I have adverted to the important role that nuclear weapons and military technology had in building the national security state. The lengths to which state apparatus sought blindly to insist on the guilt of the accused in the *Oppenheimer* and *Rosenberg* cases is instructive on this point. The judge in the *Rosenberg* case assured the Rosenbergs that they had caused the Korean War because they had "leaked" secrets to the Russians and that, in consequence, they had on their hands the blood of thousands of Americans.[117] Of course, such cases were used to justify and strengthen the security apparatus.

The attitude of protecting the secret of the bomb and using nuclear weapons as the first and final arbiter of state relations was established prior to its existence. In 1944, according to the historian Martin Sherwin, Niels Bohr tried desperately to get Roosevelt and Churchill to invite "Soviet participation in postwar atomic energy planning before the bomb was a certainty and before the war was over."[118] He had wanted the Russians to be informed of the Manhattan Project and hoped for a situation in which scientists would be instrumental in bringing about a modus vivendi in nuclear armaments. For his troubles Churchill said of Bohr:

> Enquiries should be made regarding the activities of Professor Bohr and steps taken to ensure that he is responsible for no leakage of information particularly to the Russians. I did not like the man when you showed him to me, with his hair all over his head, at Downing Street. How did he come into this business? . . . He says he is in close correspondence with a Russian professor. What is this all about? It seems to me Bohr ought to be confined or at any rate made to see that he is very near the edge of mortal crimes.[119]

So now we have followed the conventional wisdom about holding on to the "secrets of the bombs, finding means to threaten with them, constantly increasing the numbers of them until we have over 30,000 of them in place each of them greater in explosive power than those used at Hiroshima and Nagasaki."[120] We have heard often of how horrible it would be if an irresponsible leader, usually envisioned as being from a Third World country, should obtain control of nuclear weapons. But it should not be forgotten that it was the United States that used the weapons and accepted the recommendations of Stimson and others that they be used against a "vital war plant employing a large number of workers and closely surrounded by workers' homes."[121]

And while we are aware of the dangers of the nuclear arms race, our leadership continues to assert the use of nuclear weapons as a first use and first strike weapon, even as we know that at least six nations presently have them. The question that this raises is a double one. We have been told in a Supreme Court case that neither the Constitution nor the United States is a "suicide pact."[122] Yet these weapons make clear that states have become entities that hold the mortgage on the lives of the citizenry. Do we have no rights as citizens against this state of affairs? And what are the human and natural rights of a citizenry against a national security system that leads to violence, anxiety, and genocide? As Craig Comstock has pointed out, the arms race will lead to our sudden ruin; the brushfire war policy will lead to a waste of money; and fear of dissident groups, racial minorities, and the unemployed will lead to police repression: "Most serious perhaps, to the degree that we rely on these kinds of violence done in our name, we will be unable to move toward policies of cooperation (where possible), disengagement (where necessary), or political development toward a more humane society."[123]

We may begin to find insights to answer these questions by reviewing the Nuremberg and Asian War Crimes Trials so that we can comprehend proscribed behavior on the part of governments. In the Ninety-fourth Congress, Representative Robert Kastenmeier and thirty-seven colleagues introduced legislation to set up a system of personal accountability of government officials.[124] It uses the standards that the Americans had applied to the Japanese and Germans after the Second World War, including bureaucratic standards of behavior developed prior to the beginning of the Cold War. These standards can reach the entire issue of the national security apparatus because they are based not on values that are imperial in nature but on a recognition that governments must be controlled if civilization is not to be lost. This legislation begins to open the debate on national security standards. It could be used as an opening wedge to tame and transform the national security bureaucracy.

The development of scientific and technological wizardry in relation to the ability of a bureaucracy to organize the resources of the society for military and defense purposes has resulted in armaments becoming the measure of state power. But, as the armaments race deepens, so does the moral contradiction to it become more obvious. This moral contradiction is also reflected in the fact that the armaments themselves increase anxiety, distort the value and priority structure within the arming nation, and ultimately cause an interdependent link between military bureaucracies of opposing sides who use each other to rationalize their commitment to arming.

It is not too late to break this dance of death. In this context, three specific and immediate questions are to be considered: (1) If the United States were now to stop any further production of nuclear weapons and missiles, would it be any less secure? (2) Should not American government officials be held to a standard of personal accountability, as outlined in Kastenmeier's proposed bill,[125] so that aggressive war will not be a part of the national security bureaucrat's kit? (3) Should people in the armed forces be able to unionize for wages, hours, and a code of ethics that would exclude the use of genocidal weapons and participation in aggressive wars? In other words, should soldiers and sailors have the power to limit the mode of weaponry and destruction by abiding by an oath of conduct that eschews such weaponry and acts as a control over unconstitutional wars of aggression?

While such questions must now be opened and debated in society as a whole, it is still necessary to press for disarmament arrangements through the national security bureaucracies as they are presently organized. In 1961, the United States and the Soviet Union agreed to the McCloy-Zorin "eight points," which outlined principles for obtaining universal disarmament.[126] This memorandum could be used as a basis for reopening the disarmament question. In 1963 the signatories to the partial Test Ban Treaty proclaimed as their principal aim "the speediest possible achievement of an agreement on general and complete disarmament under strict international control in accordance with the objectives of the United Nations which would put an end to the armaments race and eliminate the incentive to the production and testing of all kinds of weapons, including nuclear weapons."[127]

It remains possible to set the motion for general disarmament in three stages:

As a first stage, the United States must undertake unilateral steps, such as banning future missile production as well as uranium and plutonium production. Outmoded alliance commitments that justify elaborate military forces must be transformed. A process of "agonizing reappraisal" and reconsideration must be instituted in the bureaucracy so that policy decisions for disarmament will not be sabotaged.

This will make possible a second stage that will include the disarmament of troops, nuclear weapons, and missiles from different regions of the world. Thus, for example, the nuclear free zone concept should be reinitiated for the Pacific. The context for discussion on disarmament in the second stage could begin in the United Nations Security Council with the permanent members laying out the basis for determining the questions and concerns of disarmament. Thus, in 1977 the United States, for example, should convene a United Nations Security Council meeting with a series of studies about disarmament, including the means of accomplishing and preserving it. These disarmament proposals would be debated in the council for at least a year, during which time an agreed-upon position would develop. That position would include these steps: consensus as to what nations should do on their own without inspection; the reduction of missiles and nuclear weapons, unilaterally and through negotiation; development of inspection techniques and collateral forms of inspection; budget examinations as suggested under the Helsinki agreements; and the reduction and abolition of armaments over a period of ten years. Past plans have correctly called for the staged reduction of armaments in which the great powers would reduce their forces first in the context of a worldwide disarmament and arms control plan. Less heavily armed nations would be more likely to follow suit.

In a third stage the success of so-called "confidence building" measures would cause national leaders to move to the abolition of weapons and armed forces. Such plans should now be examined by Congress in the light of current needs and realities. It should be noted that certain new plans have been proposed that bear careful study because they include the actions of nongovernmental groups and citizens. For example, the plan for general disarmament put forward by the Nobel Peace Prize winner Sean MacBride outlines actions to be taken by nongovernmental groups with transnational and United Nations organizations.[128]

The Department of Defense hopes to increase the defense budget to $160 billion per year in the next five years.[129] It is to be expected that the Soviet defense budget and those of other nations will increase correspondingly. At present, the world is spending $315 billion a year on defense.[130] No security or budgetary relief is in sight. Our choices are stark and obvious.

Conclusion

The national security state is the synthesis of state power and capitalism. Its emergence as a political form turned out to be a crucial step in keeping a level of unity within the United States as it attempted to sustain an imperial or hegemonic thrust in the world. But there has been no way for it to transcend its own internal contradictions. It has been grounded on continuous preparation for war, on a passive and receptive society that would automatically accept the judgments of the administrative leadership, on a code of loyalty to authority that would guard people against cultural diversity and ideological impurity, and on a system of economic growth that would mask the costs of armaments and empire. It has hoped to hide behind the bonapartist skirts of a president and has sought to hide its own actions from public view. None of these conditions now pertains in the United States. The national security state consensus lasted for approximately fourteen years before it became clear that its specifications had nothing to do with the democratizing process; indeed, that it was often illegal and criminal in its mode of operations. It was both natural and predictable that the democratizing process would put the national security apparatus on the block.

Why? In an important sense the United States is a Hegelian society in that people are invariably trying to actualize human ideals. They do so out of either a sense of pain with their current condition, or a sense of surplus that they would like to share with others. The process of this actualization is often humorous, sometimes grotesque and perverted. Nevertheless, the impulse is present. It is a democratic impulse that seeks a social contract in which all members of the society participate. The principle of citizenship assumes that people have individual rights and rights of participation. This process of "leveling," which began with Locke's defense of the bourgeois class so that it would be included in decision making, has found its natural historic result in the cultural, political, and economic struggles that have occurred in the United States over the last fifteen years. That Locke's ideas were meant to be restricted to men of property and wealth no longer matters. What does matter about his view is that governing depends upon the governed. Once it is concluded (and this occurred through monumental struggles of revolution, civil war, and social protest) that there shall be no slavery but rather equality between people of different color, that women are equal to men, that homosexuals have rights and are also equal, that people should have a participatory voice in their place of work, then the society is on a collision course with its state apparatus.

It has been the historic role of liberalism to distill the changes that the militancy of revolt reflects and to replace this militancy with an ordered method of bringing about change. As Chateaubriand said, "[W]e must preserve the political work which is the fruit of the Revolution . . . but we must eradicate the Revolution from this work."[131]

However, liberalism lost its mediating role and the practitioners of liberalism found themselves as political covers for the national security state. They were coopted and they became the fig leaf for imperialism. Liberals embraced the national security state as the compromise between fascism and socialism within the United States. They worked on means of organizing imperialism and of using the Keynesian principle of economic growth and defense spending as a central mechanism of avoiding class conflict. But this choice has given rise to new perplexities. Liberals have not been able to hold back the Dual State, internalize the cultural revolution of the 1960s in their thought and action, or criticize in any fundamental sense the corporate oligopoly system. Thus, the political question is whether liberals have any sort of role to play as mediators in a society whose ideological compass is broken. It would seem that they have none unless they renounce the national security apparatus and develop a full employment economy that is not dependent on the whims of corporations or the defense department. They need also realize that the democratizing process must include economic democracy and the means of holding in common what is basic to the well-being of the society. These are matters that must be debated locally, in schools, factories, churches, and neighborhood bars.

The society is at a turning point. And in this regard so is the legal profession. Either we will surrender representative democracy, embracing instead different forms of corporate fascism and bureaucratic control (military, police, and social) that cannot be halted through citizen action and democratic processes, or we (including the legal profession) will begin the difficult task of dismantling the national security apparatus. It does not seem likely to me that those who struggled in the 1960s to develop a new meaning of democracy will settle for bureaucratic or corporate fascism. And those who are neutral on the question will be less likely to acquiesce in fascist or bonapartist deformations once it is clear that they are inefficient, and that they provide only insecurity, unemployment, imperial wars, a deepening arms race, and a process of repressive exclusion that reduces politics to an empty game.

Notes

1. See generally R. Barnet, *Intervention and Revolution, The United States in the Third World* (1968); L.B. Johnson, *The Vantage Point* (1971); J. O'Connor, *The Fiscal Crisis of the State* (1973); M. Raskin, *Being and Doing* 47–76 (1971); R. Stavins, R. Barnet, and M. Raskin, *Washington Plans an Aggressive War* 199–252 (1971); Borosage, "The Making of the National Security State," in *The Pentagon Watchers: Student Report on the National Security State* 3–64 (L. Rodberg and D. Shearer, eds. 1970); Raskin, "The Kennedy Hawks Assume Power from the Eisenhower Vultures," in *The Pentagon Watchers: Student Report on the National Security State* 65–98 (L. Rodberg and D. Shearer, eds. 1970).
2. C. Mills, 2 *The Power Elite* 274–78 (1956).
3. Raskin, Book Review, 1 *New York Review of Books*, November 14, 1963, at 6.
4. G. Novack, *Democracy and Revolution* 152 (1971); M. Raskin, *Notes on the Old System* 7–35 (1974).
5. M. Raskin, *The Common Good* (1986).
6. See generally M. Freeman, *The Politics of Women's Liberation: A Case Study of Emerging Social Movements and Its Relation to the Policy Process* 170–244 (1975); P. Goodman, *People or Personnel: Decentralizing and the Mixed System* 28–49, 147–73 (1963); L. Mumford, *The Myth of the Machine: Technics and Human Development* (1966); J. Phelan and R. Pozen, *The Company State: Ralph Nader's Study Group Report on DuPont in Delaware* (1973); M. Raskin, above note 5.
7. H. Arendt, *On Revolution* 252–60 (1963).
8. G. Kolko, *The Politics of War: The World and U.S. Foreign Policy, 1943–45*, at 618–26 (1968).
9. J. Jones, *The Fifteen Weeks* (February 21 to June 5, 1947), at 28 (1955).
10. 2 D. Fleming, *The Cold War and Its Origins, 1917–1960*, at 661–706 (1961); G. Kahin, *Nationalism and Revolution in Indonesia* 344–45, 417–23 (1952); *The Vietnam Reader* (M. Raskin and B. Fall, eds. 1965); *The Price of Vision, The Diary of Henry A. Wallace, 1942–1946*, at 85–6 (J. Blum, ed. 1973).
11. P. Stern, *The Oppenheimer Case, Security on Trial* 81 (1969).
12. M. Sherwin, *A World Destroyed: The Atomic Bomb and the Grand Alliance* 209 (1975).
13. E. Janeway, *The Economics of Crisis: War, Politics and the Dollar* 28 (1968).
14. I. Howe and L. Coser, *The American Communist Party* 426 (2d ed. 1962).
15. B. Fall, *The Viet Minh Regime: Government and Administration in the Democratic Republic of Viet Nam* 5 (rev. and enl. ed. 1956).

16. B. Catton, *The War Lords of Washington* 8, 24 (1948).
17. G. Perrett, *Days of Sadness, Years of Triumph, The American People, 1939–1945*, at 173–85 (1973); A. Schlesinger, Jr., *The Age of Roosevelt: The Coming of the New Deal* (1958).
18. H. Ginsberg, *Unemployment, Subemployment, and Public Policy* 3 (1975).
19. Ibid. at 6.
20. A. Berle, *Economic Power and the Free Society* 14 (1957).
21. I. Kristol, "On Corporate Capitalism in America," 41 *Public Interest* 126–27 (Fall 1975).
22. Ibid. at 128.
23. A. Goldberg, *AFL-CIO: Labor United* 44 (1956); J. Mattes and J. Higgins, *Them & Us* 38–172 (1974).
24. P. Taft, *Organized Labor in American History* 546 (1964).
25. J. Blum, above note 10, at 266.
26. R. Barnet, above note 1, at 97–128; F. Dulles, *America's Rise to World Power, 1898–1954*, at 231–32 (1953); Paterson, "The Quest for Peace and Prosperity," in *Politics and Policies of the Truman Administration* 91–2 (B. Bernstein, ed. 1970).
27. The National Security Act of 1947 § 1016, 50 U.S.C. § 402(a) (1970).
28. A. Cox, *The Myths of the National Security State* 93 (1975).
29. Gehlen had been a senior planner for "Operation Barbarossa," the German invasion of the Soviet Union, E. Spiro [E. Cookridge], *Gehlen: Spy of the Century* 42 (1972).
30. R. Niebuhr, *Christian Realism and Political Problems* (1953). Niebuhr was the senior adviser to the Policy Planning Staff of the Department of State during the crucial early stages of the Cold War. For a sympathetic account of his pre–World War II views, see Nichols, "Reinhold Niebuhr, Prophet in Politics," in *Responsibility of Power* 370 (L. Krieger and F. Stern, eds. 1967).
31. Employment Act of 1946, 15 U.S.C. § 1021 (1970). A Senate version which committed the nation to full employment and guaranteed a right to employment was defeated in the House and deleted in conference committee. U.S. Code Cong. Service, 79th Cong., 2d Sess. 1068 (1946).
32. 15 U.S.C. § 1021 (1970).
33. H. Ginsberg, above note 18, at 9–16.
34. J. Keynes, *The General Theory of Employment Interest and Money* 129 (1936).
35. Office of the Assistant Secretary of Defense (Comptroller), U.S. Dept. of Defense, 100 Largest Defense Contractors and Their Subsidiary Corporations, Fiscal Year 1974 (October 9, 1974) (unpublished report available at Directorate for Information Operations, U.S. Dept. of Defense).
36. J. Tobin, "On the Economic Burden of Defense," in *Defense Science & Public Party* 38 (E. Mansfield, ed. 1968).
37. Labor Management Relations Act, 29 U.S.C. § 141–97 (1970).
38. Ibid.
39. Resolution of the AFL-CIO, quoted in A. Goldberg, *AFL-CIO: Labor United* 205 (1956).
40. P. Taft, above note 24, at 587–88.
41. J. O'Connor, above note 1, at 49; M. Raskin, above note 4, at 134–39.

42. J. Burnham, *Congress and the American Tradition* 129 (1959).
43. C. Mills, above note 2, at 231.
44. M. Raskin, above note 4, at 28.
45. Senate Special Comm. on the Termination of the National Emergency, Emergency Power Statutes, *S. Rep. No. 93-549*, 93rd Cong., 1st Sess. 1, 7 (1973). See also M. Raskin, above note 4, at 29.
46. G. Novack, above note 4, at 158.
47. M. Raskin, above note 4, at 18-25, 53.
48. L.B. Johnson, above note 1.
49. M. Raskin, above note 4, at 38-39.
50. See, e.g., Johnson, "My Political Philosophy," *Tex. Q.* no. 4, at 17, 17-22 (1958).
51. R. Stavins, R. Barnet, and M. Raskin, above note 1, at 194-252; "Hearings on S. Res. 21 Before the Senate Select Comm. to Study Governmental Operations with Respect to Intelligence Activities, Vol. 7: Covert Actions," 94th Cong., 1st Sess. 1-136, 148-210 (1975).
52. Ibid.
53. Exec. Order No. 9835, 3 C.F.R. 627 (1943-1948 Compilation).
54. B. Schwartz, 1 *The Powers of Government* 26 (1963).
55. T. Paine, "Common Sense: Addressed to the Inhabitants of America [A New Edition 1776]," in *Common Sense and Other Political Writings* 332 (N. Atkins, ed. 1953). *Common Sense* lays out the theory of natural rights, law, and independence which the new nation applauded. See generally C. Beard and M. Beard, *The Rise of American Civilization* 237 (2d ed. rev. and enl. 1947).
56. Alas, Chief Justice Burger in his opinion, United States v. Nixon, 418 U.S. 683 (1974), does nothing to limit either executive privilege or confidentiality. See generally, Cotter, "Legislative Oversight," in *Congress the First Branch* 25, 55 (A. de Grazia, ed., abr. ed. 1967).
57. N. Chomsky, "Introduction," in *COINTELPRO: The FBI's Secret War on Political Freedom* 3-26 (C. Perkus, ed. 1975); *Senate Select Comm. to Study Governmental Operations with Respect to Intelligence Activities, Alleged Assassination Plots Involving Foreign Leaders, S. Rep. No. 465*, 94th Cong., 1st Sess. 19-67 (1975).
58. In *COINTELPRO: The FBI's Secret War on Political Freedom*, above note 57, at 119-71; *Hearings on S. Res. 21, Vol. 6: Federal Bureau of Investigation*, above note 51, at 1151, Appendix 4.
59. See, e.g., *Hearings on FBI Counterintelligence Programs before the Civil Rights and Constitutional Rights Subcomm. of the House Comm. on the Judiciary*, 93rd Cong., 2d Sess. 10-47 (1974).
60. T. Ross, "Surreptitious Entry," in *The CIA File 93-108* (R. Borosage and J. Marks, eds. 1976).
61. D. Guerin, *Fascism and Big Business* 98 (1939).
62. *Alleged Assassination Plots Involving Foreign Leaders*, above note 57, at 234.
63. Chomsky, above note 57, at 15.
64. San Diego Union, January 10, 1976, quoted in "Newspaper Says FBI Funded Terror Unit," *Washington Post*, January 11, 1976, at A2, col. 1.
65. Ibid.

66. *Inquiry into the Destruction of Former FBI Director J. Edgar Hoover's Files & FBI Recordkeeping, Hearing before a Subcomm. of the House Comm. on Gov't Operations*, 94th Cong., 1st Sess. 59 (1975) (hereinafter cited as *Hoover Files Hearings*).

67. Mr. Nittle. [Counsel of the House Committee on Internal Security] Mr. Maroney, I see literally nothing specific in the directives of Presidents Roosevelt and Truman which informs us or the FBI as to the precise mission to be fulfilled by the Federal Government in undertaking investigations of subversive activities. Has this been spelled out in any other published or unpublished memoranda or directives?

> Mr. Maroney. [Deputy Assistant Attorney General] I think we are back to what we were talking about earlier as to particular directives to the Attorneys General from time to time.
> Mr. Nittle. I see nothing in title 28, CFR which informs us of the precise mission to be fulfilled. Wouldn't that help to inform the FBI of the scope and nature of the investigations to be undertaken?
> ...
> Mr. Maroney. The FBI has its own manual. I am trying to tell you the Attorney General has from time to time provided them with instructions as to what to investigate and what to furnish the Department in this area, but it is not wrapped up in a nice little package.

Hearings on Domestic Intelligence Operations for Internal Security Purposes Before the House Comm. on Internal Security, 93d Cong., 2d Sess., pt. 1, at 3446–48 (1974).

68. B. Schwartz, above note 54.

69. *Alleged Assassination Plots Involving Foreign Leaders,* above note 57, at 10. See also United States v. United States Dist. Court, 407 U.S. 297, 324 (1972) (Douglas, J., concurring).

70. See text accompanying note 14 above.

71. Directive of the National Security Council, NSC 5412/2, quoted in *Alleged Assassination Plots Involving Foreign Leaders*, above note 57, at 9 note 4 (emphasis added).

72. *The CIA File 190* (R. Borosage and J. Marks, eds. 1976).

73. *Alleged Assassination Plots Involving Foreign Leaders*, above note 57, at 139–69.

74. H.R. 8388, 94th Cong., 1st Sess. (1975). A memorandum in explication of the bill containing a detailed analysis of its contents appears at 121 Cong. Rec. H6396 (daily ed. July 8, 1975).

75. Ibid. at 173.

76. See NSC 5412/2, above note 71.

77. *Alleged Assassination Plots Involving Foreign Leaders*, above note 57, at 231 note 2.

78. Ibid. at 250.

79. Ibid. at 246–55.

80. Conflict of Interest Group, Institute for Policy Studies, The Disability of Wealth, An Inquiry into the Nomination of Nelson Rockefeller as Vice-President

(November 1974) (unpublished report available at the Institute for Policy Studies, 1909 Que St. Washington, D.C.).

81. Ibid.

82. Quoted in B. Schwartz, above note 54. But cf. *Alleged Assassination Plots Involving Foreign Leaders*, above note 57, at 9.

83. Alfred A. Knopf, Inc. v. Colby, 509 F.2d 1362 (4th Cir. 1975) *cert. denied*, 421 U.S. 992 (1974); "Developments in the Law—The National Security Interest and Civil Liberties," 85 *Harvard Law Review* 1130, 1134 (1972).

84. *Alleged Assassination Plots Involving Foreign Leaders*, above note 57, at 11.

85. Ibid. at 11–12.

86. R. Stavins, R. Barnet, and M. Raskin, above note 1, at 246.

87. Remarks of President Gerald R. Ford following his swearing in as 38th President of the United States, 10 *Weekly Comp. of Pres. Doc. 1023, 1024* (August 9, 1974).

88. Command Study Group, R. Stavins, Chairman, Study on U.S.S. *Gatto*, Problems of Nuclear Accidents 4 (February 1974) (unpublished report available at the Institute for Policy Studies, 1909 Que St. Washington, D.C.).

89. Ibid. at 1–7.

90. "Hoover Files Hearings," above note 66, at 36–48.

91. F. Neumann, *Behemoth* 452–58 (1942); T. Becker, *American Government, Past, Present, Future* 319 (1976); R. Stavins, R. Barnet, and M. Raskin, above note 1, at 284–85 (explaining the use of para-law).

92. M. Raskin, above note 1, at 47–76.

93. In COINTELPRO: *The FBI's Secret War on Political Freedom*, above note 57, at 9–17, 110–18.

94. See generally ibid.

95. See generally ibid.

96. *New York Times*, September 28, 1974, at 9, col. 8.

97. M. Raskin, above note 4.

98. C. Beard, "Giddy Minds and Foreign Quarrels," 179 *Harper's Magazine*, 337, 349 (1939); W. Lippmann, "What Rome Was to the Ancient World," *Life*, June 5, 1939; R. Niebuhr, *Children of Light and Children of Darkness* 10 (1944); Schlesinger, "Theology and Policies from the Social Gospel to the Cold War," in *Intellectual History in America*, 158 of Foreword (C. Stout, ed. 1968).

99. S. Adler, *The Isolationist Impulse: Its Twentieth Century* 15 (1957).

100. R. Stavins, R. Barnet, and M. Raskin, above note 1, at 289; H. Graff, *The Tuesday Cabinet* 135 (1970).

101. See generally 1 and 2 B. La Follette and F. La Follette, *Robert M. La Follette, June 14, 1855–June 18, 1955* (1955).

102. C. Solberg, *Riding High, America in the Cold War* 77 (1973).

103. A. Schlesinger, Jr., *The Vital Center: The Politics of Freedom* 156, 182–85, 255–56 (1949).

104. J. Warburg, *The United States in the Post-War World* 184 (1966). Warburg discusses the Rusk doctrine in which the United States can get along militarily or otherwise to withstand Communism.

105. H. Arendt, *Crisis of the Republic* 33–34 (1972).

106. L. Mumford, *The City in History* 533–40 (1961); Study Group on the

Federal Budget, Institute for Policy Studies, The Problem of the Federal Budget (November 1975) (unpublished report available at the Institute for Policy Studies, Washington, D.C.).

107. L. Mumford, above note 106, at 548–60.

108. R. Leckie, *The Wars of America* 858 (1968).

109. Office of the Assistant Secretary of Defense (Comptroller), U.S. Dept. of Defense, U.S. Casualties in Viet Nam, January 1, 1961–October 31, 1975 (January 15, 1976) (unpublished report available from Directorate for Information Operations, Dept. of Defense).

110. Raskin, "Towards a Modern National Security Policy," in *The Problem of the Federal Budget*, above note 106, at 51.

111. J. Blum, above note 10, at 285–86.

112. Interview with John T. Connor, Executive Vice President of the Trade and Economic Council, on NBC Television (January 9, 1976).

113. Seminar given by Leslie Minigot, Director, Institute for International Relations, University of the West Indies, Port of Spain, Trinidad, at the Institute for Policy Studies, Washington, D.C. (Fall 1975). It must be noted that there is greater official and military interest in the Caribbean ostensibly to counteract the Cuban support for Puerto Rican independence.

114. *The Village Voice*, February 16, 1976, at 85, col. 1.

115. Q. Wright, *A Study of War* 1189–92 (2d ed. 1965).

116. M. Sherwin, above note 12, at 108.

117. M. Schneir and W. Schneir, *Invitation to an Inquest* 170 (1965).

118. M. Sherwin, above note 12, at 110.

119. Ibid.

120. Center for Defense Information, *America's Nuclear Arsenal*, 1 (Winter 1975). This is a somewhat conservative estimate. In a conversation with the Director of Public Affairs for the Arms Control and Disarmament Agency, Pedro San Juan, the number of nuclear warheads of all sizes in the United States arsenal is, according to him, over 40,000.

121. M. Sherwin, above note 12, at 144–5.

122. M. Raskin, *Being and Doing* 36 (1971).

123. N. Sanford and C. Comstock, *Sanctions for Evil* 293 (1971).

124. 121 Cong. Rec. H6396 (daily ed. July 8, 1975) (introduction of H.R. 8388, the Official Accountability Act of 1975, by Representative Robert Kastenmeier).

125. Ibid.

126. Declaration of Disarmament, *Dept. State Bull.*, October 16, 1976, at 650.

127. Nuclear Weapons Test Ban, August 5, 1963, 2 U.S.T. 1314, 1316, TIAS No. 5433.

128. Proposal for a World Disarmament Conference (1975). There is to be a special session of the General Assembly of the United Nations in August 1976 to discuss comprehensive disarmament proposals.

129. Based on a $120 billion FY 1978 budget a straight line project of 9 to 11 percent which reflected a 4 percent increase per year in quantum of men and machines for the next 3 years plus 6 percent of inflation per year for 3 years. These are very conservative estimates. This essay was written in 1976. The 1990 national security budget is $400 billion yearly including defense, energy (nuclear

weapons and clean-up programs) CIA and NSA (secret budget) veterans benefits for past wars, space agency (military satellites, etc. . .). In 1990, those who call for cutting the defense budget as part of a "peace dividend" are reluctant to cut more than a few percentage points a year. One reason is that the military mission of U.S. forces in the world have not changed since the end of World War II, in 1945.

130. United Nations Association Controlling the Conventional Arms Race 4 (1976). In 1990 the world's nations are spending a trillion a year on armaments.

131. G. Novack, above note 4, at 120.

2

The Kennedy Hawks Assume Power from the Eisenhower Vultures

This essay was written as part of a study of the Pentagon that a number of students undertook at the Institute of Policy Studies in 1968. The book that resulted from this study, called the *Pentagon Watchers*, edited by Leonard Rodberg and Derek Shearer, was intended to show how university students under the tutelage of older public scholars could generate a critical analysis and stance of the operations of the presidency and the national defense establishment. The Eisenhower-Kennedy period had been portrayed in the press as a time of contrasts, although members of the governing elite were not especially overwhelmed by the difference. John McCloy, the doyen of the East Coast establishment, once defined the difference between a Democratic administration and a Republican administration as the difference between the trustees of a university (the Republicans) and the professors (the Democrats).

There were, of course, differences in foreign and national security policy between the two parties. One concerned the right's claim that China was "lost" by the Democrats and the East Coast establishment. The other was the conservative claim, as reflected in the position of Senator Robert Taft, that too much money was spent on defense, even though there was a communist enemy within.

On the other hand, a bipartisan consensus did emerge that was predicated on the slogan that political disagreement stopped at the edge of the Atlantic and Pacific oceans and that disagreements were to be managed behind closed doors. Presidential candidates received secret briefings and were told by the CIA what they could or could not make public. Regarding the debates between Nixon and Kennedy, for example, Nixon later claimed that he could have won the election had he been able to talk about the invasion of Cuba that was being planned under Eisenhower. Having been briefed, Kennedy knew there were such plans but claimed in a debate that the Eisenhower administration was not doing anything to disturb Castro's hold over Cuba. Nixon bit his tongue, argued that international law prevented the United States from intervening in Cuba, and as a result, according to him, looked soft while Kennedy looked tough.

There was also, of course, an enormous difference in aura between Eisenhower and Kennedy. Eisenhower by 1960 had become a walking national monument who had commanded millions of men in war, a five-star general, and military commander of NATO. He had also served as president of Columbia University. All this had happened to him in less than twenty years: in 1940 Eisenhower had been only a lieutenant colonel; in 1953 as president, he sought ways of placating the Old Guard of his party, people who believed the best government is best which governs least.

Eisenhower was never averse to undercutting his own program in the interests of political harmony and stability. While he was perceived as a "modern Republican," which in the 1950s was defined as a Republican who did not want to repeal the social programs of the New Deal and Fair Deal, he often sided with the Old Guard, which never gave up its interest in repealing or emasculating such social programs of the period as aid to education.

Eisenhower, the old warrior, was not a hawk. After the death of Stalin, he wanted to end the Cold War but didn't quite know how to do it. He asked speechwriter Emmet John Hughes to prepare a speech along the following lines:

> Here is what I would like to say. We are in an armaments race. Where will it lead us? At worst to atomic warfare. At best to robbing every people and nation on earth of the fruits of their own toil. . . . Now, there could be another road before us—the road of disarmament. What does this mean? It means for everybody in the world: bread, butter, clothes, homes, hospitals, schools—all the good and necessary things for decent living.
>
> So let this be the choice we offer. If we take this second road, all of us can produce more of these good things for life—and we, the United States, will help them still more. . . .

According to Hughes, Eisenhower called for withdrawal of troops on both sides, no propaganda and a new beginning, "And let us say what we've got to say so that every person on earth can understand it."[1]

But even a person as popular as Eisenhower was not able to transcend the state apparatus. Eisenhower's secretary of state, John Foster Dulles, whose brother Allen became director of the CIA, did not favor such a change in U.S. attitudes and policy. Dulles had introduced the idea of brinkmanship into international politics. He believed that it was important to play nuclear chicken, scaring the other side with the possibility of war in order to keep control over friends and allies. It should be noted, however, that direct conventional military force was used sparingly during the Eisenhower period.

John Kennedy came to the White House when he was forty-three, the youngest person in American history to be elected to the presidency. He had served fourteen years in the Congress, having won election to the House of Representatives in 1946, at the same time as Richard Nixon. Kennedy had been a navy lieutenant and was severely wounded in the war. His back injury caused him continuous pain thereafter, and it acted up at moments of great stress. For example, after his fateful meeting with Nikita Khrushchev at Vienna in the early summer of 1961, Kennedy suffered severe back pains necessitating extended bed rest. By nature Kennedy was sardonic but had a healthy respect for the existing distribution of political and economic power. Perhaps that is why he was especially pleased at having wrested the presidency from the WASP establishment, for this had never before been accomplished in American history.

Much has been made of the fact that Kennedy had significant difficulty with Congress and did not know how to get his social programs through a recalcitrant leadership of Southern Democratic and Republican conservatives. He was not convinced of his mandate, having won by so few votes in 1960. His narrow victory, however, did not stop him from creating an aura of vitality and movement, of possibility, for the American nation. In the last analysis, he embodied for the American public its vision of imperial greatness undiluted by concrete reality. □ □

While a senator, John Kennedy "exposed" the fact that there were only ninety-nine people in the whole government of President Eisenhower working on disarmament. Yet, eighteen months later, the deputy special counsel to President Kennedy noted that there were still less than a hundred people, and he asked the head of the Disarmament Agency "to find" more people working on disarmament even if it included secretaries, so that there would be an appearance of greater action in that direction. Where was most of the action at the beginning of the Kennedy administration? It was in military affairs. And this "action" transformed American society.

Almost immediately after the presidential election, in 1960, Jack Kennedy offered the position of secretary of defense to Robert Strange McNamara, an industrial manager. Within one decade, two secretaries had gone mad in the pyramid on the banks of the Potomac, James Forrestal and, according to Dean Acheson, Louis Johnson. Before offering the defense portfolio to manager McNamara, a Ford Motor Company employee who had served briefly as its president, Kennedy offered the post to Robert Lovett, a man who from the First World War "grew" with the aviation industry, investment banking, and the national security establishment, as secretary of war for air, undersecretary of state, and then deputy secretary of defense under George Marshall. But Lovett declined the Defense portfolio under Kennedy for health reasons.

President-elect Kennedy, ever mindful of his responsibilities as the chief minister of a coalition government, offered Republican Lovett the secretaryships of Treasury and State. He refused these "responsibilities" as well. It was said at the time that this investor in American national security on Wall Street and in Washington refused the three portfolios because he wanted all three of them, and that he intended to operate them from his rolltop partner's desk in Brown Brothers, Harriman. But surely that story was not to be taken seriously. The likelihood was that the war-making power of a Defense Department Secretary could cause one to be overwhelmed into madness; and Lovett did not want to take the chance. What was needed instead was a man who could systematize nuclear weapons, thermonuclear weapons, napalm, millions of men, rifles, chemical weapons, pencils, missiles, promotions, counterforce, aircraft carriers, anthrax virus, and counterinsurgency into organizational rationality. Robert McNamara seemed a natural for the job, having once been a professor at the Harvard Business School. However, it would be a disservice to Robert McNamara if we argued that he had no conscious ideology save that of the technology of organization. He burned with that quiet flame of the committed anti-Communist. After having told a Senate committee how he had become familiar with the evils of communism as a Ford Motor Company executive, he said:

> There is no true historical parallel to the drive of Soviet Communist imperialism to colonize the world. This is not the first time that ambitious dictators have sought to dominate the globe. But none has ever been so well organized, has possessed so many instruments of destruction, or has been so adept at disguising ignoble motives and objectives with noble phrases and noble words.
>
> Furthermore, there is a totality in Soviet aggression which can be matched only by turning to ancient history, when warring tribes sought not merely conquest but the total obliteration of the enemy.
>
> Soviet communism does not seek the physical obliteration of a conquered people, although it would not hesitate to do so, in my opinion, if this would serve its ends. But it does seek the total obliteration of their customs, their social structure, their political structure, their religion, and their freedoms. Everything and everybody must be remolded according to a blueprint laid down by Lenin and altered only for the purposes of ruthless efficiency by Stalin and the present-day leaders.
>
> There is nothing too sacred—friendship, integrity, church, or family—that it escapes the attention of the Soviet Commissar or the Communist bureaucrat.
>
> Soviet communism seeks to wipe out the cherished traditions and institutions of the free world with the same fanaticism that once impelled winning armies to burn villages and sow the fields with salt so they would not again become productive.
>
> To this primitive concept of total obliteration, the Communists have brought the resources of modern technology and science. The combination is formidable. Twentieth century knowledge, when robbed of any moral restraints, is the most dangerous force ever let loose in the world. And the entire literature of Soviet communism can be searched without turning up the faintest trace of moral restraint.
>
> If the free world should lose to communism, the loss would be total, final, and irrevocable. The citadel of freedom must be preserved because there is no road back, no road back to freedom for anyone if the citadel is lost. . . .
>
> I cite this material because I want you to know the spirit in which I believe the education program of our Defense Establishment should be conducted. The threat is clear and it is immediate. Our fighting men should know the positive values of the freedoms which the Nation is calling them to defend, and they should know the nature of Soviet communism, which seeks to take them away.

When he took over the position of secretary of defense from Thomas Gates, McNamara appointed over 120 task forces to look into the various programs of the department. Early in his stewardship, the Department of Defense was a hotbed of intellectual activity, where hard-core fantasists were given their chance at statecraft. Whereas a generation earlier the fantastic-minded might have gone to Hollywood to seek their fortunes in writing movies, in the early sixties many *from* California—and particularly the Rand Corporation—came to the Department of Defense. There they hawked their studies, created war games, and wrote scenarios that led to comprehensive defense policy and institutional changes. McNamara informed the House Appropriations Subcommittee on Defense that he "personally reviewed the results in detail in order to have the benefit of their advice and counsel." McNamara went on to tell the committee, ". . . we have examined all of the principal alternatives and have selected that combination of programs which we believe will give the Nation a fully adequate defense at the least cost, in the light of the threat as we view it today." He believed this view, although several years later he pointed out to the House Committee on Armed Services, ". . . we are, in effect, attempting to anticipate production and deployment decisions which our opponents, themselves, have *not* made" (emphasis added).

The strategic choices that the Kennedy administration made in its early days set the framework for a generation of defense planning. Weapons systems need at least ten years of planning, development, and programming; and each weapons system brings with it a whole social, economic, and political support system. Even if the particular weapons system is changed or diminished, the "support" system remains to continue the martial spirit and bring in new weapons. The decisions made to build up the armed forces and develop key new weapons systems, produce them, and deploy them, were generated by internal government, bureaucratic, and corporate pressures. The dynamic needed to justify our offensive military posture was a crisis-oriented foreign policy that served as the pretext for a huge expansion of American military forces. The consequences of this policy were known at the time. It did not escape attention that the Kennedy/McNamara "combination of programs" would lead to a fantastic increase in the military-social system, the nuclear arms race, and war fighting, as well as America's intervention capability. The president had stated in his special defense budget message to Congress on March 28, 1961, "Our defense posture must be both flexible and determined. Any potential aggressor contemplating an attack on any part of the free world with any kind of weapons, conventional or nuclear, must know that our response will be suitable, selective, swift, and effective. . . . Our weapons systems must be usable in a manner permitting deliberation and discrimination as to timing, scope, and targets, in response to civilian authority, and our defenses must be secure against prolonged reattack as well as a surprise first attack.''

Not only the civilian defense strategists were busy. The Joint Chiefs were asked by McNamara to establish a working group ''to study the requirements for U.S. general-purpose forces to meet a number of possible non-nuclear combat situations in various overseas *potential trouble spots.*'' Parallel studies were conducted in each of the services. Sixteen different situations were studied in Europe, the Middle East, Southeast Asia, and Northeast Asia for the purpose of determining requirements of a global policy. This study, undertaken by Lieutenant General J.W. Parker and Vice Admiral H.D. Riley, was a supplement to those studies conducted by civilians in the secretary of defense staff who studied thermonuclear war. Such plans had a powerful effect on the size, character, and matériel of the Department of Defense. After two years it resulted in:

> A 100 percent increase in the number of nuclear weapons available in the strategic alert forces.
> A 45 percent increase in the number of combat-ready Army divisions.
> A one-third increase in the number of tactical fighter squadrons.
> A 60 percent increase in the tactical nuclear forces deployed in Western Europe.
> A 75 percent increase in airlift capability.
> A 100 percent increase in general ship construction and conversion.
> A sixfold increase in counterinsurgency forces.

As a result of these improvements, the American policy makers, according to McNamara, were prepared to undertake a:

> demonstrated willingness to risk using these forces in defense of our vital interests. Here are some examples:
>
> The callup of about 150,000 reservists and the deployment of 40,000 additional men to Europe in the summer of 1961.

>   The confrontation of Khrushchev on the issue of Soviet offensive missiles in Cuba in October of 1962.
>
>   The dispatch of 16,000 U.S. military personnel to South Vietnam to assist that country with logistics and training support in combating the Vietcong insurrection.
>
>   The prompt response of the United States in sending Army and Marine Corps units to Thailand in May 1961, when it appeared that the Communists might overrun Laos.
>
>   ... continuing efforts to assist other free nations in defending their sovereignty and in building a better future for their people. Our military and economic aid to such nations, particularly those on the periphery of the Communist bloc, has given them a more desirable alternative to communism and has made them less vulnerable to Communist penetration and subversion.

The United States intended under Kennedy to develop a war-fighting capability on all levels of violence from thermonuclear war to counterinsurgency. For the policy makers it was a heady time, in which strategy became a toy of war and men sat in "situation" rooms in the State Department, the White House, and the CIA, planning and manipulating the destinies of unsuspecting millions. The military and the civilian war planners designed strategies and weapons for every option and situation they could conceive. Their tools were violence and threat, and their ideology was the Roman notion of domination. If the question of justice was considered, it was the justice of Thrasymachus, wherein justice followed the decisions of the strong.

War and Threat

The use of threat and violence as tools of national policy required the ability to escalate the level of violence if the armed forces or the planners seemed to be losing at the particular level initially chosen by the war planners. The logic of such a strategy of escalation pressed the national security apparatus to prepare for a first-strike capability against the Soviet Union. Most Kennedy strategists and military planners believed in two theories in 1961: the willingness to escalate from any particular level of violence to a higher one, and the idea that the

American people must be prepared to fight and intervene in other people's problems for the good of others and for the needs of the American state. It was believed that unless the American legions would fight in place A, they would have to fight in place B under less "advantageous" conditions. As Secretary McNamara said, "Readiness and mobility can greatly reduce requirements for general purpose forces. This is simply the principle of getting there first with the most, before the situation deteriorates and greater forces are required to recover lost ground."

A military buildup was consciously sought in order to back up the grandiose plans of the policy makers, who wished to have at their command every option no matter how unlikely its use might be. Looking back over his first years as secretary of defense, Secretary McNamara was particularly proud of "the substantial build-up in our military strength during the last three years, both for general and for limited war." He had early reported to Congress that a war-fighting capability and counterforce were central to his theory. The instruments of violence were morally neutral and were to be applied whenever and however necessary. As McNamara pointed out, "We are implementing processes at all levels of authority to insure that our response can be graded by degree, by geographic and political area, and by target type, as would be appropriate to the type and extent of an enemy attack."

War was a natural extension of bureaucratic decision making. It was the life of the state—purposive, rational, and not wasteful. Weapons were not for show; they were for use—unless threat proved to be enough. This view represented a significant change from the policies of the Eisenhower administration, which saw threat value in the brandishing of nuclear weapons but did not envision fighting wars with them. Indeed, there were no war options under the Eisenhower administration once nuclear weapons were introduced against the Soviet Union. (The war plans of Eisenhower's administration were described by Herman Kahn as a wargasm.) While Dulles talked like a brinksman, his military policies did not match his words. The great change in switching over to the Kennedy national security theory was that policy makers thought that nuclear weapons could be used as an instrument of war fighting. Thermonuclear war was no longer "unthinkable" as Eisenhower had said, or mad.

When Kennedy became president, he was told by strategists that nuclear weapons were a rational option, and unless he was prepared to use them, the NATO alliance and dreams of Atlantic community would be shattered. He was told that strategies for limited and full counterforce were absolutely essential for the Grand Design in Europe and Asia. With these strategies, he was told by his advisers, he could decide how many weapons he wanted to use, when, and where. The Kennedy fantasists believed that nuclear bombing or brushfire war or B-52 bombing or missile attacks could be "surgical." Much time was spent by the savants in the Kennedy administration talking about such "surgical" methods. The foreign policy now specifically stated the need to defend every place in the world that the leadership said needed either defending, attacking, engaging, or dominating. It was essential that budgetary constraints be dropped at the Defense Department. "Arbitrary" ceilings on defense expenditures were removed by Kennedy and McNamara. The new policy was to "recommend the size of Military Establishment and the type of Military Establishment that we believe is required to protect our national security, without regard to arbitrary budget ceilings."

The idea of active dominance was a central theme in the presidential campaign of 1960. Following its presidential nominee's lead, the Democratic party appealed to the sense of American insecurity, which required that America as a state have "purpose" and be first in everything, whether making weapons or widgets.

Kennedy argued that United States prestige, power, and military arsenal were slipping. This view reflected the position taken by technocrats and manufacturers who were taking over the operations of major American corporate interests, and who were on the frontiers of new American industry such as electronics and missiles. The impetus for the loss-of-prestige argument was first presented during 1956–57 at hearings on air power and missile preparedness held by Senator Stuart Symington. Those hearings concluded that the Eisenhower military policies had failed to maintain a preeminent lead over the Russians in military matters. The claim that there was a bomber gap and then a missile gap was a political challenge by the Democratic party to the middle-western, middle-class big businessmen who controlled the policy of the Eisenhower administration in the White House. Men like George Humphrey and Charles Wilson were unimpressed with preparedness arguments or even challenges within the Republican party to war-option mongers such as Nelson Rockefeller, who proposed to

Eisenhower military policies similar to those that were put in practice a few years later by President Kennedy. The predominant thread of the national security establishment groups that attached themselves to the Rockefeller brothers' reports and the Kennedy presidential aspirations was that technique, technology, expertise, and risk taking for war were crucial in maintaining American dominance in the world arena.

The winner mentality of President Kennedy coopted the Rockefeller position. Playing on the Soviet Sputnik success of 1957, Kennedy repeated over and over how America had to get moving again; that it did not have to *fall behind*—words that strike terror in the hearts of Americans—but could maintain dominance in all things. So, in 1960, large segments of the "educated" middle class believed in missiles, huge military expenditures, and adventures, as manifestations of America as Number One.

The Eisenhower administration, somewhat less pretentious, saw military budgets in different terms. After the Korean War ended, allocations to the Department of Defense were viewed by the Eisenhower cabinet in two ways—one, as an economic pump primer, and the other, as a political payoff to departmental agencies that wielded great power in the country and in Congress, so that they would not challenge civilian authority. The Budget and Treasury, with the president's approval, allocated a lump sum that the services could fight over and split among themselves. Thus, the payoff had particular limits.

Eisenhower tried to limit military power by arguing for balancing the budget, a slogan that means business-class control over governmental bureaucratic expenditures, whether defense or otherwise. The powers within the Democratic party during the Kennedy period denied this view. Reflecting bureaucratic and technocratic expertise, they could not believe that money expended on the military should not be immediately translated into political power and preeminence in the world.

The Country Gets a New Strategic Theory

At the end of the Eisenhower administration, strategists from the Rand Corporation and Harvard, such as Herman Kahn and Thomas Schelling, urged the idea of making military power relevant to political bargaining. In their mind, there was an inherent illogic in having nuclear weapons and not making them advantageous to political bargaining.

From their views and those of General Parrish in the Air Force, the strategy of counterforce was developed. Such nuclear war theoreticians as William Kaufman (presently at the Brookings Institution), Henry Rowen (formerly director of the Rand Corporation), and Charles Hitch (the comptroller of the Department of Defense and later president of the University of California) helped to refine the counterforce warfighting strategy. The war-fighting counterforce policy was first presented as a relevant instrument for political bargaining in the crisis over Berlin. In the spring of 1961, the Soviets were continuing to press, as they had done since 1950, to reinstate four-power control over Berlin. The Cold War in Europe was centered on Germany, with the United States trying to integrate West Germany into a mythical Atlantic community, the Soviets wishing to have a neutral Germany not committed to an alliance. The restatement of this policy by Khrushchev caused the president to respond that he was a Berliner and that the United States was prepared to "defend" Berlin or NATO by initiating the use of nuclear weapons.

After discussions with Khrushchev in Vienna, Kennedy returned to the United States, called up the reserves, hurried studies of a first-strike attack on the Soviet Union, and otherwise responded in a way that showed the grit of President Kennedy with our lives. The counterforce strategy was an important instrument in this diplomatic battle. With President Kennedy's defense message of March 1961, the handwriting was on the wall for a counterforce strategy. Much was made of the idea of command and control. While this notion was billed publicly as a way to ensure against accidental war, it was in fact an instrument for war fighting, so that policy makers would think that they could fight thermonuclear wars and control them. The hard-core counterforce planners believed in and advocated the need to be in the position of staging a preemptive strike on the Soviet Union, and some thinkers even advanced the idea of city swapping, or the "diffident" use of nuclear weapons. As a purely strategic matter, counterforce received its greatest impetus from those who saw that the ICBM could be suddenly launched, and that the speed and size of the attacking vehicle all make the task of detecting, tracking, and destroying the incoming warhead a technical problem of unparalleled difficulty. Needless to say, the superior force that had surprise on its side could, or so it was said, inflict enough damage on the other side through a disarming attack of its military bomber and missile installations, to make it unlikely that the Soviets could destroy the United States.

In situations such as Berlin, where it was decreed by the American leadership that America's vital interests were involved, this meant that the United States would have to be ready to perform a first-strike counterforce attack on the Soviet Union. Members of the White House staff such as Spurgeon Keeny and Jerome Wiesner carried the burden of the argument that no matter how many missiles the United States had, it would never have enough to carry out more than a deterrence-only strategy, because the Soviets would always have enough missiles left to destroy the urban industrial land space of the United States. Yet, by the spring of 1962, it appeared that the foreign policy of the United States, with its involvements in Vietnam, Laos, Berlin, and Cuba, was making the counterforce strategy more palatable.

The most explicit statement of this strategy came in a speech to the graduating class of the University of Michigan by the secretary of defense. In this speech, McNamara specifically advocated counterforce as the only viable American nuclear policy on the ultimate level of violence. From outside the policy-making circle but still very much within the nation's elite groups, scientists took an ad in the *New York Times* deploring the secretary's speech and its implications of an unlimited arms race that might lead to preemptive war. But there was support for McNamara's position in the Congress. Senator Margaret Chase Smith, a spartan governess and senior member of the Senate Armed Services Committee, supported the "lonely" secretary, as she described him, and urged the president to come out in support of the secretary, who had gone out on a limb for an unlimited arms race with maximum (though unattainable) options.

One recommendation of Senator Symington's preparedness subcommittee was that the United States improve its intelligence estimates of the Soviet Union. Yet it was clear, even by the early spring of 1961, that the presumed missile gap did not favor the Soviet Union, but the United States. This fact did not change the number of missiles recommended by the militarized civilians operating the Department of Defense.

In a committee hearing, Secretary McNamara was asked by Congressman Gerald Ford how seriously the Defense Department leadership took intelligence estimates. "But if we had a 25 percent downgrade in the Soviet Union ICBM threat in the next several months, would that have a substantial impact on their total destructive force as far as we are concerned?" McNamara answered Ford's comment by observing that such estimates did have "impact but not very much" on the missile programs that the Department of Defense would submit to the Congress. McNamara later commented that, had the planners known then what they did later about Soviet plans in 1961, he would not have proposed such a massive ICBM buildup. There is very little in the record of 1961 to suggest that intelligence estimates played any but the most marginal role in our attempt to build a counterforce strategy. From intelligence reports, McNamara knew that the Soviets were not ahead of the United States in strategic missiles in early 1961. Such estimates were used only to rationalize policy or to report new "threats," not to change the basic ideology of war fighting on either the thermonuclear or limited-war level.

The tragic aspect of the McNamara and early Kennedy administration advisers was their belief that technical answers could be found, so that thermonuclear war could be fought surgically and precisely. The Cuban missile crisis was thought to prove the viability of counterforce, that American missile strength had frightened the Russians into retreat. Critics of the Kennedy period suggest, instead, that Khrushchev had put missiles into Cuba in the first place in response to America's buildup of a first-strike capability.

The counterforce strategy has been a hard one to put down. It continues to live in the Pentagon and in the choices made for present-day weapons systems. During the McNamara period, the self-deception of the counterforce strategy was that it could limit damage in a thermonuclear war. Beneath this mask was the hard reality that policy makers wanted to use thermonuclear weapons for war fighting. McNamara, Paul Nitze, and others had hoped to interest the Soviets in the thermonuclear game of counterforce war fighting, but the Soviets continued to point out that they were not rich enough to aim at military targets. They repeatedly said in disarmament talks that they could "afford" only a deterrent strategy. They had only enough missiles to destroy the urban-industrial land space of the United States, and they would do this if a first strike were launched against them.

The notion of building a "flexible capability," as it was called, meant that the United States wanted the option of striking at a variety of targets, both city and military. The massive strike forces that the United States had in the early sixties—650 manned bombers on fifteen-minute alert, over 200 operational Atlas, Titan, and Minuteman missiles, 144 Polaris missiles, with the prospect of far greater numbers of these missiles—required the planners to find more exquisite ways of using such weaponry than an all-out thermonuclear holocaust.

The Soviet Union did not have, nor does it presently have, enough missiles to destroy the military targets of the United States. Thus, in any nuclear conflict it always risks destruction of its cities, but the United States then and now continues to live with the illusion of war fighting at the highest level of violence. Such habits of mind, which attempt to create problem-solving options for insoluble problems, allowed the Kennedy leadership to believe that they would be able to undertake a counterforce strategy, and simultaneously to get the Russians to accept the idea of limited thermonuclear war, in which the United States would control the escalation because it possessed enough hardware to go to the highest level. This fantasy came to be accepted also for the less-than-general war level and guided the thinking of Army planners in counterinsurgency and brushfire war. The next step up in the violence category was tactical nuclear war.

While Eisenhower attempted to argue the unthinkableness of nuclear war, strategists such as Henry Kissinger, as well as the Rockefeller brothers, men who have long had the public interest in their private hearts, attempted to find a way wherein tactical nuclear weapons could be used, and limited nuclear wars could be fought. The idea of a limited tactical nuclear war had much currency in fashionable intellectual circles during the late fifties, until various war games showed that the countries who were hosts to tactical nuclear weapons would, for all practical purposes, have been destroyed. What the great powers referred to as tactical nuclear war—war on someone else's land—was general war to the country upon which the warriors fought. War games run in the late 1950s, such as Operation Carte Blanche, showed that Europe would be destroyed in any tactical nuclear war. Such defense experts as Sir Solly Zuckerman exploded the myth of a controlled tactical nuclear war and presented that evidence in 1961 to the White House staff, but this did not deter the Kennedy buildup of tactical nuclear weapons—options, of course, had to be maintained.

The Civil Defense Madness

With the counterforce strategy came the notion of civil defense to protect American cities and larger numbers of SAC planes on airborne-alert status. Both were to create a new martial spirit in the country and the bureaucracy. If there were civil defense, then as a Stanford Research Institute report said, "will-stiffening" could be performed on the American people, and American policy rulers could be that much tougher at the bargaining table. In effect, America would merely have to advertise, and never bargain.

A favorite thought of the time, never put into practice, was the idea of population evacuation. Cities would be evacuated to show the enemy that we were invulnerable to his deterrent, which was aimed at our cities. Once we were able to "take out" enough Soviet missile and bomber bases, with nuclear weapons left over to destroy the Soviet population, the United States would be able to enforce its will at the bargaining table. If the bargainers from the other side did not go along, then the United States could destroy the "enemy," and our people could survive.

The issue of civil defense was a political one as well for the president in the early months of his administration. Nelson Rockefeller was the chairman of the panel on civil defense for the Governors Conference in 1961. He had worked hard, with advisers Edward Teller and Henry Kissinger, to initiate a shelter program in the state of New York. When he went to India, he attempted to convince Nehru of the importance of building civil defense shelters for his people in India. Rockefeller at that time was an important political figure nationally who, it was feared, would challenge Kennedy in 1964. President Kennedy ordered his special assistant for national security affairs McGeorge Bundy, to put his staff to work on the civil defense issue. The person put in charge of this effort, Carl Kaysen, wrote, with me, a study of the civil defense program that concluded that it would not work and so recommended to the president. However, the special counsel to the president, Theodore Sorenson, pressed for the program for political reasons, and it was devised by the Department of Defense and Carl Kaysen.

The Department of Defense received primary operating responsibility for civil defense from the Office of Civil Defense Mobilization. The army hesitantly took the program, making clear that it was not giving up its primary mission as war fighters. The army leadership feared that they would be reduced to a police operation, to fight off the rats and protect those with shelters from those who did not have them.

One view of those, like Kaysen, who were opposed to the program, was that it might be "insurance" but could never be more than that. The fear of the insurers was that civil defense would be seen as a "will-stiffener," causing the Russians to believe that America was preparing for a first strike. McGeorge Bundy, who might have been able to stop the program in the first rather than in a later stage, did not comprehend its consequences quickly enough to act with the kind of dispatch and force that might have stopped it. A program was put together, meant by the White House as insurance.

As some within the government, specifically Adam Yarmolinsky and then Steuart Pittman, saw their positions tied to civil defense, they presented a more comprehensive view of it through the Department of Defense.

By July of 1961, civil defense was becoming part of the American deterrent arsenal. In the White House, national security advisers had lost interest and responsibility for it. The new assistant secretary for civil defense, Steuart Pittman, said before the Senate Armed Services Committee that civil defense needed to be "a priority military assignment."

The program itself was absurd. It provided for protection only from fallout, not from fire and blast. The public itself was to buy its own middle-class shelters, although the $207.9 million requested in new funds was to provide a national program for identification and marking of community shelter spaces in existing buildings. Secretary McNamara also requested that a program be developed for the construction of shelters in new federal buildings. "This last program should also serve as an incentive for State and local governments and as a model for their buildings, schools, and offices." The federal government was going to make the conditions for nuclear war, and then the rest of the country would have to try to protect itself.

McNamara then went on to say, ". . . in order to make shelters usable, they must be equipped with the minimum essentials for survival during a 1- to 2-week period. Based on careful studies and tests, we regard the minimum essentials for survival to be five days' rations at 25–30 cents per person per day—an austerity ration with a long shelf life; 2 weeks' water supply at 1.5 cents per day per person; first-aid kits; sanitary supplies; tools to remove debris; and perhaps most important, radiation meter kits." Of course, studies showed that, even 200 miles downwind, a person would imbibe enough radioactivity to guarantee his death if he came out of his shelter after the fifteenth to twentieth day. Studies by scientists at the Atomic Energy Commission showed that the only survivors would be the rats.

Politically, the most extraordinary example of bad judgment was a recommendation of the Department of Defense that President Kennedy go on television and state to the American people that everyone should have a defense shelter. He was to sign a letter to every family in the United States, and each family was to receive a civil defense booklet, first prepared by the Time-Life people and later rewritten. This bit of statecraft madness was stopped by members of the White House staff. In Congress the program was given to Albert Thomas, who was opposed to it, and its active life ended while people from New Jersey, Washington, and Arizona debated how they were going to keep out their neighbors who did not have shelters.

The Army's New Opportunity

In 1953, the incoming Eisenhower administration brought with it a new view of how to manage national security and defense affairs. The so-called New Look meant reliance on air power, and specifically structuring our defense posture so that the United States could never again involve itself in a war like Korea. What the military and the planners might have seen as limited, the people and the politicians saw as exhausting. Consequently, the Eisenhower policy favored a reduction of U.S. forces deployed overseas. Army forces would be kept small lest we be tempted to use them to fight another Korea by conventional means. The partisans of the New Look were convinced that the United States should never again make that mistake, and set about reducing army forces to make it physically impossible even if our future leaders might be so inclined. This theory was of course predicated on the idea that if the United States did not have certain arms and armaments *in being*, it could not use them. The opposing view advocated sufficient arms to allow the leadership a wide range of options.

It is worthwhile to pause a moment on this debate. The Eisenhower administration was very concerned about budgeting and civilian control over the military. As General Maxwell Taylor described it, when he was considered for army chief of staff, then-Secretary of Defense Wilson told him that he expected obedience from the military and if Taylor had any reservations about such loyalty it would be better if he did not take the job. General Taylor averred that he could be obedient, since he had thirty-seven years' training in the art of obedience. Wilson then sent Taylor to see Eisenhower, his World War II commander. Eisenhower was also concerned about civilian control and, according to Taylor's account, spent most of that interview talking about the importance of civilian control. This was a period in which the president and his civilian advisers did not want any backtalk from the military. They did not want another General MacArthur on their hands. Generals were expected to watch carefully their p's and q's, deferring to the civilians and to budgetary requirements as laid out by the Department of the Treasury, headed by George Humphrey, a buccaneer capitalist whose low esteem of the military was famous. Humphrey had been the head of Mark Hanna Mining, and the Treasury was not much more difficult to operate than international business investment and exploration. His replacement, Robert Anderson, came from Texas, where he had managed the King Ranch. These gentlemen were agreed on the importance of limiting military operations and of control as instruments of a business class that believed in balanced budgets for their own sake and as a dual instrument to contain the military and hold down government spending and bureaucratic control that might challenge business power.

The generals who sought highest command chafed under this view of governing. They wanted wars to fight, men to use, interests to protect, and action. Maxwell Taylor, the author of the idea that less-than-nuclear wars should be fought to protect American interests, endeavored to press his point of view during the Eisenhower administration. He found few receptive ears until the last years of that administration, when he succeeded in convincing the navy and marines that if they ever wanted to fight wars again, they would have to have flexible responses, because when "push came to shove," as the saying went, the civilians would not authorize the use of nuclear weapons. There were those in the government and outside of it who believed Dulles and Eisenhower were secret softies. These men, it was said, were hiding under brinksman talk and paper alliances, but they were unable to match their talk and alliances with military force. Forward thinkers in the military field, such as General Taylor, Bernard Brodie, and B.H. Liddell-Hart agreed that the policy of mutual deterrence should give way to limited conventional wars of a smaller scale. Taylor made the argument that the U.S. military forces were muscle-bound, unable to respond, because the United States had adopted an all-or-nothing stance. Our threats to destroy the world, he said, were not credible. Indeed, had not Eisenhower once said that thermonuclear war was unthinkable?

On Taylor's mind lay the incident at Dien Bien Phu, where the flower of Western civilization, French colonialism, was lost to the Vietnamese.

The spring of 1954 was a sad time in American policy-making circles. The CIA and military assistance were not enough to save the French in Indochina. Debates ran heavy about American military intervention to save the French chestnuts, as one American senator put it, or to feed on the dying carcass of French colonialism. The decision was to stage a series of air strikes in Indochina called Operation Vulture. This view was presented to Eisenhower, who had many of the characteristics of General Kutuzov in *War and Peace*. He told the advocates of Operation Vulture that, if they could get support from leading members of Congress and the allies, he would agree to the operation. There was no chance of that happening.

General Taylor was disappointed. He saw the American failure to intervene in Dien Bien Phu in two ways. One was a failure of nerve and leadership. And the other was a failure to have the fighting equipment and armed forces necessary for intervention and engagement with the Huns of Vietnam. Taylor agreed with General Ridgeway's position that bombing intervention would not work. As Taylor points out, we were unprepared to intervene. "During these deliberations and hesitations, the need was apparent for ready military forces with conventional weapons to cope with this kind of limited war situation. Unfortunately, such forces did not then exist in sufficient strength or in proper position to offer any hope of success. In May, Dien Bien Phu fell, and in the following July in Geneva, Indo-China was partitioned between Communism and Freedom at the 17th parallel [*sic*]. This event was the first, but not the last failure of the New Look *to keep the peace on our terms*" (emphasis added).

General Taylor was not interested in respite from war, which he viewed as a continuous activity of the state. The Korean adventure was part of the overall struggle for Southeast Asia between its inhabitants and the West. He wanted to press ahead. His own views on American intervention in Vietnam from 1961 on were directly related to his belief that the American rulers had not fulfilled their "responsibilities" at Dien Bien Phu. Members of the Eisenhower administration did not accept war fighting in their doctrine. On the other hand, Taylor did not believe that the covert activities of the CIA were enough to police the Third World. His view contradicted that of the brothers Dulles, who argued that the United States did not have to intervene militarily in various parts of the world. It would be able to dominate, through covert means, that is, through the CIA, and through threats of massive nuclear retaliation. The day-to-day activity of American involvement in the world would be through the CIA, which would both spy, and control through payoffs, bribes, and blackmail—the ancient methods of rulers. What the CIA could not do, it was assumed that various forms of foreign aid could accomplish. Eisenhower's chief of staff in World War II, Walter Bedell Smith, had been in charge of the CIA from 1950, where for three years he had worked at the task of defining the mission and the organizational structure necessary to carry out overt and covert activities. The formal institutionalization of the CIA's operation as the central arm of American foreign policy was "telegraphed" by Smith's shift from head of the CIA to undersecretary of state in 1953.

"Wild Bill" Donovan, who had set up the Office of Strategic Services during the Second World War, was chosen by President Eisenhower in 1953 as ambassador to Thailand. His responsibility in that position was to set up a Southeast Asian spy control network in this area. At first he thought it necessary to undertake this task as a personal representative of the president—without diplomatic status. However, he was assured that such activities could be carried out directly through the secretary and the undersecretary of state.

The ascendancy of the CIA through the Dulles brothers and Smith during the Eisenhower period had the internal effect within the American national security bureaucracy of playing down the active use of the army for purposes of war fighting. The United States had gone through a difficult Korean "limited" war engagement, which threatened the internal power balances between civilians and the military within the national security system. Furthermore, the Republican party itself had come to power specifically denying the policies of military engagement and intervention, and pressing the need to end the military war in Korea.

By the late 1950s, some of the army general officers became concerned that war fighting, as in Korea, would no longer occur. Consequently, army budgets would be constantly cut except for those portions earmarked for assistance in building the militaries of other countries, and, within the national security bureaucracy, the CIA would grow. The major *active* use of the armed forces during the Eisenhower administration was that of commanding the Seventh Fleet to evacuate 17,000 civilians and 25,000 troops from the Ta Chen islands, which the mainland Chinese then occupied; and the U.S. intervention in Lebanon with 15,000 American troops, which were withdrawn within three and a half months.

The strongest advocates of a war-fighting capability, such as General Maxwell Taylor, thought they saw the power of the CIA growing as the army's power decreased. General Taylor's development of the limited-war strategy enabled the army officers to assert an *active* mission for the army in the face of the CIA involvement and extensive paramilitary covert activities. The chance to control the CIA and to effect a decrease in its power occurred as a result of the Cuban adventure of April 1961, which was planned and executed by the CIA. After its failure, the president assigned the task of analyzing the Cuban failure and reallocating the power of engagement and intervention within the government to General Taylor and Robert Kennedy. Needless to say, General Taylor was not an "independent spokesman," since his bill of goods was the importance of fighting limited wars. So, while the Eisenhower administration threatened total nuclear destruction and simultaneously used the CIA as its chosen instrument of intervention, the Kennedy administration attempted to reallocate power within the national security bureaucracy, favoring continuous military engagement and a ready war-fighting capability.

In 1959, General Taylor believed that the United States had to "deter general war, to deter *or win* local war, and finally to cope with a general war if deterrence fails." Taylor pointed out in an article, which the Department of Defense refused to clear, that his program of defense would be costly. "*Without making a specific estimate, one may be sure that the total bill will exceed any peacetime budget in United States history*" (emphasis added). But in exchange for this bill, we would, he thought, be able to deter general war and win local war quickly. General Taylor was appointed by President Kennedy as his chief military adviser.*

---

*A little anecdote of some importance should be told. When Taylor was appointed military adviser to the president in the early summer of 1961, his offices were on the same floor as those of the National Security Council Staff—the third floor of the Executive Office Building. When he moved in, he immediately put guards around his office and those of his staff. This symbolic victory over the Bundy staff necessitated a retaliation. The Bundy staff got guards for its offices so that one had to go through guards in order to get to their staff as well. But now there were guards on that floor within one hundred feet of each other. An arms-control agreement was called, and guard desks were now put in front of the elevators to cover both staffs.

Taylor's views were not unknown, so the president was not buying a pig in a poke. He wanted to increase American military power across the board. Not only was it necessary to be able to fight general wars through a counterforce strategy, it was also necessary to be able to fight local wars. It was expected that the U.S. Army would be prepared to fight guerrilla wars, limited wars, and general wars *simultaneously*. By 1961, General Taylor was in a position to rectify the American error at Dien Bien Phu. He was sent by the president with Walt Rostow, a deputy special assistant to the president, to Vietnam. They worked out a local war plan to save the South Vietnamese from a fate worse than death. In his first time before a congressional committee with his own program, McNamara called for adding $230 million to the limited-war budget. Secretary McNamara pointed out that the new planning of his group recognized the possibility that the armed forces would have to fight limited wars in different places at the same time: "My statement specifically states that the ability to respond promptly to limited aggression in more than one place at the same time is one of my objectives."

McNamara's view was held also by the new secretary of the army, Elvis Stahr, who later became the president of the University of Indiana. In his opening statement to the House Subcommittee on Defense Appropriations, Stahr gave the congressmen a lesson in international politics and diplomacy. He pointed out that there were "trouble spots in all parts of the globe—and the threats to freedom and survival that grimly and persistently stalk this planet are facts whose haunting reality weighs upon you. One simple truth is crystal clear: We must be prepared to deal swiftly and effectively with military adventures directed against any part of the free world. If we are not so prepared, those adventures will multiply and spread." The strategy of flexible response and brushfire war was the Kennedy answer. On the congressional subcommittees dealing with defense, there was wide agreement with this point of view. Congressman Dan Flood of Pennsylvania told McNamara, ". . . sound military planning will indicate that in your limited war the enemy is not going to be convenient and let you have one at Laos and stop; you are going to have a half dozen boils in a half dozen places."

If there was "trouble" in a certain part of the world, the United States was the fire department that would put out the fire with its hoses. If necessary, it would drown the area in the blood of its sons and the blood of the people in the brush fire.

According to Stahr, we also needed to *"strengthen our special forces. The numbers of Allied indigenous forces in the fields of counterintelligence, civil affairs, and psychological warfare—all of which are essential to complete success in such-type operations—can be stepped up."* If what was required was drowning the people in propaganda, spying, and American-style administration, so be it. We were moving again.

The army's role in the Kennedy administration was to include fighting guerrilla brushfire wars in the Third World, and mopping up after a thermonuclear war. The army would have to maintain its position as a winner even *after* a nuclear exchange. Said Stahr, "Our Army must have the capability in general war to meet and defeat aggressor forces in the wake of the damage caused by nuclear exchanges. They must then be prepared to exercise direct, full-time, and comprehensive control over the land, the resources, and the peoples of the aggressor." Translated, this meant that the United States would have to occupy the Soviet Union after a nuclear war.

What was going on in the heads of the planners? In a convoluted way, the Stahr statement represented the unshackling of the army from the leg irons of the massive retaliation strategy practiced by Eisenhower and Admiral Arthur Radford, chairman of the Joint Chiefs of Staff. Radford did not believe in conventional war with the Soviet Union. Indeed, he did not believe in conventional war with anyone. Consequently, when as the chairman of the JCS he ruled that there could be no conventional wars and that all wars thenceforth needed nuclear weapons, the possibility of building up the army as a force to fight conventional wars was virtually nonexistent. Under Eisenhower, the cuts in budget of the army were substantial. The Eisenhower army budget went from $17,054,000,000 in 1953 to a low of $9,002,000,000 in 1956. The last Eisenhower army budget was $10,293,000,000, in 1960. While cuts in the army budget were made, Radford was unsuccessful in his attempts to change the so-called "forward strategy" of the United States. The army's limited role in the 1950s, as a "trip wire" in Europe in case of Soviet attack, or as the mop-up contingent after a nuclear war in the wake of massive retaliation, hardly seemed tenable to the professional soldier. Massive retaliation, it seemed, was a cover for not being willing to fight.

For the army, it was a welcome change from the Eisenhower days when President Kennedy asked for a call-up of the reserves in his June speech of 1961, to threaten the Soviet Union or, as was stated then, to show our will and determination in defending American allies and interests. A year later, in September of 1962, the president again asked for a call-up of 150,000 combat-ready reserves over the objection of conservative and right-wing Republicans. The arguments made by Bruce Alger, a right-wing congressman from Texas on the House floor against the call-up of 150,000 reservists was that this was a phony political gesture. "As I see it, it is a terrible mistake to call up 150,000 reservists, upset 150,000 families, and places of employment. This is no answer to world neighbors or our citizens for our lack of foreign policy."

In the same debate, Melvin Laird, later to become secretary of defense, also objected to the calling up of the reserves, as did Congressman Gerald Ford, who pointed out that eleven days before the debate McNamara had stated that "the potential need for a call-up of reserve forces to meet the military requirements similar to those imposed upon us a year ago, has been considerably reduced. Our conventional capability has been greatly enhanced during that period by the addition of five Army combat divisions, bringing our total to sixteen."

However, Ford suggested—outhawking McNamara—"if you really want to make Mr. Khrushchev believe that we mean business, then we ought to give to our President the full authority to recall up to one million men, excluding those who recently served. *This would give the President a real stick to shake in the face of Mr. Khrushchev.*" These men were cannon fodder in the hands of leadership, and the Department of Defense saw armies specifically in these technocratic terms—as instruments of power for the powerful.

The Navy Polices the World

With the Kennedy administration, there came the new Golden Age of Defense for the navy as well. During the Eisenhower administration the navy had been squeezed downward. Navy men complained that their ships were getting older and that age and disuse were setting into their arsenal. The total number of warships had dropped from 973 at the end of 1956 to 812 at the end of fiscal year 1960. The number of personnel in the navy also fell during this four-year period, from 663,223 to 619,000.

The original navy estimate for the 1962 period under a budget projected by the Eisenhower administration was $1.6 billion less than the estimates put forward by the navy once the Democrats came to power and transformed the imperial purpose. The navy found itself gaining in the bureaucratic struggle for moneys by using two tactics. It could adopt massive retaliation strategy, which meant that Polaris missiles were needed to destroy the cities of our enemy. And it could simultaneously accept the flexible response strategy, since the navy was essential in fighting wars around the world.

The Senate had long favored the navy. As Senator Stennis said to Admiral Anderson at his nomination hearing as chief of naval operations, "I feel like the U.S. Navy, to a great degree the world's policeman, and a mighty good one, represents the very best traditions of the armed services as well as of our great country."

During the Eisenhower administration, the navy was the prime mover in a massive retaliation strategy, or, as it was described then, a city-busting strategy. The Polaris was the invulnerable deterrent. Yet, while the Polaris submarines were important as a deterrent, the central organizational problem for the navy was that the navy's activity as the world's policeman would disappear unless a different military and diplomatic strategy were pursued by the national security managers. Because of the need for an expanded role for the navy, it supported a new view of geopolitics, which required that the navy be able to involve itself in many little wars simultaneously.

Admiral McCain, at the beginning of the Kennedy administration commander of Amphibious Group 2 and then commander in chief, Pacific, noted to the House Defense Appropriations Subcommittee that "the spread of communism throughout the world may be likened to the cancerous growth in the human body where one does not know which vital organ will be attacked next." Consequently, said the admiral, "... we must be prepared to move to any spot in a dozen different directions in order to be in a position to 'nip in the bud' any possible trouble in its inception."

President Kennedy in his first State of the Union address had said, "in all these areas of crisis the tide of events has been running out and time has not been our friend." All over, according to the Kennedy analysis, the American empire was on the run from the communists or their friends. American policies were unsubtle, failing to use military and related power against insurgencies in a way that would stem the tide of communism. The navy view was that the Russians could be stopped if the United States could dominate the world's waterways. By playing down its city-busting policy in favor of the flexible-response policy, the navy, like the other branches of the armed forces, wanted to participate in all levels of war fighting. As Admiral McCain put it, "We have just passed through an era wherein massive retaliation has been the governing philosophy. Because of the possibility of mutual annihilation, the policy of graduated deterrence is now in the ascendancy. Seaborne striking forces, because of their unique characteristics, are the ideal instrument for the execution of this policy. These ships have a capability of engaging in everything from a nuclear exchange, to a conventional war, to a mere demonstration of force."

According to navy strategists, there was a "new sea frontier." Up to the time of the Korean War, the United States was "directly concerned with only about one-ninth of the earth's land mass. Today, this has expanded to where we may be called upon to commit our Armed Forces any place along one-third of the earth's land mass." Needless to say, such a view of imperial responsibility demanded a navy to equal such ambition. But beyond the size of the navy needed to carry out this worldwide policy, it was necessary to accept the idea that since there was a mutual standoff on the thermonuclear level, the United States needed to be able to enforce its will on other levels of violence.

The United States, it seemed, would spend vast sums of money, train men, and fabricate resources for imperial purposes that would give American policy rulers instruments of violence "in all shapes and sizes," as McGeorge Bundy so aptly put it. Because of American wealth and technological strength, it would be impossible for other nations to match the United States in its ability to mobilize for war, *remain* mobilized for it, and fight *permanent* war. The Kennedy version of the national security state was predicated on a stable but growing corporate and military structure. The state would use the young people by challenging and channeling them into accepting and prosecuting the imperial purpose. The Peace Corps was one part of a mission of national purpose and sacrifice that the children of the middle class would be able to identify with and carry out. The working class and the subproletariat blacks would be drafted and mobilized for war. The children of these classes had their tasks to perform and their roles to play. This version of the national security state played itself out in the bloody quagmire of Southeast Asia and the crumbling cities of the United States.

Notes

Much of the material in this paper is based on personal observations of the author, while a member of the Kennedy administration, and on the material presented by officials of that administration in congressional hearings during the early 1960s.

Secretary of Defense McNamara's description of the Communist threat appears in *Hearings* on Sen. Res. 191 *before the Senate Armed Services Committee*, September 6 and 7, 1961. His later listing of the enhanced military capabilities the United States had achieved under his stewardship appears in *Hearings before the Committee on Armed Services of the House of Representatives on Sunday Legislation Affecting the Naval and Military Establishments*, 1964, p. 6899.

The secretary's explanation of the need for rapid deployment appears in HASC 1963, p. 430. His discussion of civil defense appears in SASC 1962.

General Maxwell Taylor's views on the need for a flexible-response policy are fully laid out in his book *The Uncertain Trumpet* (Harper & Row, 1969).

The congressional debate on the Kennedy call-up of reserves appears in the *Congressional Record*, 1962, pp. 20501 ff.

1. Emmet John Hughes, *The Ordeal of Power* (New York: Athenaeum, 1963), pp. 103–4.

3

Ideological Premises of the United States' Cold War Policies

The end of the Cold War is giving rise to a new American myth. It is the unwarranted assumption that American policies led to the transformation now occurring in Eastern Europe and the Soviet Union, and that American leaders laid the groundwork for these events beginning with the Truman Doctrine and ending with Reagan's military buildup. The story goes that we have been led by wise men such as Acheson, Dulles, Harriman, Bundy, Johnson, and Truman, who set us on a wise course that ultimately prevailed.

But the stubborn fact is that the Cold War could have been terminated long ago had American leaders not been tied to a predominantly military response to the police barracks socialism of the Soviet Union, and had they shown more trust in the will of ordinary people to be free. Throughout the Cold War we were overwhelmed by shorthand words such as authoritarianism and totalitarianism that stopped our own leadership from understanding the fluid and turbulent changes that were occurring beneath the surface.

At the very beginning of the Cold War, nuclear weapons were seen by American leaders as the most important card to be played in international affairs. They emboldened Truman in his negotiations with the Soviets and with our own allies. He insisted that Communists be removed from the Italian and French cabinets. Having drawn a line between East and West Europe, Truman was only superficially concerned with the Soviet riposte in Eastern Europe when the Communists were removed from the French and Italian cabinets: the Soviets responded with the 1948 coup in Czechoslovakia and then tightened their security belt by turning the East European nations into their clients. They believed this to be their "right" under the Yalta agreements.

The truth is that very few U.S. government officials have cared much about the lives of East Europeans. There were some expectations of U.S. intervention, especially among those CIA operators who had attachments to particular emigré groups and among a few members of Congress who represented East European ethnic constituencies. The general "hands off East Europe policy" was reflected in John Foster Dulles's response to the Hungarian uprising of 1956. When the Hungarian people rose in authentic resistance to the Communist regime, the United States resigned itself to sending good wishes to the freedom fighters, even though the U.S. government, through the Voice of America and Radio Liberty, had encouraged revolt.

At the time, a powerful argument was made that any military intervention would be dangerous and costly and would risk the threat of world war. But in fact there were negotiable diplomatic solutions that could have gotten the Soviets out of Eastern Europe. Unfortunately, the record shows that the United States had little interest in acting on these possibilities. Harold Stassen and Valerian Zorin had negotiated a comprehensive arms missiles agreement that could have provided for the removal of Soviet forces from Eastern Europe as well as cutbacks of U.S. forces from Western Europe. But Dulles destroyed the possibility by withdrawing our initial acceptance from the negotiating table. Dulles's interest was not in ending the Cold War, or in helping East Europe politically, or in decreasing the numbers of arms and forces in Europe. In fact, his vaunted "roll-back" of the Soviets in Eastern Europe was a rhetorical ploy—aided by certain CIA activities directed by his brother Allen—to keep the pot boiling there, but never to cook anything. Dulles had the diplomatic disease of "pactomania"—that is, the building of military alliances under U.S. tutelage with the United States holding a very large nuclear umbrella.

The irony and tragedy of this historic period are that throughout the Eisenhower and Kennedy-Khrushchev era, it would have been relatively easy to "Finlandize" Eastern Europe. For example, in 1955 the concluding of the Austrian state treaty resulted in the withdrawal of Soviet troops from Austria, leaving Austria officially neutral but favoring the West culturally and in its foreign affairs. There were East European diplomatic efforts in the 1955–57 period to get the Soviets out of Poland. Picking up on Anthony

Eden's idea of a demilitarized zone between East and West, and Nicolai Bulganin's call for the removal of foreign troops from East and West Europe, the foreign minister of Poland proposed a nuclear weapons free zone comprising Czechoslovakia, Poland, and East and West Germany. But the United States had already committed itself to using West Germany as a base for nuclear weapons, so another opportunity to end the Cold War was lost. Similarly, an opportunity was lost in 1968, when a mutual disengagement policy could have saved the Czechoslovaks their independence and dignity, but the United States was too caught up in its own war of intervention in Vietnam.

When disengagement proposals were made by George Kennan in his BBC Reith lectures, Dean Acheson laughed derisively. Most American policy makers had an image of the world that assumed there was no way the Soviets would give up Eastern Europe, even though from 1949 the Soviets offered withdrawal predicated on mutual disengagement and East European nations staying out of NATO. American leaders had forgotten that the Soviets had initiated the Warsaw alliance because of the prior emergence of NATO and their fear that Germany would dominate it. Because of its cost, the Soviet's security belt of Eastern Europe was always too tight for the Russian people.

As costly as NATO has been for the United States, the Warsaw Pact has been a greater drain—both politically and economically—on the Soviets. This was understood and calculated by American policy makers, who believed devoutly that the United States could spend so much on defense that the Soviets would not be able to keep up. Unfortunately, the more we spent on military forces, the more they spent. The result was that both sides became more insecure. But it was the United States that pressed the arms race forward. As Herbert York, the former director of defense research and engineering under Eisenhower, wrote in 1970, "Our unilateral decisions have set the rate and scale for most of the steps in the strategic arms race." Part of our interest in building these arms was to get our allies to believe that we would go to war for them. Correlatively, they were to accept our policies and assumptions about the NATO alliance and Atlantic community. The latter became an increasingly fantastic proposition since the Carter presidency, as Western Europe became economically stronger and turned to itself as a common trading area.

American conservatives have told Eastern Europeans that it

was the American military buildup that caused the Soviet turnaround in foreign affairs. The fact is that Soviet scientists concluded that there was no substance to SDI as a completed active defense or as an unanswerable first-strike possibility. Their conclusions allowed Mikhail Gorbachev to reply to those in his own government who claimed it was necessary to keep the arms race going.

The major underlying security problem for Moscow is not the United States but Germany. In the early stages of the Cold War the Soviets sought a neutralized Germany controlled by the United States, Soviet Union, Great Britain, and France. The West rejected this formulation, fearing communism would find its way into Western industrialized economies. The two-state German solution was devised: "we" would control "our" Germans and "they" would control "their" Germans. But this has always been an inherently unsatisfactory solution. Now the Cold War solution regarding Germany has come to an abrupt end. It is obvious that a newly formed Germany (with Japan) will not remain subservient to the wishes of the Department of State.

Without a worldwide general disarmament program that includes the superpowers, there is no reason to believe that Germany and Japan, having won the Cold War economically, will not be independent significant military actors by the beginning of the twenty-first century. Such a political situation is not empty of danger. It is not likely that the Germans and Japanese will be more restrained toward rearmament than we and the Soviets were at the beginning of the Cold War unless a worldwide comprehensive disarmament agreement is negotiated and achieved. Before the end of World War I, some fourteen nations sought to take advantage of the Russian civil war, each for its own purposes. Those in the West who see the Soviet Union's present upheaval as an opportunity for gain for the United States had better ponder the consequences of warring armed forces and national dissolution in a nation where there are 25,000 nuclear weapons under rudimentary command and control.

It is not likely that we will be able to deal forthrightly with the present international problems unless we look more closely at what was wrong (and right) with our policy during this period. Our own glasnost is long overdue. □ □

It is not possible to understand the Reagan administration's early national security policies without seeing them in their historical, political, and cultural context. Indeed, there are important psychological ramifications to our policies for they stem from a combined and often unbalanced sense of omnipotence and impotence. We are thirty-eight years into a Cold War. The reasons for it are obscure to a new generation. And the implements of war that we now employ may destroy what we seek to protect. These simple, stark facts should give all of us pause about how rational the struggle is, whether it is in our best interests, or whether we are using the proper means of expressing our altogether important need for defense. Later in this essay I will sketch out the prerequisites for a just defense.

It is not an overstatement to suggest that the American national security system has created profound problems of insecurity for the American people. It is manifested in the hopelessness and sense of impending doom that many of the younger generation have come to feel in relation to the future. It is found in the avoidance that congressional leaders have adopted about various aspects of nuclear policy or covert operations, not wanting to know, or not knowing how to interrupt the almost autonomous nature of the nuclear arms race; and not knowing how to interrupt global policies that committed the United States to actions that seem to violate the nation's interests. Of course, it is not only Americans who are fearful. As Americans fear an increasingly awesome strategic force of the Soviet Union, so the Soviet Union increases its military budget in fear of American defense technologies, especially in the nuclear weapons and missiles area. In its first two years, the Reagan administration was gripped by its belief that the United States had to rearm to parley. The Soviets continued their nuclear and strategic buildup, laying their reasons for it on the United States. The psychological fears of governments and their citizenry have devastating consequences, for they fuel the arms race and become self-fulfilling prophecies on both sides.

The United States' national security budget and the Soviet budgets expand because of *internal* pressures within their own military, technological, and industrial elites. Both sides, pressured by their perception of the other, add to the profound insecurity felt by other nations, as well as by their own populations. The two superpowers, armed to the teeth, can hardly be called tranquil or secure nations. It is, of course, correct to point out that the Soviet difficulties are related to the mad and criminal choices its leadership made against its own people through the Stalinist era and beyond. However, another cause for the insecurity of the Russian people and the economic difficulties they face—difficulties that if transcended could lead to a more sensible internal policy in the Soviet Union—is the arms race. The historic obsession of the Soviets with secrecy grows out of invasions from other nations. In the past, its unwillingness to harbor disarmament inspectors on Russian territory was related directly to its feelings of military inferiority. This situation has changed for the Soviet Union, but it has not resulted in a greater sense of security among its leadership.

The U.S. military buildup has also helped to increase American insecurity. As Herbert York, the former director of defense research at the Pentagon, has put it, "since World War II, the power of the United States has been steadily increasing, while at the same time our national security has been rapidly and inexorably decreasing. The same thing is happening to the Soviet Union."

Politicians of the Cold War's second generation may now want to ask whether anyone benefits from the creation of this insecurity, for if no one benefits, then either there is an autonomous character to the arms race that cannot be interrupted by human intervention, or humankind is beset by a collective death wish that cannot be dealt with except through massive psychotherapy. For practical people it would be a great mistake to embrace this tragic view of history. It would be far more useful to adopt a more traditional political analysis in order to see how certain interests gain directly in terms of money, power, and status when they perpetuate the national security system. The human and venal aspects of the arms race should never be dismissed out of hand. Scientists have worked on problems of nuclear war and missile development because they are "sweet" scientific problems, and they are well paid for working on them. They are like well-trained and gifted football players who want to win at their game. They receive, of course, high status for their work. The military also receives its satisfactions from the arms race and the present national security system. In the American galaxy of power, the American military officer class has a strong political role beyond that of defense. It is not a passive player in American politics "exogenous" to the workings of the system. Anyone who thinks so should carefully analyze several processes: the role of the retired military officers in the politics of such states as Virginia, the role that a four-star general, Alexander Haig, played in maneuvering Richard Nixon out of the White House (could this have occurred without the assent of the Joint Chiefs of Staff and the Pentagon civilian secretary?), or the more traditional role that veterans' benefits play in keeping the millions of veterans loyal to the national security system, whatever its purposes and goals might be. (This is not to say that such benefits are not also economically necessary and critical to millions of people.)

Another beneficiary of the national security system is that part of industry that depends on government defense planning for sustained profits. In the business world, when a firm does not feel economically secure enough dealing with the American market because it believes that there are greater profits to be made elsewhere, the firm will seek trade or "branch factories" abroad. This we might view as horizontal expansion to escape the internal competitive market. The second way firms seek economic profitability is by vertical expansion, dealing in a closed market, where the firm sells only to one client, namely, the federal government. The defense and national security system—that is, the state—is the place where American capital can escape the disciplines of the marketplace. This part of the industrial system, best evidenced by General Dynamics and Lockheed, has long since given up competing within the United States or against international competitors.

Another group that benefits substantially are those members of Congress who avert their eyes from defense costs for regional economic reasons. They use their votes for jobs and contracts in their states because in the Cold War national economy there is no other politically acceptable way to provide for those millions of people who might otherwise directly or indirectly face economic disaster. In the Cold War period, defense spending and arms sales became a critical economic and social prop. The internal use of defense spending has an international dimension.

According to the Department of Defense, arms manufacturers, and the Department of the Treasury, an auxiliary benefit to the United States of arms manufacture is that a hard-sell arms assistance and sales program helps the country in easing trade deficits. This aspect grows more important as the United States is less able to compete with other nations in usable commercial goods. During the early stages of the Cold War, many corporate leaders believed that the American commitment to overwhelming military power enabled the United States to set the terms of world trade and guarantee markets for its goods by helping the United States rid itself of "surplus commodities" that could not be absorbed intranationally. But another role for military power was added during the post–World War II period. The new internationalists argued that acceptance of American world involvement as mediated through a strong national security state, could help divert class and race conflicts within the United States. In other words, if domestic tranquility could not be achieved through income and political power redistribution, then people's eyes could be diverted to foreign involvements and nightmares that were fueled by an overwhelming emphasis on seeing the world as a threatening place.

Until the Reagan administration, American military adventurism, whether in nuclear force planning or Third World military involvements, tended to obscure economic, regional, and racial problems within the United States. Indeed, the Cold War with the Soviet Union helped black people in their struggle for desegregation and political rights, as the armed forces became a place of opportunity for minorities. But times changed in the 1980s. Reagan's internal policies did not operate to perpetuate internal allegiance or docile acceptance of national security policies because he refused to continue a minimum equity base in the society. As a result, the costs of the national security system under the Reagan Republicans were not as palatable as under the Democrats. Whereas under the Democrats it was assumed that the national security budget would help the economy, under Reagan it was perceived by the citizenry as a major cause of internal economic decay. The expenditure of at least $1.8 trillion in the national security budget from 1982–87 was thought of as wasteful, even though the Department of Defense argued that they were revitalizing American industry. The former arguments under the Democrats, advanced by some military Keynesians, that a dollar spent on defense is as good as a dollar spent on anything else just so long as money is circulating and people are working, is finally being discredited as an economic proposition and a national security tenet. The starvation of the industrial structure—the roads, bridges, subway systems—could no longer be denied. It became especially obvious to people who travel to Germany and Japan, the vanquished of the Second World War, nations that now spend minimum amounts of money on defense, and instead put their profits and capital into industrial and technological expansion and innovation. For purposes of schematic clarity, there are four national security themes that appear to govern our daily activities in foreign and defense affairs.

Defense budgets are argued in Congress, government, defense planning sessions, and the media in terms of these four principles. Even the political mold breaker, President Reagan, defended his policies in terms of these principles.

Themes of National Security

1. Economic and Military Dominance

The United States (but not necessarily the American people) must maintain or obtain the dominant economic, political, and military position in the world. Throughout American history, this conception has played a critical role in the formation of our consciousness.

It was taken for granted, and so organized by government and business leaders alike, that the agencies of government were to be a facilitating mechanism for exploiting and controlling the resources and markets of the world, in both the short and the long term. Since World War II, American policy makers have been suspicious and sought confrontations with nations or movements appearing ideologically to challenge American paramountcy or business thrusts, wherever they might be. High government officials, who often came from the business corporate world, saw American interests as intertwined with business interests. To them, the American national interest was tied economically to American-controlled multinational corporations.

Most Third World nations believed that American national security and foreign policy consigned them to a submissive role. They believed that they were to produce goods and raw materials at low costs while committing themselves to a mode of capital-intensive technology that the United States would sell to them. These nations, including more industrially advanced ones, were encouraged to reform their social structure (even their eating habits) to lines that were acceptable to international banks, multinational corporations, agribusiness, and the U.S. national security bureaucracy. This ideology was variously known in the United States as "nation building" (1950s), "modernization" (1960s), "development" (1970s), and "structural adjustment" (1980s).

The task of government officials since World War II has been to "iron out" differences between the various business players in the international field. In the past, it was assumed by government officials that national security policy should primarily reflect military and diplomatic judgments. Economic considerations were hidden even from the actors, even though those factors were usually determinant in daily decisions. The unspoken assumptions of the Truman, Eisenhower, and Kennedy administrations were that all decisions served the gross (dominant) economic interests, whether or not they were directly represented at government meetings. This assumption did not turn out to be accurate according to the Murphy Commission, an executive and congressionally appointed group of senators, former ambassadors, and other paladins who produced a five-volume study of U.S. foreign policy at the end of the Vietnam War. In the mid-1970s, this blue ribbon commission argued that there had to be more economic and corporate awareness in national security decision making because political and military considerations determined the judgments of the bureaucracy in the national security state. The Vietnam War, for example, served no discernible economic interest. It was for this reason that in the early period of the Carter administration, attempts were made under Secretary of State Vance to organize a foreign policy that was not totally dependent on military power. He also assumed that the interests of the largest American-based corporations could be more carefully rationalized and hence protected. Vance sought to use multinational corporations as an instrument for securing trade and détente with the Russians and the Chinese.

Carter's administration seemed to believe that these corporations could be useful in organizing world trade and the economies of the Third World as well. Through policies on human rights and its willingness to accept liberation movements once they were clearly successful, the Carter administration found friends for the United States in Africa and Latin America. George Shultz, a most clever bureaucratic operator and Reagan's second secretary of state who was the captain of a great multinational corporation, was not averse to flirting with this policy in South Africa in the context of sustaining the present resource allocation between the white and nonwhite nations. This policy can be seen most clearly in the United Nations where the United States has consistently voted against those trade and economic development resolutions that might lead to a more equitable distribution between the poor and rich nations. Reagan's torpedoing of the Law of the Sea Treaty was a classic example of this policy. The American contribution to international economic development is Milton Friedman's advice: namely, that Third World nations should adopt the free enterprise system (an ideology that East Europeans were soon to entertain).

Until his second term, Reagan's foreign policy did not show the flexibility in execution that was practiced by Henry Kissinger and Richard Nixon in 1970–71. This diplomatic duo attempted to establish a new international club with rules fashioned by the most powerful. Kissinger saw himself as the major domo of this international ruling club, comprised as it was of communist leaders, capitalists in multinational corporations and banks, oil sheiks, and democratically elected leaders. He assumed that 500 people were able to control the destiny of the world and that the task of American leadership was to perpetuate this form of "stability" by finding means of intimidating or cajoling club members to hold back insurrectionary groups, liberation movements, or any serious jockeying and change in the pyramidal status among members of the club. Kissinger had assumed that this was the way to protect American preeminence. While previously it was assumed by American leaders that the Soviets and the Chinese favored insurrection and liberation movements, his operative assumption was that the Russians and the Chinese could be managed to support the status quo and the present distribution of operational power in the world. This balancing act was thought to be a condition precedent to "détente."

It is dubious that in a multipolar world this form of international politics can work its will. There are too many players and too many variables. The types of power that now exist are various, and therefore economic and military power as it is usually defined does not have the stabilizing effect that it once had. One reason is that by their very nature, arms races increase technological innovation, and therefore instability, as do free markets.

2. Non-Nuclear Military
Engagement in World Politics

The American security system has aimed at controlling animosity between rivals. It has attempted to control both sides of a dispute, mediate, or where necessary "enflame" it through arms sales. Thus, for example, in the Middle East or between India and Pakistan, the American defense policy was to sell arms to both sides and train officers of opposing sides in military and paramilitary assistance programs. The U.S. government believed that it could extend its sphere of influence through its arms and intelligence technology. It also believed that local wars could be fought to U.S. specifications by controlling the spare parts to both sides, as in the India-Pakistan dispute of 1973. Through such manipulation, the national security bureaucracy hoped to judge which nation, or which of several nations, could operate as its "deputy" in a particular region of the world. For example, Iran played the U.S. deputy in the Near East before Khomeini. Throughout the Cold War period, national security policy makers sought military bases in the Middle East ostensibly to stop Soviet intervention, but more fundamentally to keep friendly regimes in the oil-producing states.

In Reagan's first term, anti-communism was the ideological ground upon which American foreign policy played out its multifarious purposes. As important as the backdrop of anti-communism was during the Cold War, policy makers in the bureaucracy operated according to the principle of perceived national security "threat" and "mischief." Terms such as "mischief" or "threat" are, of course, highly subjective, fraught with the problems of judgment and class bias. In an expansionist period, "threat" means anything that thwarts the will of the powerful. But not everyone in a polyglot nation such as the United States is powerful or perceives in the same way. The assessment of a foreign "threat" is colored by class, race, ethnic background, and ideological spin. During an expansionist period, national security policy makers finesse the issue of threat by assuming that the United States is under *continuous* threat. And there is invariably objective, external correlation to this view because of the United States' far-flung continuous presence all over the world, and now in space. During the Kennedy period, for example, the Defense Department assumed that there were seventeen threat situations to the United States in which the nation had to be prepared to intervene. In Eisenhower's time, the New Deal type government of Jacobo Arbenz in Guatemala was overthrown because it was thought to be a threat to American economic interests. However, the U.S. intervention was played as necessary because the Soviets intended to give Guatemala economic aid.

"Mischief" situations are also grist for national security action. It is assumed that the United States must counteract the "mischief makers." Panama's Noriega, a former CIA contract agent and thorn in Bush's side, was one such "mischief maker," requiring a U.S. invasion of Panama.

President Bush had internalized the learning of Dean Rusk, secretary of state under Kennedy and Johnson, who was fond of pointing out that while we were asleep for eight hours, two-thirds of the world was awake, and some of "them" were making mischief. Iraq's Saddam Hussein fell into this category. Concepts such as "threat" and "mischief" buttress those who say that as a world power, the United States has a right of intervention to protect its definitions of its interests.

Direct Engagement

Throughout the postwar period, national security policy makers assumed that the American presence should be felt directly through permanent military engagement, or indirectly through military assistance. The direct engagement system in which American troops and weaponry are present gave national security policy makers a sense of international bureaucratic omnipotence. Prior to the Vietnam War, American policy makers believed that the presence of troops in another nation was a good indicator of U.S. power. After Vietnam, and with the Soviet invasion of Afghanistan, it began to be clear that military presence reflects great vulnerability and insecurity. For example, it might appear to interventionists that the American "influence" in Southeast Asia was greatest when Khanh and Ky were the heads of South Vietnam and when the United States had 500,000 troops in there. However, the presence of so many forces, whether in the Middle East or in Southeast Asia, may be a sign of weakness.

As a general rule, the presence of troops on foreign soil is a statement that the intervening nation has no other way to influence the course of events. The interventions, for example, of Soviet troops in East Germany were a statement of Soviet fears and vulnerability. Prior to Gorbachev, the Soviet concern was that the East Germans might follow a foreign policy that could be at odds with the Soviet Union and perhaps more congenial to neutrality or independence. This is one unstated public reason why some American policy makers are eager to keep American troops in Western Europe. American policy makers concerned about Germany in the Cold War period argued that U.S. troops must stay in Germany as a control device over future German ambitions. The United States and the Soviet Union do not want Germany playing a hegemonic role in Europe on the eve of the twenty-first century.

Increasing German independence or neutrality from the United States, according to this view, would result in economic calamity for American interests. Why this is so is not readily discernible. The reverse is more true. Even when there is no war, when troops of one nation are stationed in another, a tinderbox situation develops over a period of time. Indeed, once the Cold War ends and American troops are left behind, we may face a second "Versailles Treaty" backlash in which German political parties would campaign against Western "discrimination" of Germany. Either the military forces become the lightning rod for internal nationalist sentiment or they are the basis of a *casus belli* with competing third-party nations that view the presence of troops beyond another's border as evidence of hostile and expansionist intent. Where shifts in domestic opinion occur, American military engagement abroad places the United States in an embarrassing situation. For example, Congress was chastised by Secretary Kissinger because it refused aid to Turkey during the Ford administration.

Indirect Engagement

Indirect programs are tied either to military assistance and covert activity or to the rigging of economic credits and resource markets. Historically, the congressional Republican party argued for indirect modes of influencing other nations on the ground that it is economically and politically less expensive to train others to fight than to send our own troops. The late Senate minority leader, Everett Dirksen of Illinois, once explained American foreign policy in Asia during the Eisenhower period by saying that it was predicated on Asian boys fighting Asian boys. It is also assumed that client troops of one nation can be used in another nation to put down an insurrection. Johnson and Rusk tried this method by getting Philippine and South Korean troops to fight in South Vietnam just as Truman had done with greater success in Korea. Another form of indirect engagement is the use of military advisers and assistance to put down insurrections, such as those by the Huks in the Philippines or the leftists in Greece.

Economic and paramilitary coercion was the method of indirect engagement in Allende's Chile. A study of how international bank credits to the Allende government dried up during its three years in power while Chile continued its high level of imports shows a classic case of economic coercion. Credits and loans to Chile ended peremptorily when Allende came to power, as was the case for Sandinista-run Nicaragua. The "indirect" mode has far-reaching negative effects on long-term U.S. interests. This should have been the lesson for U.S. officials after Brazil when the United States helped to engineer a coup there in 1964. The consequence of such policies for the United States was that the country was drawn into a web of dependency. Generally, the winning group (having been spurred on by the United States) seeks military and economic assistance to defend itself against its own people. This process weakens constitutionalism and strengthens bureaucratic fascism unadorned by control by the people or parliament.

Within the United States such "victories" reinforce bureaucratic and corporate patterns that favor militarism, manipulative violence, bribery, and control "from the top." The elites that operate American national security institutions (as well as those climbing the bureaucratic ladder in them) are hardly averse to teaching—and learning from—their Brazilian, Pakistani, or South Korean counterparts. To what extent *their* patterns of violence are emulated by American bureaucratic "teachers" should be a matter of continuous concern.

Covert Operations

Some have argued that indirect engagement aids the United States in understanding the world. This argument is usually advanced by those who favor covert intelligence or covert operations run by the CIA. It should be recalled, even though international law has fallen on hard times, that there is a rule of comity among nations that denies the right of any nation-state to breach the local laws of a host nation. Covert operations invariably begin by breaching local law.

There is another argument not grounded in "mere" law that should be taken into account. Where the United States does infiltrate another nation, or builds up a spy network or economically dependent system, it will be more likely to misperceive the complex cultural and political forces of that nation. The covert national security operatives in another nation are hardly objective observers who are able to report on the activities or independent actions of the "host" nation. If another nation's system is rigged by our own operatives, we cannot begin to know the aspirations and feelings of the people of the "host" nation because we are trying to turn it into a puppet. Because of what operatives do, they are often fooled by what they see. The national security and corporate institutions undertake to control what they do not begin to understand. This state of affairs existed in Iran before Khomeini's forces toppled the shah. As former Senate majority leader Mike Mansfield reported when he was a member of the Senate Foreign Relations Committee, often one agency of the United States finds itself supporting an agency or institution of another nation at cross-purposes with those of another American agency. This happened as a matter of course during the Indochina War.

The result is that American national security bureaucrats are far from comprehending what is going on because they are interminably running into the tail of some other part of the American national security bureaucracy. For example, the people on the various tracks that operated from Washington to get rid of Chile's Allende seemed to be unknown to each other or the then U.S. Ambassador Edward Korry. Only a Pollyanna believes that this is a problem of coordination rather than one endemic to a historically sanctioned policy of meddling. While it may be much less fun for intelligence agencies, strict adherence to a policy of state nonintervention is the surest guarantee of comprehending and judging a society and its leadership actions.

At the end of the Second World War, the State Department sought to stop the creation of the Central Intelligence Agency because it would meddle and vitiate independent reporting in other nations. This view has even more merit at the end of the twentieth century than it had when it was first argued.

Alliance Decay and Congressional Reassertion in Foreign Policy

The U.S. alliance structure is predicated on a supine Congress that allows an Executive great discretion and no limits. If Congress were to assert that it did not intend to give the Executive a military blank check in advance, and that it reserved to itself the power to declare war, the present alliance system would have to be transformed, and the presidential penchant for military intervention could be curbed. Internationally, as contradictions develop within the alliance into open disagreement, as nations in, for example, the NATO alliance compete for markets among themselves and fear nuclear arming will lead to war, and as the Soviet Union and Eastern Europe change without a discernible expansionist ideology, it will be harder for the national security bureaucracy to maintain an alliance built on Cold War anticommunist and nuclear war assumptions.

At the root of NATO alliance disagreement is the growing economic independence and strength of Europe—its GNP is greater than that of the United States, and a new generation of Western Europeans sees preparation for nuclear war as detrimental to Europe's survival. It should be noted that the Soviets are faced with the same situation within the Warsaw Pact nations, although their situation is more aggravated. As a general rule, client states seek independence and will work for that goal every step of the way. This rule is even more applicable as the Soviets continue to surrender their hegemony in Eastern Europe. The underlying reasons for the alliance system are now shifting. There is little doubt that Congress will be placed in a position of reevaluating fuzzy commitments in the light of new economic demands.

3. Soundness of the Dollar

The third principle of American foreign policy revolves around the need to ensure a sound international currency system in which the American dollar is the preeminent exchange. Since Bretton Woods in July 1944, it was assumed that the dollar was the paper that was "as good as gold." Primarily because of military alliances coupled with the expansion of U.S. corporations outside the United States, the U.S. tax base and the wise use of public expenditures have both eroded.

The American middle and working classes find themselves paying taxes for the national security protection of corporate interests that are steadily leaving the United States. In the 1990s, the largest corporations with worldwide interests continue to pay less than 8 percent in federal taxes to the federal government. There have been monetary repercussions as well. As more dollars were gathered abroad in the 1970s, foreign governments and banks—including U.S. multinational corporations—cashed American dollars into gold or other currencies because of the apparent "weakness" of the American economy. The American economy was doubly penalized by the multinational corporations. They escaped taxes, required national security protection, and then bet against the U.S. dollar because it appeared to be a "soft" currency.

How to protect the worldwide power of the American dollar is a matter for different opinions among liberals and conservatives. The liberal mechanism is to circulate money through strong governmental intervention in the domestic economy. Keynesianism needs "flexible" dollars that prime the pump to obtain conditions of economic health in the society. This mechanism, plus an international economic hard-sell program of goods tailored to different markets, is assumed to be the way to continue the dollar's preeminence. But flexible dollars needed for domestic expansion lead to national and then international inflation. During the Ford-Carter presidencies, traders began to question whether dollars should be the world trading and payment medium. Speculators, nations, and corporations sought control over gold and payment in gold.

As we learned from the Reagan administration, conservative businessmen and economists would prefer unemployment at home and sharp cuts in labor costs for production, a lowered standard of living, increased tax subsidies to the large corporations and rich, and increased productivity per worker as the means to protect the strength of the dollar. Republicans are split on this strategy. The Ford administration favored sales to communist nations and higher tariff restrictions on imported goods, a program President Bush favors in his presidency In his first two years, Reagan favored unemployment and gutting social programs as the way to protect the dollar.

Both liberals and conservatives rejected the obvious way of protecting the dollar as a medium of exchange during the Cold War period. That is to say, neither cut military spending, or sought to transform the alliance system, to get corporations to pay an equitable share of their taxes, to control near-money operations such as American Express or the Eurodollar, to develop a full-employment economy, or to control the staggering amount of debt that stalks all American institutions and American people. It takes twelve dollars of debt to "turn on" one dollar of production in the United States. This condition has had a powerful role in the decline of American industry's competitiveness in the world market.

4. The Arms Race and National Security

The most dangerous side of U.S. foreign policy continues to revolve around armaments, and especially nuclear weapons. Such weapons are the ground upon which other forms of violence stand. Military and foreign policy experts remain committed to a vast panoply of weaponry and doctrine. The Pentagon still favors the concept of the so-called flexible brushfire war—adding to it the military dictum that we should "get there firstest with the mostest." Its name during the Reagan-Bush period is "low-intensity conflict." This is supposedly the way to escape the trap of defeat or using nuclear weapons and of inserting the United States as the hegemonic police power whether in the Middle East or Latin America. Official documents about nuclear arms control proclaim that brushfire war capability is necessary so that nuclear weapons do not have to be used.

While lip service is invariably given to the dangers of the arms race, there is truth to the argument that arms control negotiations have acted as a spur to arming, for such negotiations have usually revolved around one or two weapons systems as the negotiating nations were free to build up other arms areas. The value, however, of bilateral arms control negotiations in daily bureaucratic practice, is that they focus the bureaucratic mind and force choices and decisions that are otherwise made through inertia. As a result of arms control negotiations, new arguments are made that ordinarily would not be heard in government. Nevertheless, such arguments are conducted in the context of arms expansion.

In the 1960s and 1970s, the United States developed a triad of capabilities: "strategic nuclear, theater nuclear, and non-nuclear forces." On the nuclear side, the Defense Department argued that the only way the United States could continue its nuclear hegemony was through the combined strategic doctrine of deterrence and counterforce. One purpose of this strategy was to prove to those who were members of our various pact associations that the United States was in a position to use nuclear weapons for them "locally"—that is, in their geographic sector—while being able to maintain a counterforce strike against the Soviet Union. For example, the Schlesinger strategy called for missile, bomber, and submarine forces that can hit and destroy "hard" targets (in other words, counterforce), strike soft-point targets "with yield weapons" (a partially disarming attack), and sustain major attacks (deterrence) on all Soviet cities and Eastern Europe and China. Weinberger sought to strengthen this tower of Babylon in the face of the supposed *possibility* that the Soviets could perform a partially disarming first strike on one leg of our triad, land-based missiles.

The weakness in all of these strategies, from McNamara to Cheney, was that with nuclear weapons we destroy what we want to protect.

Cities and installations in allied nations including Eastern Europe must also be considered potential nuclear targets of U.S. planners. The deadly logic of nuclear war knows no geographic boundaries and U.S. defense planners include Western alliance nations as nuclear targets in the event of war, as well as antagonists.

Strategic Doctrine and Defense Cuts

The end of the Vietnam War caused people to rethink the defense budget. Indeed, it was assumed that the defense budget would drop substantially and could be reassigned to domestic programs. Politically, the Defense Department needed a strong doctrine of continued/increased defense expenditures to counteract those who thought that there was no longer a need for high defense budgets. The secretary of defense, James Schlesinger, supplied just such a doctrine. He outlined three basic choices for United States national security and foreign policy. One option he deprecated was Congress's mechanical attempt to control the high defense budget by cutting it "in such a way that the net reduction is no more than 5% of the total." Schlesinger rejected the cuts advanced by congressional liberals like Senator McGovern and the defense budget analysts from the Brookings Institution on the ground that this method would "erode" the "real military power of the defense establishment" and provide the United States only a "shadow" rather than the "substance" of first-class military power. Schlesinger argued that the United States should "make the decision explicitly rather then in a casual and impulsive fashion over a period of time." The Senate upheld its Budget Committee and cut the defense budget slightly. But the committee did not challenge any of the Defense Department assumptions or the type of worldwide responsibility that the defense budget manifests in its dollar allocations. Consequently, without changing the assumptions of national security doctrine, it was not long before Schlesinger's views about the need for a triad framed defense analysis and national security budgetary requirements. The notion of counterforce seemed to be more real with Schlesinger's triad theory. It meant overthrowing the traditional Republican reluctance at supporting high defense budgets.

The Eisenhower administration defense budget was negotiated between the president, Joint Chiefs of Staff, secretary of defense, secretary of the treasury and the director of the Bureau of the Budget. The military services were given a number that could not be exceeded, although within that number they could decide how to spend the funds they received. In some ways, this was the defense version of the Republican block grant to the states. The relative amounts were then struggled over by the various departments and agencies within the Department of Defense.

The nuclear strategies of Eisenhower's time were relatively primitive. They did not distinguish various types of targets, favoring instead a city-busting strategy, especially since the Soviet Union had very few military targets that housed nuclear weapons. Destroying the Soviet Union through nuclear war was not thought to be a credible strategy by the think-tank advisers, and indeed, they helped the United States move to a two-and-a-half strategy. It was this strategy that President Kennedy and Defense Secretary McNamara sought to implement. The reason for this strategy was, ostensibly, the number of threats to the United States and its allies that would have to be fought at the same time or sequentially. During the Kennedy period, the defense budget was written for a war doctrine that assumed the United States would be able to fight a non-nuclear war and two nuclear wars simultaneously for 120 days.

The seeds of the unlimited level of the arms race on the strategic and limited-war level were sown in the Kennedy-McNamara period. And while that period led to tragedy, the transubstantiation of the Kennedy/McNamara policies by Reagan/Weinberger tasted of farce. Secretary Weinberger rejected the two-and-a-half war strategy for one that favored an open-ended military strategy so that more than two and one-half wars could be fought simultaneously. Thus, his assumptions demanded an open-ended mission for the military departments. They must be prepared to fight any and all types of war—simultaneously. And therefore they must have a budget to match. Yet, paradoxically, the Weinberger doctrine made clear that there would be virtually no circumstances in which the United States would go to war unless there were total support from the American people. This position was modified by Bush and his secretary of defense, Richard Cheney, who believed that the American public could be "massaged" into war through military action and some form of international legitimation.

When he was secretary of defense, James Schlesinger stated that there was a "strong connection between the safety, interests, commitments, and foreign policy of the United States on the one hand, and the size, composition, and development of our defense establishment on the other hand." In the post-Vietnam period, Schlesinger made clear that reduction of the defense budget must be based on a "clear recognition that we will not be able to fulfill our responsibilities." Richard Cheney made the same arguments at the end of the Cold War.

Our secretaries of defense have not readily grasped the fact that foolish missions cannot and should be not be fulfilled. Indeed, the continued direction of the arms race and intervention so destructive of world civilization and our own internal economic needs, is the classic case of losing touch with what our needs and responsibilities are. We should not be afraid to reexamine our alliance systems so that we come to recognize them as means and not ends. NATO did not become the catalyst to a United States of West Europe or a United Atlantic community. Nevertheless, it could be the beginning of an arms control and disarmament arrangement with Warsaw Pact nations that could result in military disengagement from Europe and the building of world civilization.

Since 1945 the American military excursion abroad has cost several trillion dollars in defense and alliance building. These funds and the bureaucratic structures that were built must give way to new strategies of security.

Alternatives

The reader of this essay will wonder whether any tendencies of the last generation in American foreign policy can be used as a basis for new policies. In considering such a question it is necessary to decide the framework and forum in which foreign policy should be conducted. While there is much to criticize in the United Nations, its organization, and the vast differences among nations, including their many hypocrisies, the fact is that the United Nations is now the place where several human aspirations can be made practical. It is, for example, the organization where nations can debate the meaning of decolonization, disarmament, and economic equity in such a way that the entire world's needs can be taken into account. As alliances are revised, the chance for coordination and consultation among nations could take place within the United Nations. Consequently, the United Nations could again emerge as the central forum for the carrying out of American foreign policy. Iran, Japan, Germany, Brazil, India, and Nigeria would be added to the U.N. Security Council. Why is this important? The fact is that there must be an international political framework for conducting national foreign policy, a framework that recognizes the changing world order and can coordinate plans and compose differences simultaneously. A new framework with expanded membership in the Security Council could set limits to nationalist behavior. Since 1958, the United States has felt itself isolated in the United Nations. It is now able to break out of that isolation as a result of the end of the Cold War. One way is to initiate discussions on how each nation might implement General Assembly resolutions in their respective foreign policies. This could result in generating a world common law that would open up political disputes to being handled according to world precedent. Obviously, there are numerous U.N. resolutions that do not fall into anyone's interests, nor do they speak to American needs. On the other hand, there are many that do. Consequently, a review of General Assembly resolutions should now be undertaken to see how or whether they could in fact become guides to U.S. national action—how the United States voted on the resolution notwithstanding. Hence, a joint congressional review group of the Foreign Relations Committees of the House and Senate should study U.N. resolutions to ascertain whether and to what degree the United States could and should conform to them. As important as such an activity is, implementing this proposal would merely indicate a change of attitude. In fact, any changes in foreign policy must grow out of the realization that there are new needs, aspirations, and forces within the United States that can lay claim to the American national interest.

It can no longer be a given of American foreign and national security policy that the habits of the past are good enough for securing American freedom in the future. The principle of nonentangling alliances that President Washington laid out in his Farewell Address may be more relevant to our current internal crisis than all the tub-thumping that is heard about the need for American military involvement around the world.

As I have indicated, one of the major problems of the last generation was caused by the assumption that the United States has permanent attachments or ties to particular nations that permanently define its interests. Indeed, in this generation the United States also tore up another piece of advice from President Washington, that military weapons should be made in the United States for the American armed forces. Prior to the Second World War, American diplomats and politicians viewed permanent overseas attachments as antithetical to the United States and its interests. The Second World War and then the Cold War changed this doctrine of American foreign policy. Our leaders identified those nations with whom they made commitments irrespective of their ideology with the concept "Free World," a term coined by Henry Wallace during the Second World War. It is necessary to study and rethink the assumptions that drive the United States to make such alliances and commitments, for they are costly and dangerous. There are several issues on which the relevant congressional committees might reflect in determining the utility of the alliance conception. What have been the benefits, risks, and costs to the American people of these alliances? Would we have been more secure, and the world more secure, had we pursued a policy of no permanent attachments? What obligations under the U.N. Charter should frame a new independence and new internationalism that would define American foreign and national security policy?

Hanging over all of these questions is the issue of disarmament. In part, the arms issue grows out of political tensions. But just as surely, armaments, and especially nuclear and strategic arms, have become an autonomous aspect of international politics.

In the United States, mass public opposition to the arms race was quiescent until the Reagan administration. This quiescence resulted in inertial arming. The United States developed well over 25,000 nuclear weapons. Our military strategists insisted on making the low-yield nuclear weapon an "ordinary" weapon that would be treated conventionally. By making nuclear weapons "everyday" weapons, the United States integrated them into our various armed units for possible use in limited wars. Military strategists are enamored of first-strike options on the strategic level as well as first-use options. Elsewhere I have raised the question of legality involved in the use of nuclear weapons. What is important to ascertain is whether the Nuremberg obligation and various U.N. declarations are applicable (as Richard Falk and others including myself have suggested) to nuclear war questions, and whether such ideas can be made part of the lives of bureaucrats, citizens, and policy makers. It is my contention that defense and disarmament must be conducted in the framework of international law, strong moral proscriptions, and popular pressure. Otherwise, there is no chance for a constitutional common defense that adheres to law and morality. In this context, I asked four questions in 1975 that are still pertinent:

> If the United States were now to stop any further production of nuclear weapons and missiles, would it be any less secure? Should not American government officials be held to a standard of personal accountability outlined in various laws so that aggressive war will not be a part of the national security bureaucrat's kit? Should people in the armed forces be able to unionize for wages, hours and morality setting forth a code of ethics which would *exclude* the use of genocidal weapons and participation in aggressive wars? In other words, should soldiers and sailors have the power to limit the mode of weaponry and destruction by abiding to an oath of conduct that eschews such weaponry and acts as a control over unconstitutional wars of aggression?[1]

While such questions must now be opened and debated in society as a whole, it is still necessary to press for disarmament arrangements through the national security bureaucracies as they are presently organized.

In 1961, the United States and the Soviet Union agreed to the McCloy-Zorin "eight points," which outlined principles for obtaining comprehensive disarmament. This memorandum can be used as a basis for reopening the disarmament question.[2] It should be noted that the signatories to the partial test ban treaty proclaimed that "their principal aim (is) the speediest possible achievement of an agreement on general and complete disarmament which would put an end to the armament race and eliminate the incentive to produce and test all kinds of weapons, including nuclear weapons." It remains possible to set the motion for general disarmament in three stages.

The context for discussion on disarmament must now begin in the U.N. Security Council with the permanent members laying out the basis for determining the questions and concerns of disarmament. Thus, the United States, for example, should take the lead in convening a U.N. Security Council meeting with a series of studies about disarmament, the means of getting it, and the means of keeping the peace in the world. These disarmament proposals would be debated in the council for at least a year, during which time an agreed-upon position would develop. That position would include these steps: what nations should do to reduce missiles and nuclear weapons on their own without inspection; developing inspection techniques and collateral forms of inspection; budget examinations as suggested under the Helsinki agreements; and *the reduction and abolition of armaments and military forces over a period of fifteen years.* Past plans correctly called for the staged reduction of armaments in which the great powers would reduce their forces first in the context of a worldwide disarmament and arms control plan. Less heavily armed nations would be more likely to follow suit.

In the meantime, there are two changes that in fact would shift dramatically the costs of the armaments system in the United States. The first is to reinstate an excess profits tax on defense and national security contracting. Presently, the contractor is able to lay off other corporate costs on defense projects, and is able to guarantee financial solvency through higher than reasonable profit returns. A defense contracts renegotiation board similar to the kind that operated for over a generation as an instrument to repatriate profits should again be reinstated.

The second consideration of a budgetary nature is to tie salary schedules in defense corporations to those in the federal government. Thus, the government would not pay for any salary of a defense corporation official that exceeded the federal government's Defense Department pay scales. In the last analysis, however, major savings (over $150 billion yearly) can only be sustained through mutual disarmament and reducing the open-ended responsibilities of the American defense establishment.

The question remains whether there are precepts that could now be used prior to disarmament to guide our policies through a complex and bewildering period of transition.

The first precept is that a national security policy for the United States must defend its land, people, and institutions. Second, the United States cannot assume that military alliances are perpetual. Shifting alliances always occur among nation-states. Consequently, the United States would do better to understand the importance of limiting its military commitments to alliances and seek other modes of military security. It should move to reconstitute the Military Committee of the United Nations to prepare a world security arrangement. The third precept is to avoid the danger of allowing national security to be captured by narrow economic, ideological, or other interests that do not speak to the real security of the nation.

If these precepts are applied, the defense budget can be transformed, since it will then fit into a just defense view of U.S. aims in the international arena. By a just defense I mean a mode of social protection that recognizes that international institutions such as the United Nations also have such a role, and accepts the principle that governments and people must operate according to moral standards of conduct and not surrender to the madness of proliferating military technology. A just defense requires establishing ways for nations to exercise their right of self-defense properly. Its use should be limited to times when a nation is attacked, and the means should be circumscribed by international law. Military measures that cause ecological damage on an international scale and harm future generations, for example, should be proscribed.

Notes

1. *IPS Budget Study*, no. 1, ed. Marcus G. Raskin.
2. I have written an updated version of the McCloy-Zorin framework. It appears in *Winning America*, ed. Marcus Raskin and Chester Hartman (Boston: Southend Press, 1988).

4

A National Security Manager Tries to Explain

I worked for McGeorge Bundy when he was President Kennedy's special assistant for national security affairs. The relationship did not last, and while we were mutually respectful, we viewed the world from different perspectives. I remember the first day he introduced me to Walt Rostow, his deputy. Bundy said that I was to be their conscience. I have often wondered about that half-joke and its meaning. Those aware of the operations of modern states know that a government official who is seen as a "conscience" is immediately put aside as a nag who is considered ignorant of the harsh realities of governing. As in all ghetto cultures, those who lived within the national security culture were limited to thought, language, and options that outsiders would have immediately concluded were narrow and even absurd. And so it seemed to me. I had thought a certain quality of wisdom and judgment would characterize those professors who had come from Harvard. But they saw governing as a series of operations and transactions that were to be carried out in the rigid grammar of the Cold War. Bundy was no exception, although in my opinion he had hoped for much better. Like others, he was broken by the Indochina War, which was to have been proof of the effectiveness of the limited-war strategy, a doctrine brought forward by the Kennedy advisers into the Johnson administration.

Bundy hoped for a career that would reflect his capacity for hard work, his willingness to keep confidences, and his intellectual gifts. The reward for such service was the position of secretary of state. It must have struck him as ironic that an immigrant courtier, Henry Kissinger, should become Nixon's national security adviser, and then secretary of state. Bundy had championed Kissinger for tenure at Harvard over the great political scientist Hans Morgenthau, but he later sought to curtail Kissinger by insisting to President Kennedy that Kissinger not have direct access to him. Kissinger's position as an insider was saved in the 1962 period from Bundy's wrath by White House staff members Arthur Schlesinger and Carl Kaysen, who recommended that Kissinger be made a consultant to the National Security Council staff. Of course, it was the Rockefeller family, especially David and Nelson, whom Kissinger had served with such zeal, that procured Kissinger his place in the highest circles of government.

Bundy, the Boston Brahmin, was unable to play the courtier game very successfully. Nevertheless, his bureaucratic style fit well with that of Kennedy. Both of them believed in informal meetings and were happy to rid the National Security Council of the various boards within boards comprising representatives of the various agencies of the national security apparatus that seemed to be merely bureaucratic and nonaction-oriented. Eisenhower's Operations Coordination Board, which the Kennedy administration dismantled in its early days, was one such unit that acted as a brake and rationalizer of national security activities.

A word should be said about the function of the national security adviser. There is a story by Henry Miller in which he describes the prostitutes of Paris as denizens whose loins come to know every social class of the city, from murderer and thief to judge and priest. The national security adviser is like the Paris prostitute, for he comes to know every activity of the government, the legal and the criminal, as he attempts to guide and structure each into coherent policy. This is not an easy task, and it is a hard one to explain to fellow citizens, as Admiral Poindexter, Reagan's national security adviser, found out when he tried and failed to explain himself to a federal jury. ☐ ☐

Although they haven't said so publicly, since the Vietnam War McGeorge Bundy and Robert McNamara have sought redemption and rehabilitation for their government service. Relatively young men during the Kennedy and Johnson years, they were among a handful who were instrumental in building up the war-making capacity of the United States beyond anything Dwight Eisenhower thought necessary or useful. They flirted with arcane nuclear strategies pressed the United States into the Vietnam War as well as other interventions. They personified that part of the American culture that sees itself as "tough" guys—people who clothe bureaucratic and class interests in ringing rhetoric and miss-the-point analyses.

Perhaps for reasons of conscience, these activities sent Bundy and McNamara into a more eleemosynary line of work, Bundy as director of the Ford Foundation and McNamara as head of the World Bank. Whether or not the same habits of mind that led them astray in the government plagued them at these institutions I do not know. It is not unfair, however, to say that as government officials they helped to set the nation on a course from which it has yet to recover.

Bundy is now professor of history at New York University. As part of his attempt at redemption and explanation, he wrote *Danger and Survival, Choices about the Bomb in the First Fifty Years* (1988). This book is a goldmine of information written by a gifted establishment regular. By "establishment regular," I mean a person who may disagree with reigning authority on tactics but never disagrees on ends. He will never veer far from the establishment, knowing that the penalties for seeking to attack the assumptions of a social system are very great. Therefore, the regular's conclusions will always appear reasonable in a frame of reference that may be quite mad. He will rein in his best moral and intellectual instincts for a stance thought to be "responsible," "realistic," and always safe. Establishments thrive on such men (and women), for they are dependable in terms of both policy advice given and how historical evidence is arranged and assessed. Occasionally, as in the cases of McNamara and George Kennan, an early proponent of covert wars, their outlooks and hopes change for the better. Bundy's hopes are more narrow than those of his erstwhile colleagues. He hopes that as a result of understanding how "fateful" nuclear decisions are made, it may be possible for

> the two superpowers (to) stay clear of war with one another, and if they go on reducing their common nuclear danger, it is not wrong to hope that a time will come in which they learn how to get beyond the age of survivable overkill. If and when they do that, I believe the achievement will rest on a politics of trust that exists on neither side today. In the long run only mutual trust, not arms control as such, can end any military rivalry "although" strategic stability can over time make important contributions to trust.

One may inquire if mutual trust was the establishment's goal—why was it that Bundy et al. were not able to achieve that objective during the Kennedy-Johnson period? After all, Khrushchev cut his troop levels by over one and a half million and pressed for general disarmament. Why was that not used as an indication of the beginnings of mutual trust? Because "strategic stability" for U.S. policy makers has been a code word for technological superiority militarily and huge defense budgets laced with the idea of American domination in most areas of the world. If this conclusion is not correct about American policy makers, then Bundy's book should leave the reader flabbergasted at the shortsightedness of leaders and their incapacity to mobilize ideas and directions that would yield an alternative to nuclear armament. Of course, other nations, notably the Soviet Union (as well as China, Great Britain, France, Israel, Pakistan, and possibly India and South Africa), now share the dubious honor of being nuclear noose pullers. But no national leaders (including, I may add, scientists and technologists) bear the responsibility for humankind's present situation as much as our own. This painful fact has been made more obvious with Gorbachev's attempts to loosen that noose even as the Bush administration seeks to find advantage in the stale policies that see nuclear weapons as threat, deterrent, or the conspicuous waste described as weapons modernization.

As an establishment regular, Bundy believes that there is no choice but to ride the whirlwind of nuclearism and military intervention. Lurking behind these judgments is the theological gospel according to Reinhold Niebuhr (not, unfortunately, Dietrich Bonhoeffer, who would have been more instructive for statesmen)—namely, that we live in an immoral world that offers the statesman no option but to choose evil, albeit a lesser one.

The Niebuhrian justification was the principal Cold War ideology that allowed government officials to undertake activities for reasons of state that in fact could never be approved on moral or legal grounds. That justification made sonsofbitchs of us all as we piled on more nuclear weapons and missiles of all shapes and sizes all the while devising genocidal or cataclysmic nuclear strategies.

Although Bundy expresses some hope, his fundamentally tragic view is one that asserts that human possibility for the best or the better, if it exists at all, is exceedingly limited. With this attitude, the policy maker is relieved of the responsibility of finding and acting on those legal, political, and moral alternatives that renounce the framework that dictates an evil course and builds toward a common good. Bundy's Niebuhrian view in practice means that the actions that are taken are those that risk the least for the individual statesman in terms of his class and place in society. Perhaps unconsciously, the statesman-policy maker lays off the risk on the nation without the people understanding this sleight of hand. What is worse is that, like priests of old, the policy makers trained in the Cold War do not understand how, as part of a caste, they have become the problem.

When, at Reykjavik, Reagan and Gorbachev seemed prepared to sign an agreement in principle about getting rid of nuclear weapons and setting up the means of pursuing that goal, the establishment's nuclear priesthood, which has provided the doctrine and continuity as the national security state's general staff, savaged both leaders for their unworkable utopianism. Here was a case in which the nuclear reality could have been shifted, but the nuclear priests of the establishment (among others, Kissinger, Scowcroft, Schlesinger, Nunn, and even Hoffman) rallied around the continuation of the mindless arms race. They burlesqued the zero nuclear option because they feared that the whole structure of our national security system and their place in it would have to be transformed.

This structure and political/scientific culture belies Bundy's belief that nuclear weapons in practical terms are unimportant, for he doesn't adequately assess the culture, habits of mind, and institutions that have formed themselves as political power bases since the Second World War. Unfortunately, embedded in the national security culture is fear of renunciation, for it believes in the usability of nuclear weapons and their value as political threat. After all, what else is deterrence than, ultimately, a warrant for use? Nevertheless, for a moment at Reykjavik there was the possibility of nuclear abolition, but it did not even register on Bundy's intellectual radar screen. There is no mention of this event in Bundy's book, where disarmament is given similarly short shrift.

Disarmament and arms control (of which Bundy is a proponent) are not the same, although in the popular press they are often thought to be so. In the summer of 1955 an agreement between the West and East on disarmament, especially in Europe, appeared likely. But as a result of Dulles's distrust of the post-Stalin leadership and a misplaced belief in a scientific and technological fix that would make the United States "invulnerable," Dulles undercut the initiated agreements between the U.S. and Soviet negotiators. Parenthetically, the world has been held in thrall by a science and technology that promises fixes and cures through manipulation of nature. Congress is held hostage to the next fix and the next "modernizing" weapons gimmick. The military, weapons technologists, and defense corporations each egg the other ever-onward to more complex weaponry. There is only tangential discussion in Bundy's book about this phenomenon and the role of the weapons laboratories in *keeping* the arms race going. Of course, policy makers see scientists, as the phrase goes, as never on top but only on tap. This is especially true when scientists try to stop the weapons-making process.

Perhaps the most poignant case concerns Robert Oppenheimer, a preeminent nuclear priest who found himself expelled from the national security state he helped create. Oppenheimer was totally imbued with the philosophy of the "lesser evil." This helped him justify his role in making and using atomic weapons. However, by 1952 Oppenheimer was adamantly against the hydrogen bomb on the grounds that it was strategically unnecessarily and morally repugnant. Oppenheimer paid for his apostasy. He was pronounced a security risk by his political masters. Two others fared better during that period. Enrico Fermi and Isidore Rabi favored a moratorium on nuclear weapons development and hoped that the United States would offer to sign with the Soviet Union and others an agreement not to go forward with the testing and production of the H-bomb, a policy that Bundy would have prescribed had he been in the government at that time.

The American policy maker's neurosis—namely reading events in the world according to vacillating views of our impotence and omnipotence—assured that the Edward Teller–Adam Ulam hydrogen bomb would be made. A decade later when an agreement banning nuclear tests in the atmosphere was signed in 1963 it was too little and too late. It was the lesser of two evils, that is, between testing and not testing in the atmosphere, but the brutal fact was that nuclear testing underground increased by a factor of three, pressing the nuclear arms race to new heights. This was the price Presidents Kennedy and Johnson paid to the Joint Chiefs of Staff and certain members of the Senate to assure their support of the atmospheric nuclear test ban agreement. There were better alternatives at the time.

One such alternative not discussed by Bundy, for example, was offered by the Swedish government. Indeed, the Americans and the Soviets were very close in terms of the number of inspections that each side expected of the other for fulfilling a comprehensive testing agreement. Instead the Kennedy administration chose the course of least resistance, which did not interrupt the arms race. Such arms control agreements are doomed to fail from the get-go because they are piecemeal and assume a course correction in national security policy instead of an alternative direction that is continuous and sequential.

Politically, an "arms control" agreement invariably comes with the cost of military and defense contractor bribery. Witness the case of the hapless Jimmy Carter, who in order to get support for a SALT II agreement from conservative senators acquiesced in a needless 5 percent increase yearly beyond inflation in the defense budget. He still didn't get the agreement, betrayed as he was by the senators and Soviet intervention in Afghanistan. His failure added strength to the Paul Nitze–Eugene Rostow faction identified with the Committee on the Present Danger, a group Bundy rightly identifies as ideological hysterics. In any case, the arms race throughout the Cold War period seemed to operate on its own track, irrespective of political détente between the United States and the Soviet Union. As Marek Thee of the Norwegian Peace Research Institute has pointed out:

> [Even] in the relatively most promising period of detente, between 1971–1979, marked with the conclusion of the SALT accords, global military expenditures increased (in constant 1980 prices and exchange rates) by 133 thousand million US dollars, about the same amount as during the Cold War years of 1948–1955. In parallel, the number of nuclear warheads in the arsenals of the two superpowers grew between 1972–1980 from 10,409 to 18,931—a rise of 83% although megatonnage was reduced as missiles were made more accurate.[1]

There is an inevitability to the arms race that Professor Bundy accepts. Nevertheless, Bundy correctly points out the foolishness of the Star Wars position but offers nothing but controlled nuclear arming as an alternative. Perhaps this is understandable. "Owls," as arms controllers called themselves during the Reagan period, sought to fit themselves and their weaponry within a superpower imperial definition of national security that accepted the fundamental validity of past decisions made by authority.

In Bundy's version of the Cuban missile crisis, which he views on one level as a great success, the reader is left to believe that the option chosen was the most sensible. Bundy had favored the rejected option of limited bombing. Part of the reason that the conclusion of the event looked successful to the United States was that neither Kennedy nor Khrushchev ordered nuclear war, hardly a standard for diplomatic excellence. Bundy does not describe adequately either the astounding U.S. nuclear and conventional buildup that led up to the Cuban missile crisis or Operation Mongoose, the Kennedy administration program to destroy the Castro government.

American ships and planes were on the alert, armed and triggered with nuclear weapons. Tactical nuclear weapons—unbeknownst to Bundy (and the president?)—were placed in Guantanamo *during* the missile crisis. One wonders if such weapons are still present in Cuba. Given Bundy's theological predisposition he would tend to write off the Cuba question as "tragic." He chose not to see how the personal choices that were made by men in government, their fantastical notions of military buildup as threat, tit for tat escalation, and their decision to assassinate Castro by whatever means (which, as national security adviser, Bundy would have been aware of) served as the foundation for the Cuban missile crisis.

Establishment regulars like Bundy, who are plagued with a nagging Puritan conscience and sometimes flirt with uncommon ideas, are often at odds with their best instincts as well as the demands of logic in matters of public policy. When in power they are imperial dialecticians who believe that to have peace they must prepare for war and be engaged in low-level conflict. However, the genocidal war preparations in which Bundy acquiesced while in government were undertaken with his fingers crossed.

Professor Bundy leaves the impression that he is a closet nuclear pacifist who cannot bring himself to say so. He knows, as do the rest of us who have dealt with this grizzly business, that for deterrence purposes, no more than 100 to 200 nuclear weapons are needed to destroy the urban industrial land space of the Soviet Union. (We are thought to have 30,000, with the Soviets having 25,000 and the French, British, Chinese, and Israelis probably sharing another 5,000 to 6,000 weapons.) Even knowing of its exceedingly limited validity, Bundy continues to espouse the arms control/arms race game by stressing the importance of survivable missiles so that the United States could ride out a first-strike attack on its land-based missiles. By doing so, he avoids the obvious point that survivable missiles can also be used first. Other nations will invariably see all nuclear weapons and missiles as potential first-strike weapons. That is why de Gaulle said his nuclear weapons policy was aimed at *all* other nations including the United States, even though the Kennedy administration had helped the French in nuclear weapons development, a point the historian Bundy does not cover.

The question of whether nuclear weapons would be used by the United States in "defense" of other nations has been a central consideration of U.S. security policy ever since American leaders decided to open the nuclear umbrella and supposedly brought other nations under that umbrella. As Bundy points out, de Gaulle never believed that the United States would use such weapons in the defense of Europe. Bundy does not answer de Gaulle's concern directly, although he does suggest a no-first-use, long-pause position before these weapons be used in Europe. It is understandable that he should be skeptical about the first use of nuclear weapons, for war games that have been run since the late 1950s suggested that Europe would be in unrecoverable ruins in the case of such a war. One wishes Bundy had championed this position as a White House adviser during the Kennedy-Johnson period when the United States stuffed so many tactical nuclear weapons into West Europe.

A condition of nuclear ruination could obtain even without nuclear weapons on the European continent. It should be noted in passing that in Western and Eastern Europe nuclear reactor plants are quite exposed. A sustained non-nuclear attack on these plants would do enormous unrecoverable damage to the European continent. The NATO alliance, so dependent on mystification, never expected an attack from the Russians and nothing today suggests that it should. Yet, with no rhyme or reason, we have pumped thousands of nuclear weapons into Western Europe to join a force of 300,000 U.S. troops.

Contrary to Bundy's point of view, it is time for general disarmament and disengagement by the superpowers from Western and Eastern Europe. The public at large is bored with the Cold War, which is like an overpriced meal. We are finally beginning to learn what the real costs are as we suffer from a terrible case of war-making indigestion.

Bundy is more than aware that nuclear and military decisions have been founded on secrecy and deception. Our national security policy has been based on the faulty premise that those who make the decisions have special information and wisdom that necessitate evasion and lying to the public. The parallel ideology of "loyaltyism" destroyed the possibility of independent thought and action on nuclear issues inside or outside of the government. For example, in the era of the *Rosenberg* case and loyalty commissions, both plain citizens and high government officials who were not specially "licensed" to participate in the nuclear debate feared that they would be accorded enemy or criminal status if they pressed their dissent too hard or sought to violate the "need to know" doctrine of security.

Indeed, since the first days of the Manhattan Project those who held doubts about nuclear arming took considerable personal risks. Leo Szilard, for example, was prepared to risk his reputation to assure that atomic bombs would not fall on Japanese cities. His arguments fell on deaf ears in the halls of great power politics, where loyaltyism and secrecy merged with the principle of the lesser evil. Although Bundy would like to make the dropping of the A-bombs on Hiroshima and Nagasaki part of a lesser-evil argument because they were needed to end the war with Japan, the evidence does not support such a claim. The choice was between evil and a lesser good, to coin a phrase. Gar Alperovitz in *Atomic Diplomacy* and P.M.S. Blackett in *Fear War and the Bomb* is closer to the mark and Bundy is surprisingly obtuse and wrong in discussing the decision to bomb Hiroshima and Nagasaki. Government officials saw the use of the atomic bomb as a very powerful card that would render the United States omnipotent in international politics. In the context of its use on Hiroshima and Nagasaki (but not when he discusses it in relation to the British Maud Report of 1940, which kicked off the entire nuclear bomb enterprise), Bundy overlooks the fact that policy makers from the very beginning believed the bomb to be their genie for ultimate power. While Einstein and Szilard in 1939 saw nuclear weapons research as a deterrent against the possibility that the Nazis might make a bomb, U.S. military and policy makers never saw nuclear weapons as a deterrent. They saw nuclear weapons primarily as instruments to be used to dictate victory over others, either in war or Cold War.

Bundy does not adequately explore the fact that Soviet entrance into the war would have caused a quick collapse of the Japanese. Even the Japanese army generals would not have long sustained their zeal. It could hardly have been a secret to the Japanese that the Soviets were going to come into the Pacific war after the end of the war in Europe. (That was why the Japanese approached the Russians before their entrance in the war with questions around the terms of surrender.) Truman's views about the Soviets were well advertised, and it is hardly debatable to suggest that a primary reason for the use of nuclear weapons was to stop the Soviets from becoming a senior player in reshaping Asia after the war, even though before the Alamagordo nuclear test, the United States wanted the Russians in the war. And of course the Japanese hierarchy had no interest in having the Soviet Union run a piece of the Japanese empire, which was the likely outcome of war with the Soviets.

Thus, there was an interest in using the bomb on the Japanese as a means of making the Soviets more pliant. Indeed, this method of indirection was employed twenty years later during the war in Indochina, when bombings were used as "signals" to adversaries in Hanoi, Peking, and Moscow. Such schoolboy cleverness at "signaling" encouraged the "tragic" generation to make numerous wrong choices and disastrous moral judgments. One of these was the military intervention in Vietnam, which stemmed from a kind of hubris felt by the military and the militarized civilians after the "success" of the Cuban missile crisis.

Professor Bundy stresses the irrelevance of nuclear weapons to the real choices policy makers face in their everyday work, arguing that such power turns out to be useless in the solution of diplomatic problems, even in intimidating other nations, as both the Americans and the Soviets have found out on numerous occasions. Yet, as Bundy knows, leaders are emboldened to act in crazy ways when they think they have superior conventional and nuclear force. While Kennedy appeared to want to get out of Vietnam, the advisers who lived after him and the Joint Chiefs of Staff concluded that the Soviets would stay in their sphere of influence thus emboldening the American interventionists to believe they could act with conventional military impunity in Indochina without the Soviets actively engaging. This calculation was primarily correct, but for reasons of conceit, racism, and imperial blindness the calculations of the establishment regulars did not figure on Vietnamese capacities.

Except in the case of Israel, Bundy does not tell the reader which mortal dangers are so great that they would cause leaders, including himself, to use nuclear weapons. If it is specific danger to one's nation, what is that danger? If, as Bundy seems to believe, there should be a moral, political, and ethical fence around nuclear weapons, they should be proscribed by law. That law should apply to individuals in government who have mass murder as part of their strategy. One would think that with Bundy's beliefs a strong element of personal responsibility would surface around the question of planning nuclear war. But that does not seem to be the case.

When writing the history of this period, Professor Bundy leaves part of the record blank. His book thus is a bit like a Soviet encyclopedia. He discusses neither the attempts (insufficient by my standards, but nevertheless made) to press for general and complete disarmament nor the relationship of weapons of mass destruction, crimes against humanity, and aggressive war to the Nuremberg judgments. After all, there is no way, as he points out so convincingly, that nuclear targeting can avoid population centers. There is therefore no way that they can be used except against innocent populations, a war crime. And if in some miraculous way they could be used in a controlled first-strike attack, this would commit the attacker to an open-ended arms race and a form of preemptive and preventive war that also falls well within the genocidal and aggressive war framework laid down at the Nuremberg trials. Yet Bundy does not mention any of these considerations, nor the larger question of how or whether international law can or should be used as a means of moving humanity to a somewhat different sphere from that of global deterioration caused in part by Cold War, foolish use of resources, and puerile dreams of the perfect defense.

Bundy does not mention the fact that time and energy were spent by some members of two U.S. administrations in attempting to answer Khrushchev's proposal for general and complete disarmament, nor does he discuss the U.S. riposte. What is truly tragic is that this was another missed opportunity that would have changed the character of international relations. Ironically, had one side or the other just signed off on the other's plan, both would have been far more secure a generation later.

The McCloy-Zorin framework for general and complete disarmament, the American and Soviet treaty proposals, and the internal memoranda by President Kennedy arguing that general and complete disarmament was the only way out of the arms race were important historical events on which others in this and the next generation could build. But Bundy lets those choices for survival drop down the memory hole as if they never existed.

Instead of building on positive aspects raised in the past, Bundy presents us with the dubious proposition that the further we are in time from the 1945 use of nuclear weapons, the less likely humanity is to use them and therefore we really don't have to change direction. The problem with this claim is that it flies in the face of a more tangible institutional reality.

Bundy claims that nuclear weapons were at no time seriously contemplated by leaders. This claim can only be supported by championing the most narrow reading of what goes on in modern governments. Bundy's thesis does not adequately take into account the fears generated in other nations by such "planning" and by nuclear force sizes, although curiously, he mentions this concern as a reason for the arms race. Furthermore, his thesis is based on the idea that literally hundreds of thousands of people organizing, planning, developing, and then fashioning armed forces around nuclear weapons do not really count, that there is no institutional imperative for their use, and that all that counts is their actual use. Professor Bundy appears to believe that what goes on around nuclear weapons is masturbatory or symbolic, in the realm of the psychology of perception. As one might expect, he poohpoohs the nuclear weapons of others without being prepared to apply the same arguments to the United States: namely, that other nations use their nuclear weapons only as show and as a way to be taken seriously in the world, but that in reality their weapons have no diplomatic or political effect on others and can therefore be dismantled unilaterally.

Bundy's assumption is that a president in his lonely splendor is and should be the prime decision maker in matters nuclear and military. But his own examples, murky as the situations were, suggest that U.S. presidents believed that they gave orders to do certain things in the nuclear field to no avail, as nothing happened in response. I have in mind the removal of U.S. missiles from Turkey, which Kennedy thought he had requested. But the missiles were not removed and while Bundy may think Kennedy didn't ask for their removal, that does not appear to have been either of the Kennedy brothers' understanding of what happened.

Bundy's understanding of presidential history and of the questions of command and control are more in keeping with Tolstoy's Napoleon than with his Kutuzov. The latter knew that a soldier running the wrong way in a battle can set off a panic and that all the commands of a great leader are reduced to nothing in the face of decisions made by others who may be far lowlier in station and less exulted in outlook. Bundy assumes that the president of the United States has the decision-making power and wisdom to destroy the world on his say-so; indeed, this is what enables us to think we have set up a rational control system. One would have to know more about a president's capacity and the capacity of the bureaucracy to stop a president's go orders. Bundy implies that Nixon's secretary of defense and the Joint Chiefs took away Nixon's nuclear powers during Watergate—was this a military coup against Nixon? This example notwithstanding, the president's war-making power (not authority) is total, given the means at his disposal.

There is, of course, something quite crazy when a political system turns over to one person the power to destroy the world in a few minutes. Unfortunately, there is nothing in Bundy's more than 600-page account that would lead anyone to think there is anything wrong with this centralization of power, which holds the American people and other nationals hostage. Surely this mode of statecraft has no roots in the American constitution or in any social contract theory that emerges from the Anglo-Saxon tradition. Yet Bundy does not evince any awareness of the crisis in democratic political systems brought about by nuclear weapons. Obviously, I am not suggesting that decisions on when to use nuclear weapons be left to the military, but I am saying that there is a profound contradiction between the democratic right to participate, deliberate, and choose on the part of the citizenry and the right of a president to commit suicide for the world.

There is another facet of nuclear weapons policy noteworthy in Bundy's book by its omission. Nations that have acquired nuclear weapons suppress the actual human and material costs of the nuclear weapons industry. They are more comfortable with the view first intimated by those who prepared the Maud Report in 1940 that "whoever possessed such a plant would be able to dictate terms to the rest of the world." For too long the costs of nuclear strategy were hidden from the citizenry.

One would have thought that Bundy would have discussed the relationship of the bomb and nuclear strategy to nuclear military waste. The question's omission creates the unstated assumption that the hundreds of billions of dollars in cleanup we now face as a result of "deterrence" and our nuclear strategy are a trivial concern. While the question is one that was not considered publicly until 1988, the fact is that the government has been aware of this terrible problem for years.

There is, of course, a way that one of Bundy's policy recommendations could have helped to open the door to this question: the matter of the importance of openness and truth. Had there been public debate and limits on secrecy, it is less likely that today's and future generations would be faced with the problem of nuclear military waste. And there would have been a more material aspect to the theory of "deterrence." Instead deterrence retained an airy meaning intended as a "rational passive threat" designed to induce fear in other governments.

There are other lacunae in Bundy's book. Some of our more celebrated "nuclear thinkers" gained their early reputations developing crackpot concepts of limited nuclear war. Bundy does not mention the human effects of testing their ideas: for example, the high cancer rates among soldiers who were used as nuclear cannon fodder to test harebrained schemes of tactical nuclear war. Bundy does show disdain for his former colleagues at Harvard, Kissinger, Brzezinski, and by implication, Sam Huntington—all former high-ranking members of the National Security Council—for their attempts to make nuclear weapons a usable instrument in war. Brzezinski and Huntington developed so-called decapitation strategies that meant destroying the leadership and command centers of the Soviet Union. It was then presumed that the Soviet Union would dissolve into separate nations. (Ironically, one of Gorbachev's troubles concerns national dissolution; for the rest of the world the question is what would it mean if nuclear weapons fall into warring armies in the Soviet Union or national independence-minded nations that seceded from the Soviet Union?) Bundy sees his former Harvard colleagues and Rand Corporation theorists as playful bright children who are unable to tear themselves away from destructive games of nuclearism and nuclear strategy. Of course, he too has been caught in that game.

Bundy believes that at this stage in the history of nuclearism no "responsible" American leader would risk the destruction of our cities, no matter how few. Nevertheless, during the Cold War presidents and their staffs were not averse to playing around with such ideas. During the Berlin crisis of 1961, President Kennedy ordered a top secret first-strike study, which was conducted by the Defense Department and several close advisers. He learned that a successful first-strike attack would still have meant that several millions of Americans would be killed. Would a future American president risk American cities, and even if not, how do the people stop such a catastrophic series of events except by laws making such studies illegal when public funds are used?

What becomes increasingly clear through the nuclear age is that the real deterrent to the first use of nuclear weapons by the United States is the American people. This political fact was understood by Nixon, who, according to Bundy, may have been stopped from using nuclear weapons by "preemptive" popular demonstrations. Without those demonstrations, nuclear weapons might have been introduced to win the Vietnam War. This is an important insight that should not be lost to any future peace movement. Just as street demonstrations in Eastern Europe brought change there, it is likely that the more than one million people who protested in New York in 1982 Reagan's nuclear policies and military buildup pushed him to return to the negotiating table with the Russians.

Like the nuclear age itself, each section of Bundy's book poses enormous issues of morality, scholarship, and political action. But finally, these issues come down to two questions for the reader and citizen. The first is what is the responsibility of the government official with regard to nuclear weapons and the arms race? The second is what is the responsibility of the historian in writing about these matters when he or she knows that underneath the nuclear weapons question is a combination of fear, threat, and the systematic preparation of genocide?

These two questions are interrelated, especially for those who live their lives as scholars and public officials. Bundy rightly places great emphasis on truth as the antidote to unclarity and misinformation. But if this point is to be taken seriously, it will be necessary to rid ourselves of the secrecy system surrounding nuclear weapons, surveillance, and all those "infrastructural" activities that have created the national security state. It means that policy makers will be required to reexamine the military technological imperative, which assumes a most peculiar belief, namely that we trust nuclear weapons and not people, even though the arms race within and between nations is an astonishing exercise in human trust, one that goes well beyond prudence. To adjust to the post–Cold War age, government officials will have to start without the faulty ideological and theological baggage of the last two generations. They will have to encourage ideas and alternatives that will flow at every level of society in order to change the character of the international security system.

There is a personal aspect to these matters for government officials and statesmen. They need to be clear on renunciation, that is, what they won't do under any circumstances because to take such action would be nothing less than a crime against one's own nation and humanity generally. The politician, scientist, and government official's responsibility is to make such statements publicly and to press for self-denying legislation. Such clarity would have helped the nuclear freeze movement counter those experts and politicians who trapped that movement into the game of seeking a mutually verifiable agreement when the United States was making nuclear weapons the way sausage makers make baloney. The marshalling of facts and past events requires that all of us consider seriously those forces that attempted alternative directions that are either forgotten or thrown onto the ashheap of history. Part of the historian's role is to assure a future for humanity. This requires that she or he knows what is fatal in the national security structure; that is, what does not allow for the best policies to emerge, what perpetuates nuclearism, imperial behavior, and the war system.

If these questions are not posed by historians at this stage in the twentieth century, then their histories will condemn us to repeat the errors of the past. That is what I fear Bundy's book does. His project, to get the establishment paladins to shift away from a reliance on nuclear weapons, does not point us to a way out of the war system. Instead, Bundy asserts the need for the United States to continue in the war and defense system cycle with conventional forces and alliances. But these elements of the war system feed each other and preserve a place for nuclearism.

Without recognizing that a shift in world consciousness is taking place—a political fact that both Gorbachev and the American Catholic bishops seem to understand—our national leaders remain unwilling to pass up the potential of untying the knot of the nuclear noose. The paladins will continue to think that nuclear weapons deter and threaten, that they are cheaper than ground troops, and therefore that they should retain their place as the central element in our defense capability. They will champion new attempts at technological modernization of nonnuclear killing devices and will claim that these ideas guarantee world stability. They will conduct arms control negotiations as a means of keeping demonstrators off the streets and showing that, like the players of the Bead Game in Hermann Hesse's *Magister Ludi*, they are the keepers of stability and peace. And they will claim that nuclear weapons are an important element of stability in an increasingly unstable world plagued by arming, little wars, and superpower hubris.

Bundy and his friends will have to use their considerable gifts and resources to find ways out of a war system to which they so generously contributed if they are to leave a legacy that is more than a series of little good works.

Note

1. Policy paper prepared by Marek Thee, senior research analyst (retired) of the Norwegian Peace Institute and former Polish ambassador (1988).

5

From National Security State to Democracy

A fundamental question about democracy is whether it is able to organize and keep in place large-scale associations that not only have their own specific interests but are able to present and press alternatives for what the shape of the nation should be in order to serve and create a common good. Democracy, as the means of modern participation and deliberation, is most profoundly meaningful where people possess not individual and privacy rights against the society and the state but participatory rights as citizens within the economy and the political structure, and where these rights include the power of deliberation and implementation. Democracy therefore eschews those activities and functions of state power that inhibit public deliberation and discourse.

The national security state has different purposes. The national security state prizes secrecy, not openness. And it accepts the framework of imperial manipulation. As a general matter the guardians of modern states are interested in "guiding," educating, or containing the participation of civil society so that it does not "get out of hand." The American national security state operated with little criticism throughout the Cold War. There was passive acceptance of its purposes on the part of the American citizenry, who believed, in general, in an Enemy Other that appeared to be an adversary worthy of our collective anger (though we were not engaged in any large-scale war). The business leaders of the nation were prepared to accept the costs of the national security state and its usefulness in keeping peace at home and stimulating business abroad.

In 1990, none of these so-called objective conditions for the continuation of the national security state exist. Both in Europe (including the Soviet Union) and the United States, the citizenry at large see no reason for the continuation of the national security apparatus that emerged since World War II. At best there is indifference to this state apparatus. In the United States, the vision of the Soviets as the Enemy Other has dissolved, the ostensible reason for NATO no longer exists, and the shape of the next enemy will change constantly. In the short run the drug problem may be used by American leaders as a way to "legitimize" U.S. intervention as American military forces seek to "interdict" and use the drug issue as a rationale for policing other nations. Or "instability" in Eastern Europe may be used to justify the continuation of NATO. Or American policy makers will say that the United States must keep large forces around the world to control local conflicts, stop aggression, and control oil in the Middle East, or it must inhibit the rise of Europe as an independent military power with Germany as the fulcrum against other nations, especially the nonwhite Third World and Japan. Or American policy makers will say, as American generals and planners already do, that Japan must be stopped economically and militarily. But these rationales for the continuation of the national security state will be expensive and self-defeating for they will cause, not cure, the ills that we must address as an American civilization that is part of an emerging world civilization.

The American business community, especially that part concerned with export and international trade, will come to see the national security state as a hindrance to the sale of modern communications and technology. We already have the cultural and technological seeds for an entirely different international system that no longer relies on military forces and hardware, with an understanding that cooperation, not competition, is the fundamental answer to developing a peaceful economic and political world order.

The question is whether there is enough popular power within the American body politic to dismantle the national security state. Part of the answer to this question relates to whether elites and movements accept nuclear weapons as a given of all future life and the security of Americans. If these weapons are seen as essential to the society—either to national manhood or to international relations—then it is unlikely that we will be able to rid ourselves of the national security state, for nuclear weapons demand a particular social system that is undemocratic, secretive, and elitist. Democracy cannot emerge from modern weaponry. Standing armed forces are incompatible with the existence of a republic as well; this is a principle long understood in American thought but lost during the Cold War to dreams of Pax Americana.

What is clear as the Iron Curtain rises is how weak the Soviets have been, how the Cold War could have ended long ago, and how much we need an international system that does not rest on military force or even on global corporations. What should also be clear is that democracy does not rest on the premises devised during the Cold War to operate and generate military conflict and control, whether for the United States or for other nations. There is another tradition in American political thought and practice, one that builds on a true internationalism and seeks democracy. Such ideas should now move to center stage. This essay is meant to formulate a national security policy that is linked to our new situation and that begins from democratic purposes.

The essay was presented as a lecture on national security and foreign policy at Kenyon College in 1985. It was revised (lightly), given the world historical transformations of the late 1980s. ☐ ☐

Since the Great Depression, a fierce struggle has been waged over the nature of American government and the character of American society. This struggle took on more elaborate and complex dimensions as a result of the Second World War and the powerful, seductive impulse of worldwide American responsibility.

Without necessarily knowing it, protagonists for power in the United States struggle around three forms of government. The first group assumes that the United States is a republic. Its proponents take literally the Constitution, which guarantees the United States a republican form of government; that is, a government that is representational if not representative, limited, and in practice responsible to the most prudent and well-born among us. Its leading proponent after the Second World War was Senator Robert Taft of Ohio. He believed in a limited defense budget. Indeed, he sought to convince President Eisenhower at the beginning of Eisenhower's first term in 1953 that the United States defense budget should be restored to a pre–World War II level. In post–World War II terms this would have translated into a yearly defense budget of some $10 billion. Taft sought limited involvement in alliances and feared the activism of Dean Acheson. For example, he thought NATO derogated from the United Nations and that it would lead to an endless arms race or worse. He argued that the fundamental conception of the United Nations was to guard against the reassertion of blocs and alliances whose participants might think of them as defensive but whose antagonists would find them threatening, and therefore would generate counter-response. Senator Taft feared that military and foreign expansion would defeat the republic, bring about a strong state, and result in noncompetitive, state-administered markets. As we shall see, Taft also feared the United Nations and its idealistic, democratic, and decolonizing aspirations.

The second theory of the modern American state is that of democracy. This notion, perhaps best reflected in the perspectives of such liberals as Justice William O. Douglas, hoped for greater participation of all people within the United States (inclusivity) and a limited unilateral U.S. military role in the world, a buildup of the United Nations as an instrument for the solution of disputes and the arising of economic and social standards, and a system of human rights guarantees domestically and abroad within the context of a rational international legal framework. According to this view, the question of what democracy is in the United States was answered through efforts against slavery, for voting entitlements, and for protection for labor.

The social struggles of the 1960s were an attempt to democratize the United States, bringing people into the public space, as it were, and putting forward new arguments and considerations for what a democracy was to be. The struggles in the 1960s for a reconstitution of authority and participation were carried on in our educational and social institutions and covered such issues as civil rights, equality of opportunity, even equality, and the transformation of previous forms of domination (white over nonwhite, men over women, humanity over nature). The assumption in economic terms was that new conditions had to emerge if auto workers, Mississippi tenant farmers, and oil barons were to be citizens of the same nation. The democratic view also found voice in confronting the undeclared war in Vietnam. In the Vietnam case, the structural democrats and structural republicans joined together—for example, Senator J. William Fulbright and other senators who were not part of the movements of the 1960s but were committed to a republican form of government. They believed that wars without purpose or interest would of necessity derogate from congressional and constitutional authority. Lyndon Johnson was caught, on the other hand, between his populist democratic tendencies and the "requirements" of maintaining empire, contradictions in the modern age.

The two conceptions, the democratic and the republican (using those words in their structural rather than political party sense), are used by a third form, the national security state. It is this form that in fact is the most expansionist of our period. Its links to military technology, nationalism, conflicts, and wars for interest or mystification have overwhelmed the two other forms because their adherents have accepted the national security and foreign policy assumptions of the national security state. This state formation, while it appeared to help such democratic proponents as Johnson and Hubert Humphrey, in fact destroyed them and their dreams.

The national security state emerged at the end of the Second World War. Of course, throughout much of its history the United States indulged in far-flung assertions of military intervention for rectitude and interest: "*From the halls of Montezuma to the shores of Tripoli*" and China, the United States had already made its might felt. But in 1947 it was apparent that the United States needed a state structure to take over responsibilities from empires that disappeared as a result of World War II. It was taken for granted by our leaders that the United States would always be involved in conflict; that it had worldwide responsibilities; that it needed a large standing force for that purpose; that it needed secrecy to protect its policies and weaponry; that it needed weapons of mass annihilation as instruments of threat and "deterrence"; that henceforth the struggles of the United States would be continuous, involving large-scale intelligence operations, covert activities, military assistance, government planning of the industrial sector where it touched upon defense questions, and the guiding of the universities and laboratories toward a continuous state of readiness for war. Forswearing George Washington's advice that the United States should have no permanent hostile enemies, United States leaders concluded that the country was in a battle not with evil leaders but with evil itself, namely, communism, and even if it were not involved in that Manichaean struggle, it continued to have military responsibilities in areas of the world deemed unstable. In this framework, American national security leaders learned to be relatively prudent within certain clearly defined objectives. The fundamental goals of *Number-Oneism*, selective anti-communism, and the use of force to guarantee the flow of markets and resources, together with the belief that American security rested on nuclear weapons and a "forward defense" system, were not seriously challenged until the palpable failure of the Vietnam War. However, the imperial Cold War ideology continues as the dominant strand of our public policy experience; indeed, the fundamental goals of Number-Oneism and the use of force to guarantee markets and resources were never challenged but were made part of our way of life.

That both political parties were captured by the national security state while continuing to sing the tunes of republicanism and democracy is itself a fascinating story. Suffice it to say here that it has been over a generation since any substantial number of members of either the Senate or the House have been willing to ask what effects the defense budget has on other priorities, or what effects secret agencies such as the National Security Agency—an agency that spends well over $10 billion a year—have on the character of the republican or democratic form, given the fact that the NSA has no public charter, nor is one contemplated that is public and legal.

The problems now faced by the American people as a result of forty years of mistaken international policies emanating from the center, the right, and the left (which arouses itself only in extreme crises) can no longer be overlooked in the light of changes in the Soviet Union, the United States, Eastern Europe and remilitarization "caused" by Iraq. One can only work for some new definition of sanity and prudence emerging from the center, the libertarian right, and the left that will enable the United States to move beyond what seems to be a mindless strut to colossal misjudgments that could still lead to a general war or to depleting little ones caused by ethnic rivalries, virulent nationalism, and the clash of civilizations.

Until now, there has been enough material "fat" to celebrate foolish events as victories and to manage public opinion in such a way that the American people salute myths and images rather than understand reality. If we continue to praise blunders and the assumptions that led to those blunders, we may be sure that the United States will decline precipitously as a nation and will miss the chance of building a very great American civilization. We will also miss the chance of helping world civilization pull itself away from the precipice of disaster. (I might add at this point that while wars go on all over the world, the arms race is predominantly a white-race phenomenon, with well over 70 percent of the arms expenditures spent by predominantly white nations.) We will also miss the chance to create a democracy whose aim is the common good.

Obviously, creating such a democracy is not an autarkic affair without relevance or relationship to the rest of the world. Consequently, we are required to generate a foreign and national security policy based on principles that are not unknown in international affairs, but surely are not central to the international politics as presently pursued by the United States. The foreign policy that I describe may be thought of as a triad of themes that resonate with one another.

The first theme of the triad is that there must be more action by citizens and the people in international and national security affairs. Since people are the subject actors of modern history, they must be more than the objects of nations or the nuclear hostages of leaders. I start from the democratic assumption that each citizen is entitled to the same quality and amount of defense. Thus, the Mississippi tenant farmer, the Rockefeller or Scaife, the Kansas schoolteacher, the Detroit auto worker, and the Los Angeles hippie are all entitled to the same amount of protection. If the rich or their holdings are given more defense or a particular group is overrepresented in the decision about what should be defended, then the common defense and national security that is embraced retains an elitist and skewed bias.

The second theme of the triad is that a strong United Nations is a necessary and central organizational invention that should not be degraded by alliances or by groups of nations that scoff at an international social, economic, and legal order. A revitalized United Nations can serve as the authorizer of international action and as the way to limit dangerous actions of nations.

As the third theme, the United States must operate out of a fundamental understanding of itself. It must not assert unbridgeable adversarial status toward any other nation and be "threat-oriented" in its analysis of world affairs. It must recall the sage advice of George Washington and conduct its day-to-day relations without passionate attachment to any specific alliance or cabal. Yet American leaders must have the vision that a world civilization with pluralist cultures can and must come into being.

Such themes may appear irrelevant in a world of nation-states where, at best, sovereigns or governments define their responsibility to their own people, not to others; where the currency of political leadership is power and force; where nations are bedeviled by modern weapons and alliances that have long since lost their relevance. But policies predicated on power and force as well as global alliance divisions are woefully incomplete. Each nation is increasingly dependent on every other nation in order to satisfy its needs. (The more developed a nation is, the more dependent it is on other nations.) Every nation is hostage to the decisions of other nations' military and political leaders. Every part of the globe is a microphone and television relay station for another culture. Transportation, communications, and technological and aesthetic creations fill the world's spaces. In other words, material and spiritual conditions drive every nation and ideology to be part of the same world historical process. Each person and nation seeks subject-actor status, not to be determined as objects of others but as subjects with others. This is why a truly international framework must be celebrated rather than savaged, for it speaks to this need by including all the world's people; why hostile military alliances have only pathological relevance; and why exhausted ideologies are laughed at, East and West.

It has taken close to five centuries for the world to catch up with the insights of Grotius, namely, that the basic premise of modern international relations and law must be predicated on the bonds of community and natural law. The law of the universal community of humankind was meant to govern the actions of states. But this law has to be created and forged through the crucible of pluralist ideologies and cultures.

The technological facts of the twentieth century, the horrors of world war as well as regional war, and the genocidal actions of governments stricken with misguided purpose or even governments singlemindedly committed to just causes mandate the populace to demand that governments apply universal principles of equity and caring in international relations. Such an application is not as Pollyannish as one might think. Humane ideas have a chance in practical terms if the United Nations and its resolutions are given policy and legal priority in the internal affairs of nations so that they are taken seriously and become the basis of actions in day-to-day activities. Without sacrificing any of its "vital interests" (which body in our nation should decide the meaning of this mystical phrase?), there is no reason why the

United States cannot adopt a foreign policy that accepts most United Nations resolutions as American policy and accordingly accepts liberation movements and proposes and accepts plans for world economic development, for disarmament, and against apartheid. Indeed, it should not take too much to show that embedded in these concerns are the vital interests of most Americans. And they can be staked out as a system of world law with other states.

It can be argued with justification that there is a rather flimsy character to United Nations resolutions and that they are less than useful as a basis for world law, as for example in the case of the anti-Zionist resolutions. Some would say that they carry almost no operational significance and are merely a rhetorical flourish behind which *realpolitik* functions. It is painfully true that the sort of internationalism that dominated many of the United Nations' activities since World War II was little more than a mask for partying and spying. But this reality can be shifted.

International rules can legitimate the domestic behavior of nations in confronting injustice in their own land. Basic international treaties, the human rights covenants, and many of the United Nations resolutions can give sustenance to groups seeking to secure their rights. In the United States, actions by pressure groups supporting disarmament and world economic development would find backing from United Nations statements, resolutions, and rules internalized into American law. For his own reasons President Carter continued this legitimating process by signing the Covenants on Economic and Social Rights in February 1977 and sending them to the Senate for ratification. Liberals and the left in the United States were unaware of the profound effects these covenants could have had on American politics had the Senate ratified them.

In the physical sciences it is thought that two seemingly opposite explanations or methods may have the same relevance or power in bringing about understanding and scientific progress. In this regard the principle of nonintervention, or what George Washington called "no passionate attachments," is a noncontradictory and de facto complementary road to a new international order of peace and equity. If those directly concerned with foreign policy accept the limits of the nation-state, then its practitioners must be prepared to forswear certain types of behavior as violative of international decency and the principles of internal equity and stability within the United States. The three themes

I have mentioned reject the notion that foreign policy is a thin sheath to mask the nuclear sword or an instrument that saves the United States the trouble of coming to grips with its internal contradictions, its consuming habits, or its unwillingness to defend itself directly against attack except through nuclear weapons.

A Proposal and a Policy

In the last twenty-five years certain proposals for comprehensive disarmament have been put forward within the Arms Control and Disarmament Agency and by members of the Kennedy White House staff, myself included. The most ingenious proposal was advanced by Louis Sohn, in which disarmament by the United States and the Soviet Union was to proceed in each nation by geographic zones. Each nation would inspect only the particular zone under consideration. This proposal continues to have merit, with some variations. Any proposal of a comprehensive sort must combine elements of graduated reciprocal reduction of weapons and practices that are most threatening to adversaries. Thus, to fulfill this condition, in the first stage of an agreement and preliminary to any inspection, the two superpowers would remove weapons from the respective arsenals that they intended to junk.

Each nation would perform such disarmament independently, except that the right of inspections by one's respective nations would be granted and guaranteed through the United Nations, unless the host nation prefers outside inspection either from the United Nations or an agreed-upon third party. During this preliminary stage, joint arrangements would be made so that inspection techniques and collateral forms of inspection through technical means would be operated as part of an international satellite system controlled through the United Nations. Superpowers would be likely to junk particular weapons because they are thought to be outmoded, because of pressure from their own people from economic, legal, or moral reasons, or because a new form of security must be found.

These three reasons would operate within the United States. The American military would be challenged to formulate a non-mass-destruction defense system that is in direct defense of the United States. It would reject the use and buildup of weapons of mass destruction under the Nuremberg and United Nations charter principles because they violate the laws of war.

Presently, the military and technological development of modern statecraft does not take into account the legal nature of the weaponry designed and produced. But nations should, and enough law has been forged through the crucible of war and international politics to make such statements more than the optimistic pretensions of utopians. Thus, under the language of the charter of Nuremberg, strategies such as counterforce, or so-called second-strike deterrent strategies aimed at population centers, could be classified either as crimes against humanity or as crimes against peace. Individuals and groups that involve themselves in the planning, production, and implementation of such strategies would be in danger of being categorized as criminals. Implementation of the proposed U.N. Charter of Security (starting with a freeze on arms research and arms—a holiday from armaments building) as well as arms control and disarmament negotiations must be conducted in the framework of the Nuremberg charter and with the understanding that what is being discussed is not merely strategy and quantitative or qualitative comparison of arms, but crime masquerading as policy or defense.

As crucial as the question of what is a legal and moral national defense is the question of what is to be defended, in what manner, and by whom. Less than one-third of the defense budget can be thought to relate to the defense of the United States. The rest of the budget may be assigned, as Earl Ravenal has pointed out, to the defense of Europe, Asia, and Latin America.[1] The U.S. defense and hardware system is linked conceptually to our alliance system, which is supposedly the seamless, circular web of defense for the "free world." In this seamless web one segment justifies another segment. In practical terms this means that the national security bureaucracy obtains bases and alliances for the defense of our weapons and surveillance systems, which are in turn needed for the defense of our bases and alliances. The cost of this mode of defense in FY 1988 was $295 billion, of which $125 billion could be pegged for United States defense. If the United States changed its nationalist strategy to one of world security, it would be in a position to reduce its defense budget by one-half in the very earliest stages of the new security process. Indeed, it would be able to devote far more resources to civilian reconstruction than could the Soviet Union, just because the Soviet Union is landlocked and fears invasion through Siberia and Europe.

In the United States a revised national defense structure should be erected on four participatory mechanisms, the conclusion of an international security arrangement notwithstanding: (a) a participatory tax system in which each taxpayer within limits would "vote" his or her preference according to the function of the government; (b) a defense banking system in which regions of the United States would be allocated weaponry and armed forces for their defense on the basis of regional defense plans but would remain under centralized control; (c) an agreement between state governors and regional planners that would be reviewed on a regular basis as to the needs and costs of defense: these arrangements would be carried out as a corollary to international negotiations to end the arms race, and with the understanding that all local and national defense activities would be performed in the context of international security and disarmament agreements once such agreements are signed; and (d) passage of a constitutional amendment that no American government can surrender to another nation that invades the United States, and that any government that does so is traitorous.

It is of some importance to spell out this last point. A constitutional amendment on the common defense would make it clear that no other nation could occupy the United States. In practical terms this amendment would be understood as part of a solemn declaration of continuous guerrilla war against invading forces, occupiers, and collaborators. Such a provision should be incorporated into international agreements—for example, the suggested international security agreement and the United Nations charter itself.

A similar provision meant to secure the Yugoslavian people from any invader or collaborator is found in the Yugoslavian Constitution. If such a provision were enacted into American law and became the new pledge of allegiance in the schools, Americans would discover that they had significant and direct responsibility to resist invasion or collaboration with enemies if war occurred on United States soil. It would help us resist the antiseptic system of believing that wars can be fought on the soil of other nations exclusively.

Although the strategy I suggest is a defensive one, it is totally unyielding in nature. Its effectiveness is greatest in the context of an international security arrangement where the assumption of international politics switches from aggressive action in military affairs to a clearly defined strategy of self-defense. It specially means that no nation can be a world military power except in the context of internationally accepted security arrangements.

When we consider the physical security of the society and the forward strategy the United States has pursued, we should recognize an astonishing fact: the more funds that are spent on the military, the less secure Americans become as a nation. And correlatively, the more the United States participates in the arms race, or leads it, the more other nations find it necessary to do the same, or we become their mercenaries.

The great power arms race has had a profound exemplary effect on the Third World, where there is an 18 to 30 percent yearly increase in armaments capability. The implications of such arming are an increase in the ferocity of border wars which are economically exhausting causing further war and invasion, the militarization of neighboring countries, and the interlocking of the military elites in small countries to the military and technological elites of large powers. They operate according to obedience and hierarchy—for example, in the communist countries where party organizations, or in the Catholic nations of Latin America where the church had, until Vatican I, laid out principles that secure obedience and resist reform. The modern geopolitical result is that armed forces and states are involved in strategies for minerals, goods, and so on that supposedly define each nation's place in the international pecking order. This mode of international politics sees the struggle for power as continuous, whether fought by means of war or of threat. Military actions are not considered value questions that have profound ethical consequences. But neither antagonist feels secure. The present American security system downplays the need for a democratically oriented armed force, and therefore armed forces are inherently less useful than we think—as Vietnam showed.

The history of twentieth-century armed struggle suggests that to be successful, armed forces have to be relatively democratic and participatory, reflecting a cooperative spirit and the group feeling of having been wronged. As Western powers have learned, the technology that combatants employ is secondary in importance to the spiritually democratic practice that they follow daily.

By transforming the emphasis of American war making from weapons technology to our common defense, I mean to recognize the entitlement of the armed forces in the context of international legal standards. The military's task becomes more prudent and less pathological. It is to provide protection for the land, people, and institutions within the United States as it passes through major social changes. The military's economic entitlement is decent living conditions, civil liberties, and pay for the nonofficer class at the level of skilled workers with participatory rights. Consequently, a democratic reconstruction in defense will mean the extension of labor unions to include the armed forces, necessitating a revision of the Thurmond law, which stops the labor movement from organizing a union in the armed forces. As part of their negotiated labor position, members of the armed services would underscore their allegiance to the judgments at Nuremberg, their refusal to use nuclear weapons (which open officers and armed forces personnel to charges of genocide and war crimes under international law and the 1977 Geneva protocols, initiated by the United States and 115 other nations), their commitment to the constitutional procedures necessary before armed conflict can be undertaken, and their support of a no-surrender pledge.

A modern democracy requires its military and defense organizations to formulate plans for the actual defense of the United States. These plans would have to be consistent with principles of personal courage and respect for noncombatants, which means refusal to resort to weapons of mass murder, and acceptance of a planning process with the goal of accepting and implementing a world system of security. The planning process should be initiated in study groups on all levels of the national security bureaucracy and in the war and defense colleges. Attempts at consciousness raising in the military and national security groups will begin the double process of transforming and rebuilding so that civilization can step away from the precipice of militarism and nuclear war. The choices are now more stark than ever: they are counterforce, deterrence, and a forward-base strategy that commits the United States to an ever costly world imperial role ($400 billion in FY 1991 for national security).

The national security budget figures are especially upsetting when we realize that present military preparations have little or nothing to do with protecting or directly defending American society. Whereas the Reagan administration committed itself to a forward-offense position in which engagement and military intervention were seen as crucial to American interests, a defense system that seeks to reflect the common good calls for an entirely different set of assumptions. The doctrines of launch on warning, preemptive first strike, and unilateral military intervention must move to the scrapheap of history.

General Principles for Security

What, then, are the general principles that should undergird the foreign policy of the United States, especially as it enters its own rejuvenation? Perhaps these principles could bind bureaucracies, diplomats, and politicians in the period of reconstruction.

1. The policy of noninterference in states or symmetric interference in their affairs is the most difficult to achieve during a period of unequal access to fast communications and technology as well as imperial ambition, and human rights pretension, and especially given the character of American and Russian foreign policy since 1945. Since 1948 the principle of noninterference has been a relatively important one that has determined limits and defined the way in which sovereign states intended to deal with each other. It starts from the assumption of peaceful coexistence and cooperation of sovereign states. The U.N. Charter offers protection for individual and group human rights, to be achieved through the peaceful processes of international law. There can be no intervention in the territory of another state by the United Nations or any other state except when the offending state is the aggressor, threatens the use of force, or has violated its obligations under the charter. Collective action may occur only with the affirmative vote and authority of the Security Council. Under the charter, military actions, boycotts, and so on can be undertaken by a nation only when such actions are supported by the Security Council or when the General Assembly has sanctioned their use, and they must be done for obviously accepted and humane practices. Unless the world goes utterly mad, United Nations collective responsibility will not champion apartheid or genocide. But even in the most seemingly noble cases, the United States must preserve its option not to join a peace-keeping force. Great powers should be the last to intervene militarily if at all, in any situation, even when the action is collective. In this sense it was up to the U.N. Security Council's military staff committee, not the United States, to develop a collective plan of action against Iraq.

The same principle must apply to unilateral covert activities. Covert activities are merely another name for the intrusion of one nation into the life of another, violating the laws of the host nation. They almost invariably involve criminal activity, from bribery and theft to murder. Such modes of intrusion increase instability in the host country and then in the intruding nation as well; for both these reasons, nations have attempted to fashion an international law that accepts the principles of nonintervention. The rule of comity, as it was called, is even more important during a period of international social transformation. Observing this rule and recognizing its importance as an instrument to keep the peace will be especially difficult in a period when newly emerging rules that require action opposing genocide, apartheid, and protection of human rights become the norm.

The alternative to this view is an unhappy one. It is the perpetuation of a "left" imperial system that will be no more attractive than the status quo systems the United States organized and sustained for thirty years after the Second World War. In this regard, it is likely that the Soviet-Cuban activities in Africa will be no more successful than interventions tried by the United States for its clients, nor will the Soviets look any more noble or rooted to the wretched people of Afghanistan or the frightened people of Eastern Europe than do Napoleon's attempts at the beginning of the nineteenth century to spread the ideals of the French Revolution in Spain, Russia, and Egypt.

Spreading an imperial system has negative effects on the intervening nation's body politic. Early twentieth-century British writers showed that states that sought colonies deprived their own populace for the elixir of empire. While particular commercial classes might have gained from British imperialism, by World War I it was clear to most politicians in England that imperialism was a wasteful enterprise that stopped England from coming to grips with its own need to reindustrialize. The hubris of Cuba's involvement in a two-front war in Ethiopia and Angola has had grave negative economic and social consequences for its people.

The Cold War brought an exception to this rule. At the beginning of the Cold War the United States began to change its official stance on domestic apartheid because of its world competition with the Soviet Union. But the ugly underbelly to imperial involvement has been more important. The imperial system is a means to deny one's sense of law and justice, for it treats the other or the enemy as an object, not part of the common law of civilization. Those who operate an imperial system find themselves hiring and encouraging thugs to undertake all manner of degradation from assassination to wiretapping to bribery and other deformations of statecraft. This form of pacification and containment was first used in the United States on the poor and the outsider domestically and then was exported abroad and used on other nations to teach or tame them. (In this the United States has been no different from other empires.) But the methods used on those we did not see soon came home. They were applied more widely on all segments of the society, even those who for a time held state power. It was not long before those who held power within the state competed with each other and used that power on each other.

The shift from shock at this behavior by the end of the Indochina War and Watergate to justification of it through legislation is truly an astounding turnaround. This justification, as laid out in the new charters for the FBI and the CIA, and the direct justification of covert activities by Congress makes a mockery of our own legitimate public structures such as Congress and the courts. When the intelligence apparatus is able to deceive the public constitutional forms, when false budgets are submitted to Congress, when agents and informers are to remain "nameless" under penalty of law, and when activities are conducted that are in the service of small cliques, we know that we have left a democratic stage for the rule of the national security state, which knows only its own rules and those of its leadership, and whose leaders see constitutional forms as ornamental to the real purpose of arranging power for an imperial purpose.

While the process of dismantling the national security state is necessary for the common good, it should be understood that this process is linked to the development of a more rational national security system. This will be a complex but necessary political feat. It requires working with members of the armed forces, retired officers, and veterans' organizations, who will help in defining national defense as an activity to be performed in the context of personal accountability standards as laid out in the United Nations Charter, the Nuremberg and Tokyo trials, and the genocide treaty.

2. There are modes of engagement and joint interference that I would construe as "positive" peace keeping. They fall into two categories. The first is that of joint accountability systems in which, for example, the United States and China checked on the "minorities" problem in the Soviet Union, and the Soviets, Latin Americans, and Africans did likewise for the United States, with all attempting to find ways to take into account the critiques of the other. This issue will become more important politically over the next generation in each nation as the Russian-Asian population continues to increase at a faster rate than the Russian-European population, while the Chicano and black populations within the United States also increase faster than the

Caucasian population. The second category concerns areas of joint enterprise in which economic aid is given to a third group or nation under rules laid out by the host nation and that of the United Nations Security Council. As part of a joint system of interference/noninterference accountability, the United Nations' conciliation and mediation system should be greatly expanded. Individuals and groups would fulfill this function on the international scene both as advocates of internationally accepted standards and as mediators of disputes.

The University of the United Nations should be mandated to train teams of regional conciliators who would prepare plans and take over conciliation functions in disputes referred to them by the General Assembly, the Security Council, or the disputing parties. The conciliation service would operate under the secretary general according to resolutions of the Security Council and the General Assembly. The United Nations University should now take on the obligation of teaching and setting out certain types of curriculum materials and problem questions that would become courses of study in universities and schools of diplomacy and international relations within member states. The purpose is to denationalize diplomatic problems to the extent possible in order to generate a cosmopolitan consciousness among both practitioners of diplomacy and elites. It would concentrate on problems of civil war and ethnic conflict.

3. Under Article 43 of the U.N. Charter, the Security Council was mandated to set up a military committee that was to produce an international security plan. This work was interrupted by the Cold War. International rules concerning intervention and disarmament security are utterly necessary if we are to escape a major war. One should note that it is not only the Soviet Union that has practiced intervention since the end of the Second World War.

Given well over a dozen wars and interventions since 1975, it is more necessary than ever that we alter our international system, which has broken into one of international military autarky. Either the U.N. Security Council, with agreement from the General Assembly, or the secretary general should call for the substantive reconvening of the military committee. It would review various international arms limitation arrangements and treaties that are meant to change, then limit, and finally proscribe war as a means other than for defense of one's own territory. The military committee would explore the feasibility of U.N. border detachments replacing national armed forces on borders.

Consonant with such changes is the requirement that the United States and other major powers transform the present alliance systems by independently withdrawing troops and naval forces from different parts of the world as the international security and disarmament plan is implemented through the United Nations or as political conditions change. As an international security agreement is negotiated, the United States would take the leadership in proposing that the NATO and Warsaw Pact nations pursue regional arrangements in arms control and disarmament within the context of the international security plan. NATO and Warsaw Pact nations would become a joint disarmament entente, for example.

Is it naive to think that the Security Council and the General Assembly may be brought into planning, managing, and transforming the alliance system so that it becomes part of collective self-defense and international security rather than the reflection of world confrontation and tension? If it is, then such naivete nevertheless has a realistic basis, in light of the costs of the arms race and the fact that the alliance system—in the sense that Dean Acheson and Jean Monnet or Molotov and Ulbricht formulated it—is coming apart. Thus, there is no question that Poland, France, and West Germany pursue foreign policies toward each other that cross and undercut the traditional confrontational lines of alliance systems.

In the quiet of their offices, Kremlin and State Department diplomats are concerned that both parts of Germany may pursue their own foreign policies, cut loose from their sponsors, or even unify independent of them. And European nations know that tactical limited modern war means their utter destruction. Their very survival is dependent on finding a course that steers them away from the alliance system and nuclear confrontation, just as the Soviet Union must continue to find a way either to demilitarize Germany or to develop an entente with it that will give the Soviet Union economic aid. This feat can be accomplished best in a worldwide security arrangement. The question that goes begging for an answer is whether the bureaucratic structure of the NATO, Warsaw, Comecon, and OECD alliance systems could be used to perform the joint activities of development and disarmament. International civil servants and the bureaucracies they serve could become important actors for peaceful transformation if they would reflect a transnational consciousness that is tied to an emergent pluralist world culture and is rooted in the building of a world community.

On a regional basis, Western Europe appears to be relatively successful in controlling its states' animosities toward one another through joint democratic planning and international intercourse by means of cultural activities such as communications, food, music, and travel. This consciousness could spread to all of Europe in the proper security context of disarming.

From the point of view of American security, the issue is whether alliances that were initiated in the post–World War II period and that sought to determine or to stop social transformation both abroad and in the United States have any value at a time when the United States is beginning its own transformation. The policy of bipolarism and the *cordon sanitaire* relationship to Russia and Eastern European states are peculiarly inapposite, and their merit has fallen apart in the face of political, cultural, and communications changes that have occurred in Europe. (Parenthetically, had the United States accepted the Rapacki and Kennan plan of disengagement a generation ago, Poland and Eastern Europe would not be perpetually on the edge of repression, and the West would not feel impotent.)

There is nothing to be gained from any policy that attempts to isolate another nation except when there is general agreement among all the nations of the world. It is merely recognizing reality that the task of American foreign policy during its own necessary social transformation is to keep friendly relations with all nations through the United Nations system and to help them adjust as we pursue our own internal agenda of developing a modern democracy.

Note

1. Earl Ravenal, "The Dialectic of Military Spending," in *The Federal Budget and Social Reconstruction*, ed. by Marcus G. Raskin (Washington, D.C.: Institute for Policy Studies, 1978), p. 145.

6

American Idealism, War Crimes, and a Law of Personal Accountability

This essay was written in 1971 as part of a book called *Washington Plans an Aggressive War*. Cowritten by Richard Barnet and Ralph Stavins, the book itself is an analysis of how the U.S. bureaucracy and leadership made war in Indochina and how the rules that it followed were imperial claims that had no basis in law or international law. Our study of the *Pentagon Papers* and more than 300 interviews with principals and bureaucrats involved in the war led us to this conclusion. In 1967 a number of activists including Seymour Melman, William Sloane Coffin, Ben Spock, and I presented to the Department of Justice a 300-page book called *In the Name of America*, prepared by the National Council of Churches. This book was a compilation of alleged violations of international law and war crimes by the U.S. military in Indochina. As part of our visit, we had participated in a draft card collection ceremony on the Justice Department steps. These draft cards (including my own) were also presented to the Department of Justice. In a meeting inside the department, I had suggested to the associate deputy attorney general that the charges against our government officials of war crimes be investigated. The Department functionary was not amused by the draft card turn-in or by our impertinence. And a few months later we were indicted for conspiracy to get others to evade the draft. Three of the defendants were acquitted (I at the trial level), and the cases of two others were reversed and remanded. The Department of Justice did not bring any further action against them.

The so-called Nuremberg defense had been raised throughout the Indochina War—especially in draft resistance cases—to no avail. After my acquittal, I decided to do an even more careful study of the character and structure of the war and its relationship to the Nuremberg principles. I had long been attracted to the idea of personal responsibility, perhaps as a result of two influences. One was Professor Quincy Wright. I assisted him at the University of Chicago as his reader in international law. Wright was the leading international lawyer of his generation and had been the U.S. adviser to the Nuremberg trials. The other influence, I suppose, was an existential one that had to do with the fact that freedom demands constant responsibility for one's actions thus constraining individual freedom. Obviously, people's actions and lives are contingent on others. Contingent freedom notwithstanding, the individual must call on those humane attributes within himself or herself which encourage the person to confront the obviously inhumane and beastly. I do not hold with those who believe that confrontation against the Indochina War was solely an act of conscience, depending on those interior voices that could only be heard by the individual. I believe that objection to war stems from being a citizen and objection to it is part of the legal and social process. I hold that ideas of personal responsibility and freedom inhere in the evolution of the law and in increasingly obvious standards of justice that define citizenship itself. Certainly the bitter experience of tens of millions in the Second World War was that ways had to be found to control leaders and states. If disagreement with states could only be dependent on individual heroic acts of conscience, then this degrades the possibility that there could ever be a cumulative advance in the moral and legal standards of world civilization. War and its preparation are a collective matter and therefore to confront it is a social task mediated through those aspects of the law that already embody the most humane attributes of civilization. To argue individual conscience is to miss the point that there is a fundamental set of rules and laws already existing that govern civilization and that can be called upon and applied. □ □

The people are told that responsibility for the Indochina War cannot be assigned and that we must take care not to search for scapegoats. Members of both political parties insist that everyone is responsible— that anyone in a position of responsibility in the government would have done the same.[1] Whether one is the senator from Mississippi on the Armed Services Committee, the president, a general, a tenant farmer, a special assistant to the president, a soldier, or a taxpayer, one is responsible. Some say the policies of the Indochina War are a natural extension of American foreign policies since 1940; others say, since the beginning of the United States. And to some extent such statements are true.

Yet we know that the leaders who directed the state did not see Americans as either wanting to be involved in Indochina or wanting to develop a situation that would result in colossal moral and political failure. Dean Rusk has made clear that the responsibility did not rest with the Georgian tenant farmer or, for that matter, even with the racist ax-handle wielder:

> Scratch the skin of any American and you find he wants to take care of his own affairs and not get involved. . . . There is no imperium in Americans—at least not in the post-war period. . . . Acts of will since World War II have not erased the institution of isolationism.[2]

Rusk is correct, of course. The imperium was built into the structure by its governing leaders. To make the "internationalist" (read "imperialist") response automatic, leaders knew they would have to "scare hell" out of Americans and build a bureaucratic apparatus that, by its nature, would be engaged all over the world. The apparatus created the day-to-day commitments and interests that people felt they had to maintain and protect. The "acts of will" to which Rusk referred were actions and policies taken by men operating as a government behind the shield of state necessity.[3] It was no longer possible to advocate the law of imperialism in the age of decolonization. And since no moral or legal case for imperium could be made, American imperial leaders resorted to ersatz law and morality as the cover for their actions. Para-law and pseudo-morality became important ingredients in their attempts at "educating" others to their view of imperial responsibility. Law became a shield in justifying action, since people would not consciously believe they were performing illegal and immoral actions—for whatever cause. People and power crave legitimacy.

Armed with para-law, the leaders took the people to places they did not want to go and caused them to perform acts from which they will not easily recover.[4] Yet it would be wrong to think that the men who decided did so hoping for disaster and evil results, at least as they related to the United States.

The actions of American leaders and the structures they maintained were designed to rationalize military and economic requirements to ensure American imperial "responsibility" and dominance.[5] Attempts were made to arrange governing so that the state's wars would not impinge on the rest of the government or on the people and their ways of life. American foreign policy has sought to avoid war among the Great Powers, if possible, without yielding the position of American dominance. Fighting continuous war in the lands of the poor and wretched was acceptable, and to some extent was the way the ruling elite thought American dominance would be maintained. The nagging policy problem was to find a legal rationale for such behavior. By John Kennedy's term it was decreed that to prevent the big war the American imperium would have to fight a series of "little" wars. It was not expected that such wars would be harmful to the American society; indeed, they would be useful economically and socially—even prestigious. Johnson also adhered to the idea of continuous limited war. According to Eugene Rostow, Johnson was impressed by the example of the British, who for so long were able to fight wars at the edge of their empire. "We have to get used to the idea," he said.[6] He did not want to make war total; to have "parades or bond drives." For Johnson and his advisers, as for Kennedy, it was to be a hip-pocket war in which the privileged would maintain their privilege and the poor would find advantage and opportunity by fighting in Vietnam.

As Secretary McNamara assured one historian, the American escalation was "an automatic response to North Vietnam's counter efforts to achieve its objectives."[7] There is no escape, as Eugene Rostow has said; there is no easy escape from the kind of policy we have pursued since 1947. The paralegal rationale for the policy would be found somewhere in the propaganda sections of USIA, the Defense Department, and the CIA.

The blacks would achieve equality of opportunity through joining the armed forces, learning to strut, as Daniel Moynihan suggested. For the middle class, sacrifice was not to be "real" but merely rhetorical, and the entrepreneurial-minded might find a way to make money, whether in leasing slot machines in Vietnam or in making special floodlights for jungle lighting. The war itself would be a sport, a diversion at most. And it would be presented to the people as a daily television "news" spectacular. The frolic of the leadership, with its talk of "freedom" and "determinism" and "fighting to maintain justice and freedom in Southeast Asia,'' was to be shored up by an everready brushfire war armed force. The droning of everyday life would be relieved with the purpose and determination of the leaders. The will of the leaders would remove the private tedium of a society that, many privileged mandarins thought, was too caught up in personal pursuits. The national purpose, which the ruling mandarins wrote about in the pages of *Life* magazine (1959) and William Bundy sought as the secretary of the Eisenhower National Goals Commission, was to be found in the rice paddies of Vietnam and the bawdy houses of Saigon.

War, however, has a way of getting out of control, especially when it is institutionalized through "firepower," high technology, and orders issued in language that obscures the consequences. The people who were the objects and instruments of this policy found that all of their petty but somewhat rational compulsions, desires, and interests were turned inside out in the name of a purpose and rhetoric that had only mystical meaning. The bubble burst and that primary taskmaster, Reality, interfered with the dream sequence sold by an American ruling elite.

It is at such a point that people who favor traditions grounded in everyday life attempt to set the framework of political and legal discussion. The logical and moral search for generality and symmetry is not easily denied. What might have been described as a heroic war is reevaluated in the light of the stubborn judgments that Americans made upon others a generation ago. Thus, even American war makers become murderers, and heroes become villains. As the American prosecutor at the Tokyo trials, Joseph B. Keenan, said,

> It may seem strange to include charges of murder in an indictment before an international tribunal. But it is high time, and indeed was so before this war began, that the promoters of aggressive, ruthless war and treaty breakers should be stripped of the glamour of national heroes, and exposed as what they really are—plain, ordinary murderers.[8]

We should not fear such a reality principle, since without it there is ever-greater likelihood of violent degeneration in American society.

Official War Crimes and Demilitarist Principles

The problem of America's imperial structure and its present propensity for continuous war making can only be resolved if the United States proves able to develop public conscience and power that build on positive aspects of American life. Radical changes in national security policy and structure do not require an overwhelming, convulsive change in American domestic life, since the national security state itself has few roots in the society. It is of no value to the blacks in Harlem, the Chicanos of the Southwest, or the upper middle class in Westchester County that the United States has a CIA, TAC, SAC, and MIRV. The business elite even doubts that the national security apparatus is "responsible"—that is, that it has a business consciousness.[9] As governor of Wisconsin Pat Lucey said, if Melvin Laird, Nixon's Secretary of Defense, had to get the Defense budget through the people of Wisconsin, he would most probably fail. To democratize defense and security functions that have been viewed as mystical, "too complex," and beyond the comprehension of the people, would have the effect of breaking the power of the national security apparatus. The dismantling of this apparatus could be accomplished through political and legal means. Perhaps the Indochina War can be the basis of a citizen-initiated corrective process that stems from the kind of power and conscience that is crucial to reconstructive change.

These are not new concerns for American society. At the end of World War I, leading American pragmatists in politics and philosophy sought ways of holding elites personally responsible for their actions. John Dewey argued that people should outlaw war and eliminate the government's power to wage it. Senator William Borah, as chairman of the Senate Foreign Relations Committee, proposed a resolution in the Senate

> . . . that it is the view of the Senate of the United States that war between nations should be outlawed as an institution or means for the settlement of international controversies by making it a public crime under the law of nations, and that every nation should be encouraged by solemn agreement of treaty to bind itself to indict and punish its own international war-breeders or instigators and war profiteers under powers similar to those conferred upon our Congress under Article I, Section 8 of our Federal Constitution, which clothes the Congress with the power to define and punish offenses against the law of nations.[10]

It was this resolution that led to the Kellogg-Briand Pact (also known as the "Pact of Paris" of 1928), the treaty that sealed the fate of the defendants at Nuremberg. One of the counts against the German leaders was planning an aggressive war, an action specifically prohibited under the "Pact of Paris." War was outlawed as an "instrument of national policy," and the treaty specified "that such a war is illegal in international law and that those who plan and wage such a war, with its inevitable and terrible consequences, are committing a crime in so doing."[11] The pact categorically outlawed all forms of war. The American secretary of state, Frank Kellogg, refused to accept a French proposal that would have limited the pact to wars of aggression. He said that if the pact "were accompanied by definitions of the word 'aggressor' and by expressions and qualifications stipulating when nations would be justified in going to war, its effect would be very greatly weakened and its positive value as a guaranty of peace virtually destroyed."[12]

The Allied and especially the American position at Nuremberg was that "any resort to war—to any kind of war—is a resort to means that are inherently criminal." As Jackson said, war by its nature leads to killings, deprivations and destruction, although "honestly defensive war is, of course, legal and saves those lawfully conducting it from criminality."[13]

By World War II, American leaders attempted to define war crimes and responsibility for war making. Yet they were caught in the contradiction of nation-states: that of making war to stop war, that of fighting militarism with incipient militarism. Revisionist historians have seen in World War II roots of American efforts to exert imperial control over the world's falling empires and those vanquished in that war. But such a reading is not sufficient to understand the positive aspects of American social thought and action. There was another impulse in American statecraft at the end of World War II—an impulse that carried forward the populist, antimilitarism strain in American public life. War was still viewed as a crime in the United States. This ethic, this sensibility, found its way into expressions on war crimes and the need to end militarism which, until the Cold War began, dominated American thought. The international law espoused by the United States at the end of World War II meant that war was proscribed as a method of settling disputes. And by incorporation, leaders and bureaucrats were to be held in strict account. In 1945–46 American leaders argued that it was only through personal responsibility, through the acceptance of objective legal and political standards, that leaders could be held responsible. Imperialism was not seen as the fundamental purpose of American statecraft, and tests were to be applied that would assure an anti-imperialist mode. When he signed the charter establishing the Nuremberg Tribunal, Justice Jackson used striking language in this regard:

> The legal posture which the United States will maintain, being thus based on the common sense of justice, is relatively simple and non-technical. We must not permit it to be complicated or obscured by sterile legalisms developed in the age of imperialism to make war respectable.[14]

Francis Biddle, the American member of the Nuremberg Tribunal, in late fall of 1946 proposed to President Truman that the time had come for the drafting of a code of international law that would affirm the principles of the Nuremberg Charter. Biddle told the president that although war is not outlawed by "such pronouncements," men learn to detest war more than they otherwise might because they see its criminal character. "Aggressive war was once romantic; now it is criminal," he said. "For nations have come to realize that it means the death not only of individual human beings, but of whole nations, not only with defeat, but in the slow degradation and decay of civilized life that follows defeat."[15]

> I hope that the United Nations, in line with your proposal, will reaffirm developing the principles of the Nuremberg Charter in the context of a codification of offenses against the peace and security of mankind.[16]

In December 1946, the U.S. delegation proposed to the United Nations General Assembly the principles of international law recognized by the Charter of the Nuremberg Tribunal and its judgment:

> The Committee on the Codification of International Law established by the resolution of the General Assembly of December 1946 to treat as a matter of primary importance plans for the formulation, in the context of general codification of offenses against the peace and security of mankind or of an international Criminal Code, of the principles recognized in the Charter of the Nuremberg Tribunal and in the judgment of the Tribunal.[17]

This remains unfinished business.

The Cold War interrupted the development of the law of personal responsibility for leaders.[18] The ending of the Cold War could point to the reassertion of that interrupted direction in international and domestic affairs. A new generation seems to have turned totally against the militaristic ethic and craves a definition of personal responsibility. The end of militarist values leaves a clear void in American public life that could be filled by the ethic of personal and group responsibility.

After World War II, members of the American government persuaded (or forced) the Japanese and Germans to do more than punish the guilty for war crimes. They attempted to move these societies—including Austria—to renounce militarism and ultranationalism as their dominant mode of life. Militarism and ultranationalism were seen as the conditions that created war and war crimes. Various officials were purged or retired from areas of responsibility. Unless means are found within the United States to do the same, without bloodshed and with an understanding of why this is required, we will find a society in which the values will so greatly diverge and the practice of morality will be so clearly vitiated as to lead to the kind of total degeneration and decay that Biddle said was the inevitable result of war as an instrument of national policy.

It is useful to review some of the standards that the U.S. government applied to both Germans and Japanese to build a society that would be free from militarism and ultranationalism. I will refer to only a few of those rules, laws, and directives that could help in examining the present condition within the United States. Some of those standards (inspired and insisted upon by Americans) should be applied internally as our own society finds itself in the hands of a militarized governing elite whose major response to the problems of the world seems to be a continuous violent engagement with it.

The entire American governmental system embraced the standards of war crimes that were promulgated at the end of World War II. As Telford Taylor put it,

> the United States Government stood legally, politically and morally committed to the principles enunciated in the charters and judgments of the tribunals. The President of the United States, on the recommendation of the Departments of State, War and Justice, approved the war crimes program. Thirty or more American judges drawn from appellate benches of the states . . . conducted the later Nuremberg trials and wrote the opinions.[19]

Americans believed that only through the imposition of war-crime standards would it be possible to stop statesmen who embarked on war for whatever motive or purpose. "But the ultimate step in avoiding periodic wars, which are inevitable in a system of international lawlessness, is to make statesmen responsible to law."[20] The Yamashita case contemplated that such personal responsibility would apply internally to American officials. Whatever the wartime leaders of the United States were, they were not fools. As Justice Jackson said, "while this law is first applied against German aggressors, the law includes, and if it is to serve a useful purpose it must condemn, aggression by any other nations, including those which sit here now in Judgment."[21] But most important, as it applies to the present internal domestic situation, he noted that *"We are able to do away with domestic tyranny and violence and aggression by those in power against the rights of their own people only when we make all men answerable to the law"* (emphasis added).[22]

The Operations of Demilitarist Principles by the United States Government

The avowed purpose of the occupation of Germany was to destroy nazism and German militarism. President Roosevelt outlined the American policy in a series of wartime addresses, declaring that the militarists who bred war would have to be removed from public life:

> We shall not be able to claim that we have gained total victory in this war if any vestige of Fascism in any of its malignant forms is permitted to survive anywhere in the world.[23]

In one of his last speeches, Roosevelt outlined the need for the "eradication of militaristic influence from public, private, and cultural life." This policy included war-crime trials, the dismemberment of the military, and the transformation of the laws and institutions of Germany, Japan, and Austria. There was a strict proscription of militarism, whether it came in uniform or mufti. The concern at Potsdam was the same on July 26, 1945:

> There must be eliminated for all time the authority and influence of those who have deceived and misled the people of Japan into embark-

ing on world conquest, for we insist that a new order of peace, security, and justice will be impossible until irresponsible militarism is driven from the world.[24]

These were not, according to John Montgomery, "partisan declarations" or "inspirational readings." Militarism and nazism were defined, and there was a concerted attempt to develop a concept of justice and a political theory.

The fundamental directive by which the United States attempted the transformation of Germany was JCS 1067, which outlined a plan and general objectives for a non-nazi, nonmilitaristic Germany:

> Essential steps in the accomplishment of this objective are the elimination of Nazism and militarism in all their forms, the immediate apprehension of war criminals for punishment, the industrial disarmament and demilitarization of Germany, with continuing control over Germany's capacity to make war, and the preparation for an eventual reconstruction of German political life on a democratic basis.[25]

In Japan, directives were issued with the same purpose:

> persons who have been active exponents of militarism and nationalism will be removed and excluded from public office and from any position of public and substantial private responsibility.[26]

The Joint Chiefs of Staff directive noted:

> Any persons who held key positions of high responsibility since 1937 in industry, finance, commerce or agriculture . . . [were assumed to be] . . . active exponents of militant nationalism and aggression.[27]

In effect, the military government was to bring with it as representatives of the victorious nations a social transformation that would replace the war-making elites.[28] U.S. occupation authorities prepared a six-page questionnaire covering the public and private lives of individuals under investigation. Any falsification was held to be grounds for prosecution by the American military government court, and could be punished with sentences of two to five years' imprisonment. By June 1, 1946, more than 1.6 million Germans—one out of ten in the American Zone—were processed. According to the original author of the denazification program, Elmer Plischke, some 23 percent of those who filled out the questionnaires were removed or excluded from office.[29]

On March 5, 1946, the uniform "Law for Liberation from National Socialism and Militarism" was set forth by the German leaders in the American Zone. It had the full support of the American military government. The purpose of this program was to develop the legal and social processes needed to transfer authority from those who had been part of the German regime between 1933 and 1945 to

> those who will establish a free, peaceful and democratic society. . . . The only way to develop the roots of a free society was to destroy the influence and authority of those who favored Nazism and militarism.[30]

The first article called for liberation from national socialism and militarism so that a "lasting base of German democratic life could be initiated." According to this article, this could only be accomplished by

> excluding from public life all those who are guilty of having violated the principles of justice and humanity, or having selfishly exploited the conditions thus created.[31]

According to the principles laid out in the March 5, 1946, law, the Allied purpose was to eliminate militarism, its conduct and ideas, from the public economic and cultural life of the people (Article II). Five categories were established under Article IV: (1) major offenders, (2) offenders (activists, militarists, and profiteers), (3) lesser offenders, (4) followers, and (5) persons exonerated. The October 12, 1946, directive of the Allied Control Council ordered the

> punishment of war criminals, Nazis, militarists and industrialists who encouraged and supported the Nazi regime. Their internment, imprisonment, or restriction of their activities.[32]

In examining the criteria used to identify offenders, one finds that the strict standards applied by Americans to other societies are fully applicable to American conduct in Asia. In other words, the idea that standards of international legality or morality do not exist within the bureaucratic or legal context turns out to be patently false.

Under Part 2, Article II, of Control Council Directive no. 38, ten criteria were used to define a major offender. A major offender was one who could be charged with war crimes of the most serious nature. Several of these criteria seem directly applicable to our present situation. Anyone who

> in the occupied areas treated foreign civilians or prisoners of war contrary to international law; anyone who is responsible for outrages, pillaging, deportations, or other acts of brutality, *even if committed in fighting against resistance movements* [emphasis added].[33]

This clause is of importance since some commentators have attempted to justify an all-is-fair philosophy against resistance movements, whose combatants do not identify themselves as such. The Americans promulgated a view in Germany that resistance movements had to be treated with the same attention to rules of war as armies in "proper" insignia and badge. The callous idea that the NLF could be destroyed through the Phoenix program by murder of the infrastructure, by direct assassination, burnings, etc., could not be countenanced under America's own standards as applied to the Germans. Under Section 8 of the Major Offenders clause:

> Anyone who in any form whatever, participated in killings, tortures or other cruelties in a concentration camp, a labor camp or a medical institution of asylum. . . .[34]

qualified as a major offender. As of May 1971, the U.S. government had admitted to between 5 and 6 million refugees in a country of 17 million people as a result of its own policies in Vietnam. In October 1967, the *New England Journal of Medicine* carried an article saying:

> The destruction of villages, the uncontrolled movement of groups of people and the squalid conditions in the camps have broken the natural barriers to the spread of disease . . . a rising incidence of under-nutrition, especially among children . . . tuberculosis . . . intestinal parasites, leprosy . . . malaria have been major causes of morbidity . . . ; plague . . . cholera also have grown greatly in number.[35]

Under Article III, Number 2, a war crimes offender was deemed to be "anyone who exploited his position, his influence or his connections to impose force and utter threats, to act with brutality and to carry out oppressions or otherwise unjust measures." The national security managers saw threat, force, and brutality as their primary means of carrying out their purposes in Vietnam. It is not possible to conclude otherwise from such memoranda as those that passed between staff and cabinet officers in the White House, Department of Defense, CIA, and State Department.

Militarists were viewed as offenders who caused and made war. The Control attempted to establish

> a common policy covering . . . the complete and lasting destruction of Nazism and *militarism* by imprisoning and restricting the activities of important participants or adherents to these creeds. [emphasis added][36]

Militarists were those who "sought to bring the life of the German people into line with a policy of militaristic force." They included "anyone who advocated or is responsible for the domination of foreign peoples, their exploitation or displacement" as well as those who "promoted armament" for these purposes. They also included those who "disseminated militaristic programs . . . serving the advancement of militaristic ideas." Profiteers who suppressed minorities or made "disproportionately high profits in armament or war transactions" were also viewed as offenders.

In each of the categories (major offenders, minor offenders, lesser offenders, and followers) the sanctions were stringent, ranging from death, imprisonment for life, and fifteen years at hard labor for major offenders to probation, jail terms, and loss of public employment for the lesser categories. To be "exonerated" it was necessary for those who had been in power or in the Nazi Party to show that they "actively resisted . . . and thereby suffered disadvantages."[37] The civil service was to be patterned on basic American democratic models, which meant that "the new civil service system will prohibit the maintaining of secret personnel files."[38]

In Germany, the United States insisted on a denazification process that resulted in 50,000 cases a month being heard by about 545 tribunals in the American Zone. These were basically kangaroo administrative courts that offered little, if any, chance for response, although a "defendant" who was not cleared by such tribunals was unable to occupy any position of importance. As of June 1949, some 947,000 cases had been processed in the American Zone. Montgomery suggests that the denazification system was a "gentler means" than would have been used if a natural revolution had taken place in Germany. He points out that

> in a genuine revolution, the victims of tribunals have to be buried; in Germany they merely suffered fines or temporary employment restrictions or, at worst, a brief internment period.[39]

The State-War-Navy directives to General Mark Clark pertaining to Austria[40] followed the antimilitarist, anti-ultranational and anti-Nazi directions applied to Germany and Japan. The basic American objective was to develop a "free, independent and democratic state," which meant the elimination of "Nazism, Pan-Germanism, militarism, and other forces opposed to the democratic reconstitution of Austria." It was concluded that war criminals would have to be apprehended and that all political and social service organizations that were Nazi- or militarist-inspired would have to be dissolved. Those who actively supported "organizations promoting militarism or who have been active proponents of militaristic doctrines" were to be excluded or removed from government service. In this task the American occupying force was to effectuate "the total dissolution of all military and paramilitary organizations together with all associations which might serve to keep militarism alive in Austria." The purge extended to those who "took an active and prominent part in the undemocratic measures of the pre-Nazi regime." Procedures were set up to "facilitate the conversion of industrial facilities to non-military production" and to abolish "all semi-official or quasi-public business and trade organizations of an authoritarian character." This directive also called for a "policy prohibiting cartels or other private business arrangements" which controlled the economy.

A White House press release on September 22, 1945, stated the policy that the United States government intended to adopt toward Japan:

> Japan will be completely disarmed and demilitarized. The authority of the militarists and the influence of militarism will be totally eliminated from her political, economic and social life. Institutions expressive of the spirit of militarism and aggression will be vigorously suppressed. . . . The Japanese people shall be afforded opportunity to develop for themselves an economy which will permit the peacetime requirements of the population to be met.

The demilitarization policy followed by the Americans in Japan was more benign than the one followed in Germany. In the first post-surrender directives it appeared that the United States would imprison various Japanese who would have qualified as militarists and ultranationalists, if not as war criminals, but this approach was rejected on grounds that the changes the United States was interested in making in Japan fell within the preventive rather than the punitive category. The major purpose was "the removal of leadership tainted with war responsibility from the political, economic, and social life of Japan—that under a new leadership not so tainted, democratic growth might be possible."[41] Seven categories were established.

In the major directive laid down by the American military government in Japan,[42] the Japanese government was required to remove officials of the national government and

> Bar from reappointment and from election to the coming Diet, anyone who falls with the following categories . . . :
> A. War Criminals.
> B. Career and Special Service Military Personnel; and Special Police Officials; Officials of War Ministries.
> C. Influential Members of Ultranationalistic, Terroristic or Secret Patriotic Societies.
> D. Persons Influential in Imperial Rule Assistance Association, Imperial Rule Assistance Political Society, etc.
> E. Officers of Financial and Business Concerns Involved in Japanese Expansion.
> F. Governors of Occupied Territory.
> G. Other militarists and ultranationalists.[43]

The immediate result was great consternation among the "old reactionary hierarchy," General Whitney, chief of the Government Section in Japan, described the directive (SCAPIN 550):

> blasting from their entrenched positions in the command posts of the government all those who planned, started and directed the war, and those who enslaved and beat the Japanese people into abject submission and hoped to do the same with all the world.[44]

The American directive and SCAPIN 448, which ordered the closing of all ultranationalistic societies and forbade the establishment of new ones, produced a cabinet crisis in Japan. Since the military government's order was meant to provide removal by categories of individuals, the Japanese government proposed to appoint an "Executive Commission of Inquiry to determine upon *prima facie* evidence whether the careers and activities of the persons in question deserved their removal and exclusion from office" within the meaning of the directive. The Shidehara government asserted that it would move quickly in such cases:

> As the examination of each case comes to an end, the government will at once notify the person charged of the findings of the committee and if they are satisfied of his guilt, they will proceed forthwith to his removal and exclusion from office as directed, if he has not by that time spontaneously resigned.[45]

The report of the Government Section of the Supreme Commander of the Allied Powers noted that the Japanese proposal sought to change the administrative process of removal and exclusion to a judicial one. The result would have been to require a legal case "against each individual and trying it before a quasi-judicial body."[46] The response of the Government Section of the Allied Commander was that the directive itself was not

> punitive (as the Japanese proposal implied) but, on the contrary, it is preventive. It is a necessary precaution against the resurgence of Japanese expansionist tendencies; therefore, until after the directive has been complied with, "individual guilt" (which requires inquiries into *intent* as distinguished from *act*) is irrelevant.[47]

The American government did not object to the establishment of a commission of inquiry that would make recommendations to the Japanese government, provided that the individual was first removed from public office. One case shows the extent to which the American government in Japan intended to hold to account leaders who were not viewed as war criminals. In April 1946, Hatoyama Ichiro won an election to the Diet and was thought to be the obvious choice for premier. The Americans objected, claiming he should be excluded from public office on the following grounds:

> a. As Chief Secretary of the Tanaka Cabinet from 1927 to 1929, he necessarily shares responsibility for the formulation and promulgation without Diet approval of amendments to the so-called Peace Preservation Law which made that law the government's chief legal instrument for the suppression of freedom of speech and freedom of assembly, and

made possible the denunciation, terrorization, seizure, and imprisonment of tens of thousands of adherents to minority doctrines advocating political, economic, and social reform, thereby preventing the development of effective opposition to the Japanese militaristic regime.

b. As Minister of Education from December 1931 to March 1934, he was responsible for stifling freedom of speech in the schools by means of mass dismissals and arrests of teachers suspected of "leftist" leanings or "dangerous thoughts." The dismissal in May 1933 of Professor Takigawa from the faculty of Kyoto University on Hatoyama's personal order is a flagrant illustration of his contempt for the liberal tradition of academic freedom and gave momentum to the spiritual mobilization of Japan which, under the aegis of the military and economic cliques, led the nation eventually into war.

c. Not only did Hatoyama participate in thus weaving the pattern of ruthless suppression of freedom of speech, freedom of assembly, and freedom of thought, but he also participated in the forced dissolution of farmer-labor bodies. In addition, his endorsement of totalitarianism, specifically in its application to the regimentation and control of labor, is a matter of record. His recommendation that "it would be well" to transplant Hitlerite anti-labor devices to Japan reveals his innate antipathy to the democratic principle of the right of labor freely to organize and to bargain collectively through representatives of its own choice. It is a familiar technique of the totalitarian dictatorship, wherever situated, whatever be its formal name, and however be it disguised, first to weaken and then to suppress the freedom of individuals to organize for mutual benefit. Whatever lip service Hatoyama may have rendered to the cause of parliamentarianism, his sponsorship of the doctrine of regimentation of labor identifies him as a tool of the ultranationalistic interests which engineered the reorganization of Japan on a totalitarian economic basis as a prerequisite to its wars of aggression.

d. By words and deeds he has consistently supported Japan's acts of aggression. In July 1937 he traveled to America and Western Europe as personal emissary of the then Prime Minister Konoye to justify Japan's expansionist program. While abroad he negotiated economic arrangements for supporting the war against China and the subsequent exploitation of that country after subjugation. With duplicity, Hatoyama told the British Prime Minister in 1937 that "China cannot survive unless controlled by Japan," and that the primary motive behind Japan's intervention in China involved the "happiness of the Chinese people."

e. Hatoyama has posed as an anti-militarist. But in a formal address mailed to his constituents during the 1942 election in which he set forth his political credo, Hatoyama upheld the doctrine of territorial expansion by means of war, referred to the attack on Pearl Harbor as "fortunately . . . a great victory," stated as a fact that the true cause of the Manchuria and China "incidents" was the anti-Japanese sentiment (in China) instigated by England and America, ridiculed those who in 1928 and 1929 had criticized the Tanaka Cabinet, boasted that the cabinet had "liquidated the (previous) weak-kneed diplomacy toward England and America," and gloated that "today the world policy drafted by the Tanaka Cabinet is steadily being realized." This identification of himself with the notorious Tanaka policy of world conquest, whether genuine or merely opportunistic, in and of itself brands Hatoyama as one of those who deceived and misled the people of Japan into militaristic misadventure.

f. Accordingly, in view of these and other considerations not herein recited, the Imperial Japanese Government is directed to bar Ichiro Hatoyama from membership in the Diet and to exclude him from government service pursuant to SCAPIN 550.[48]

The Japanese position seemed designed to protect individual rights but also to destroy militarism and ultranationalism. Justice Minister Yoshio Suzuki said:

> It is our solemn duty to purge those who led the people into waging war. Needless to say, we must do so voluntarily. If anyone disapproves of this, he does not know the present position of Japan. It is regrettable that there are people in this country who do not consider the purge question sternly enough. In Germany 100,000 people have been thrown into jail and one million fined, sentenced to menial labor, their property confiscated, deprived of their civil rights or sentenced to hard labor. In our country, however, those who precipitated the nation into war are only barred from public office, which, we must explicitly bear in mind, is due to General MacArthur's generous occupation policy. For this reason, although we are sorry for them, those who fall under the purge directive must be brave enough and have enough sense of honor voluntarily to assume the moral responsibility. There is no other means, I am convinced, to restore international confidence in our country.[49]

In Japan, only 210,287 persons were removed and excluded from office, as opposed to 418,037 in the U.S. Zone in Germany.[50]

As can be seen from the number of people excluded from office, the American government went to great lengths to purge other countries of militarism. American leaders believed that certain elite groups, namely the militarists and ultranationalists, were responsible for war making, and that unless modes of exclusion from the political life of the nation occurred, there was no way that a meaningful transformation of the society could occur that would allow for more humane and pacific impulses to achieve any support in the government.

One may disagree with the negative and simplistic view of the transformation of society embodied in these postwar measures, but such disagreement does not connote that in America no penalties need attach to people who make and threaten war. One can object, too, to the cynicism of the victor who forces his way on the vanquished and attempts to set the terms of life for him. Indeed, wars and revolutions are not usually instruments of justice. In war and revolution, people, justice, and public moral virtue are the casualties. As Hans Baerwald has pointed out,

> The key has not been found which might open the secrets to the manner in which the liberal democratic way of life (and its political, social, and economic institutions) might be transferred to societies in which it did not emerge as part of an indigenous process.[51]

Fortunately, we are not concerned with that question here. *We are, rather, concerned with how citizens within their own society, of their own free will,* undertake the transformation of their own elite groups and set rules of punishment and restitution when their elites operate outside the law.

Democracy degenerates when its leaders and bureaucratic elites are drawn continuously from a pool of people who have been consistently wrong, politically and morally, about their values and purposes. A society that consistently draws on such leaders invariably deprecates—and punishes—those who have made correct judgments from the beginning. Opponents of America's war in Indochina have paid heavily for their opposition with trials, jail sentences, police surveillance, detention, and blacklisting. As the war continued, the government escalated its repression of critics, including those in the military who rebelled against insane orders and requests—until it became impossible to order them about. The federal employees who now openly oppose the war and American imperialism are invariably on the edges of the government even as their position proves correct in an assessment of the American relationship to the world, and even as the Senate itself favors a nonimperialist turn and attempts to end the war through cutting off appropriations.

Repression directed against those who have been correct in their instincts and views on the war is likely to continue and cause greater conflict between large segments of the people and the governing structures, unless a new public policy results in promulgation of a series of laws for civilians, government workers, and policy makers that reassert the proposition that governments must not become criminal enterprises. America must publicly and legally affirm the principle that those who were morally and legally wrong were those who generated and prosecuted the war—not those who struggled against it. From this point of view, it would be intolerable to permit criminal wrongdoers to benefit from their actions and continue their control over governmental life. In the *Constitution of Athens*, Aristotle pointed out that the friends of the tyrants, "with the usual leniency of a democracy," allowed them to remain in the city of Athens. *But even there they were not rewarded with continued control over the democracy.*

Our imperial war will not end until forces within the United States are able to overcome the elite groups and institutions that assume continuation of the war in one form or another and the established habit of mind that assumes that aggressive war making is a legally accepted way of conducting foreign policy. The Vietnam War (and its offshoots, Laos and Cambodia) will not end successfully for the American people without the transformation of those institutions that allowed the war to be made, and the deposition of those elites who manned the institutions. Conversely, if the war does end, American society will be far different from what it is today. The elite groups that made the war and benefited from it cannot be expected to emerge from such a ten-year conflagration with their power intact. New groupings in American society will bring forward their own leadership and values, pushing aside, at least for a time, present elite groups. It is only natural that such changes should occur.

Elites that control societies can be expected to suffer punishment if they lose at war or revolution. The question American society now has to face is whether it is possible to move aside an elite group that enforced institutions of war making on the American people, without resorting to totalitarian revolution.

An important legal step to be taken is the development of a system of enforceable standards that can be applied to bureaucrats and men of power. In the literature of revolution, it is taken for granted that when elites lose the will to rule, they can be overthrown. But democratic reconstruction requires different standards. When elites rule badly, without moral purpose or wisdom, without any sense of understanding of what they are doing, they must be compelled by popular and legal means to stand aside. The first step in creating a revitalized democratic society must be the development of a system of laws that sets the limits of action for leaders of the state. Such rules must be clearly stated and understood as having real meaning; they must be supported by a system of enforcement procedures. The second must be the adoption of procedures for removing from office those who breach that system of laws.

The question of what is to be done with this leadership will be a test of whether or not American society is creative and humane and whether those groups that were denied justice can do justice to others while they dismantle those institutional structures that developed war and genocide to the point that they have reached in the world culture.

Lévi-Strauss, in his remarkable book, *Tristes Tropiques*, talks about the North Plains Indians who were known as the most cruel of societies. Nevertheless, they developed a humane form of punishment that did not sever the social links of the individual. An Indian who broke the laws of his tribe was sentenced to the destruction of his belongings, his tent and his horses. Yet, when that occurred, the police were indebted to the law breaker. They were required to compensate him for the harm he had been made to suffer. In this way, the criminal was put back in debt to the group and he was obliged to acknowledge the way the community undertook to help him.

> These reciprocities continued, by way of gifts and counter gifts, until the initial disorder created by the crime and its punishment had been completely smoothed over and order was once again complete.[52]

Toward a Future Accounting

After World War II, the American government forced and persuaded the Japanese and Germans to renounce militarism and ultranationalism as their dominant way of life. To this end, hundreds of thousands of persons were purged or retired from areas of responsibility in the Japanese and German governments. The United States now finds itself in a similar position. It now must find the means, within strict legal limits, to retire from public life bureaucrats and policy makers who see violence as the primary means of American policy making. Unless such means are found, we will find that American society is one in which there are no communal values that tie the society together. The values will be so different among groups and the practice of morality so personal as to clearly vitiate the chance for a peaceful society. Instead, the chances for total degeneration will geometrically increase.

New standards must be found to deal not so much with what has happened, as with what will happen in the *future*. We may reject laws that have an *ex post facto* quality, or that become bills of attainder. There is no need for such purge tactics in the United States. It is crucial, however, that we devise standards that tell government officials in reasonably precise terms what they can and cannot do. The Uniform Code of Military Justice and the field manuals define such limits for the military. Civilian officers of the government who deal with foreign policy and national security must not be left without standards to which they are held.

As a political matter, officials of the government who served in high positions during previous administrations, who acted to fan the flames of war and disaster, and who developed bureaucratic structures that allowed for such a situation to develop, need not be reappointed. Indeed, any political party platform should now include a clear statement that it will not appoint those who pursued a policy of war in Southeast Asia to any future cabinet, subcabinet, or policy-making position. The Senate Foreign Relations Committee could begin to serve notice on any presidential aspirant or president that there is little likelihood that any person directly involved in the Indochina War will be recommended by that committee for Senate confirmation.

The issue is not a partisan issue. It is a question of the standards of citizenship within the body politic. During the occupation of Germany after World War II the United States insisted that the various parties of Germany—and then the Germans themselves—develop a code of behavior that would be applicable to all Germans as citizens of Germany. The German representatives of the various political parties—Christian Social Union, Social Democratic party, Communist party, Economic

Reconstruction party, and Free Democratic party—all joined with the German government to support the Law for Liberation from National Socialism and Militarism. They drew a proclamation that developed a definition of citizenship that separated itself from the national socialist and militarist period of German life. It is this lesson upon which we can draw.

The power to declare war and the power to define offenses against the Law of Nations is left, constitutionally speaking, with the Congress. In 1947, when the public debated the meaning of war crimes, international lawyers argued for the development of laws that would make such crimes punishable within national courts. As one commentator wrote, the government of the United States "should not allow the slow processes of international agreement to defeat its sincerity of purpose."[53] Now, in the 1970s, the question of such a code cannot remain an item of unfinished business.

Some have argued that states are incapable, by definition, of keeping the peace, and that citizens must find a means for doing so.[54] John Dewey contended that the institutions of the state are so saturated with the war mentality that to regard the state as a major instrument for maintaining peace is a contradiction that can never be resolved in practice. But, as we have seen, there was an antimilitarist mood within the American government after World War II. Many officials were convinced then that another war had to be avoided, and that leaders had to be controlled. But those who took that position either resigned or were driven out by the new militarism that mushroomed during the Cold War years.

In 1947, with the National Security Act, the American government blurred the distinction between civilian and military operations in national security and foreign policy. Foreign policy became an instrument of conflict, and national security was judged in terms of military and paramilitary strength and the government's willingness to engage in their use. The federal government became an instrument of the national security state as the militarized civilians employed the resources of the society for covert operations, forced refugee programs, bombing missions, and nuclear war tactics. The militarized civilians escaped any code of law under which they could be held accountable by the citizenry or the Congress. Americans found that their leaders took the fork in the road that was marked by the flag of imperialism and paved with signposts that said that raw power was law.

Since 1963 the transformation of values within the American society has meant that there is a conscious wish on the part of an active public to retrace those steps, because of its own heritage and hopes and because of what has become obvious to all: that war is a crime in itself, that murder or organizing for it on a small or grand scale can no longer pass as high policy. The people are concerned with how the state is to be held in check and how power is to be held accountable. Those who have argued that the nation-state system is obsolete, and by its nature immoral, may be theoretically correct. But there is nothing to suggest that in the present there is a believable alternative. The question remains as to how the several branches of government within the United States, and the people, are able to end criminality masking as government. This can and should be done through lawful means. What recourse do the people have against elites other than law?

Notes

1. Liberal Americans who think of problem solving—that is, technical solutions to questions that one would rather not regard as having moral consequences—find it difficult to think of guilt and innocence, right and wrong. It is rarely up to a citizen to decide under what form of government he will live. Yet with modern weapons the question of responsibility to decide moral questions becomes even more crucial. It becomes a citizen's responsibility to alter the consequences of despotism. And where he fails it may be said that he shares a generalized form of guilt—the guilt of nonfeasance. But this form of guilt and responsibility is hardly the same as the kind of guilt shared by those who hold operating power and use it to destroy others. They have more than a "metaphysical" guilt; it is legal and criminal. When a society averts its eyes and refuses to understand why such men are specifically guilty, so that such deeds can happen again almost immediately, the guilt of the society becomes collective.

2. Henry P. Graff, *The Tuesday Cabinet* (Prentice-Hall, 1970), p. 135.

3. It should be noted that the state is made of papier-mâché when it comes to absolving an individual of acts performed in the state's name. As Quincy Wright has said, "The State cannot protect its agent from the consequences of his act if he acted outside the State's competence under international law." There is no legal competence to commit wars of aggression. *American Journal of International Law* [AJIL] *42* (1948):410.

4. Senator Hatfield inserted into the *Congressional Record* of April 6 and April 7, 1971, testimony of soldiers in Vietnam who claimed they committed or were forced to commit atrocities. E2825–E2902 and E2903–E2936.

5. When we analyze the national security apparatus, we see that those involved by their roles and functions are responsible for: (1) setting of manpower and material requirements, (2) the acquisition of resources, (3) the development of a technology, (4) the operational plans for the use of such forces and material,

(5) the certifying of external threat and interest, (6) their actual use, and (7) the setting in motion of forces within the society that keep the imperial direction going. These seven purposes are the fundamental activities of the national security apparatus.

6. Eugene Rostow, "LBJ Reconsidered," *Esquire*, April 1971.
7. Graff, *The Tuesday Cabinet*, p. 32.
8. *Department of State Bulletin*, May 19, 1946, pp. 846–47.
9. In his testimony before the Senate Foreign Relations Committee, Thomas Watson, the head of IBM, on the effects of the Indochina War on business, stated: "Let me illustrate the point concretely by giving you a rundown of actions against IBM properties in various parts of the world during the last six weeks. In West Berlin, nearly all the windows in one of our buildings were broken by young rioters. Then gasoline was poured about it and it was set on fire. The windows in one of our Dutch facilities were broken by students. Our branch office in Cologne was attacked by protesters against the Vietnam War and the windows smashed. A powerful bomb was discovered just before it was timed to explode in an IBM Argentina office. Just a few days ago, we received bomb threats at our Amsterdam and Paris data centers. And here at home we've had many bomb threats and one actual bombing at 425 Park Avenue in New York City—our eastern regional headquarters." *Impact of the War in Southeast Asia on the U.S. Economy*, Senate Committee on Foreign Relations, April 15 and 16, 1970, pp. 21–23.
10. Senate Resolution 45, December 12, 1927. 69th Congress, 477, Part I, as quoted in Marcus G. Raskin, *Being and Doing* (New York: Random House, 1971), p. 72.
11. Nuremberg Tribunal Judgment found at *AJIL 41* (1947):172–333.
12. Note to the French Ambassador, February 27, 1928. This view should be compared to John Dewey's view as found in *Intelligence in the Modern World* (New York: Modern Library, 1939).
13. Found at *AJIL 41* (1947):64.
14. *Department of State Bulletin 12*, 311 (June 10, 1945):1076.
15. *Department of State Bulletin 15*, 6 (November 24, 1946):956.
16. Department of State Document No. 2783, August 1947.
17. Ibid.
18. In 1947, Lord Wright, the chairman of the United Nations War Crimes Commission, stated in his foreword to the fifteen-volume series on war crimes, "I cannot sufficiently emphasize what I regard as the great importance of these reports from the point of view of the future development of International Law as applied to war crimes. . . . These reports will show, for the practitioner or the student, the particular problems which had arisen and how in practice they have been dealt with and also show to the historian of the laws of war the practice of courts in applying those laws to particular cases." But these volumes are virtually nonexistent in the United States and have had no impact on American law. This state of affairs was a result of the Cold War.
19. Telford Taylor, *Nuremburg and Vietnam* (Quadrangle Books, 1971), p. 34.
20. Opening statement at Nuremburg, 1945, by Robert Jackson, Department of State Document No. 2783, 1947.
21. Ibid.

22. Ibid.
23. Department of State Document No. 2783, August 1947, p. 2.
24. Ibid.
25. JCS 1067 found in Department of State Document No. 2783, p. 82.
26. *Political Reorientation of Japan, September 1945–September 1948*, Report of the Government Section, Supreme Commander for the Allied Powers (Washington, D.C.: U.S. Government Printing Office, 1971).
27. Department of State Document No. 2783, p. 82.
28. No elite will admit to aggressive war. Each will invent a threat that has to be dealt with through military means which leads to great war. For example, it is entirely likely that the executive committee of the National Security Council at the time of the Gulf of Tonkin would reply that they were reacting to aggression. But such a view can be disproved, from the facts. More important, we begin to understand aggression when we note the relations between Germany and Poland at the time of the outbreak of war in 1939. Quincy Wright, *A Study of War*, vol. 2 (Chicago: University of Chicago Press, 1942).
29. *Denazification Law and Procedure, AJIL 41* (1947):811.
30. *Occupation of Germany—Policy and Progress, 1945–46*, Department of State, p. 9. Note Article I, March 5, 1946.
31. Ibid.
32. Ibid.
33. Ibid.
34. Ibid.
35. "Civilian Casualty and Refugee Problems in South Vietnam," *Findings and Recommendations of the Subcommittee to Investigate Problems Connected with Refugees and Escapees, of the Committee on the Judiciary*, United States Senate, May 6, 1968, p. 9.
36. Control Council Directive No. 38, found in *Occupation of Germany*, Department of State, 1947, p. 123.
37. Ibid., pp. 127–29.
38. Ibid., p. 187.
39. John Montgomery, *Forced to Be Free* (Chicago: University of Chicago Press, 1957), p. 25.
40. *Department of State Bulletin*, September 1945.
41. Hans Baerwald, *The Purge of Japanese Leaders under the Occupation* (Berkeley: University of California Press, 1959), p. 16.
42. *Political Reorientation of Japan*, "Removal and Exclusion of Undesirable Personnel from Public Office," SCAPIN 550, January 4, 1946.
43. Ibid., vol. 1.
44. Ibid.
45. Ibid., p. 17.
46. Ibid.
47. Ibid.
48. Ibid., vol. 2, pp. 494–95.
49. Ibid., vol. 1, p. 45. Statement part of article in the *Yomiuri Shimbun*, December 5, 1947.
50. Montgomery, *Forced to be Free*, p. 26.
51. *The Purge of Japanese Leaders*, p. 106.

52. Claude Lévi-Strauss, *Tristes Tropiques* (Adler, 1968).

53. George Finch, "The Nuremberg Trial and International Law," *AJIL 41* (1947).

54. Antiwar students have pursued the pragmatist tradition of direct action independent of the state by promoting a separate peace treaty.

7

Integrity and the State: Sartre, Solzhenitsyn, and Sakharov

I did not know Jean-Paul Sartre, but he once did a service for me during the Vietnam War that stemmed from his political commitment. When the so-called Boston Five (of which I was a member) were indicted for conspiracy to urge young men of draft age to resist the draft, Sartre came to my defense in Paris at the urging of the distinguished historian Gabriel Kolko. He held a press conference and, like Martin Luther King, Jr., immediately signed a complicity statement saying, "If they are guilty I am guilty."

Sartre saw life as an unfolding project in which decisions and choices determined the meaning of one's freedom. We get clues from any particular situation in which we find ourselves, but it is our interpretation of that situation that defines how we will act with our contingent freedom. This understanding of politics and the situation preserves personal independence but it condemns the person, as it did Sartre, to being the outsider.

I wrote the essay on Sartre in this chapter in 1980, on the occasion of his death. I doubt if Sartre believed in the concept of citizenship, for in it lies the double idea of human and social bonding. He doubted the eighteenth-century ideal of citizenship beyond class. For him, struggle (class and otherwise), I suspect was at the heart of human relationships. He was an intense moralist in his politics, always being at, if not of, the scene of struggle, making moral witness. He counted as immoral those who professed a rational morality, much as the friend of his youth, Paul Nizan, had felt about professors of philosophy.

The professors of ethics, Sartre pointed out in his introduction to Fanon's *Wretched of the Earth*, were nowhere to be seen taking a bop on the head for anyone in the Third World. They never put themselves in jeopardy. He saw these bourgeois gentlemen as part of the world of sadomasochism that made human existence a living hell. Sartre understood full well the betrayal of socialist ideals in the hell that the Soviet Union had created for its people.

It is one thing, however, to understand in an intellectual sense the problem of betrayal and suffering. It is quite another to live it. That was the experience of Solzhenitsyn and Sakharov.

In an important essay on ethics, the theologian Dietrich Bonhoeffer, who was hanged by Hitler, makes the point that a greater evil is caused humanity by those who are evil but act under humanitarian ideals than by those who are more avowedly evil. In this sense Stalin and his regime reflected this most profound devilish quality, for they besmirched the human possibility in this century. Nevertheless, it should not be forgotten that it was the Soviet people who carried the brunt of the war against Nazi Germany, and we in the United States were very pleased indeed to have Stalin's Soviet Union do so and be our ally for that purpose.

The politics of Alexander Solzhenitsyn are not my politics. He is a Russian nationalist who doubts democracy, criticizes the softness of the West, and otherwise seeks to relieve Russia of responsibility for any of its troubles, which are supposedly the result of Western influences. Such ideas at present have a strong following in the Soviet Union among the followers of Pamyat, who are nationalist, antidemocratic, and anti-Semitic. In their own way, they continue Stalinism. The argument I made in *Ramparts* in 1974, reprinted here, I would still make today. It is a human rights argument, which attempts to guarantee people their humanness. It does not mean that I agree with either Solzhenitsyn's vision or Sakharov's politics.

The same argument could be made about Andrei Sakharov, who in recent years has been promoted as a secular saint in the West and in the Soviet Union. Shostakovich was once asked what he thought of Sakharov. He said that he could not have great respect for those who handed the tyrant the capacity to destroy the world during the day and at night wrote brochures against it. Sakharov was the father of the hydrogen bomb and accepted the need for a Soviet bomb, working to make such a weapon in conditions that might be best described as a velvet concentration camp. He became a dissident years later, helping literally thousands, after he saw the madness of nuclear war and the dead end that the Soviets had come to as a state. Yet, while he believed in disarmament and human rights, and spoke and worked for them, his anger against the Soviet Union before Gorbachev was so great that he encouraged the United States to go forward with the MX missile. Sakharov deserves praise with one hand clapping. ☐ ☐

Sartre: A Life in History

In the 1950s we believed that our dilemma and that of our parents' generation was captured best by the French existentialists, and it was best articulated by Jean-Paul Sartre, the man of engagement who did not stop, and whose life seemed to epitomize the antibourgeois intellectual and writer. Depending on one's point of view, Sartre was either "spread too thin" or a Renaissance man. He was all over the political and cultural map, lecturing, writing novels, plays, and books of philosophy, editing a journal and even starting a movement. He did not seem to lose any time to unproductivity and alienation. While he could write about these states, talk and even organize around them, one felt—just by looking at his record of accomplishment—that none of this was really *his* problem.

In that sense he was like the child of another class, a ruling class who gave up other ways of looking and thinking about the world in order to identify with the rest of us. He understood that the writer's responsibility was not to escape the *Angst* of his time—not because one couldn't but because he or she was morally embargoed from doing so. Of course the real pain felt by Sartre and the others was caused by nuclear mushroom clouds, concentration camps, war, depression, and the likelihood of new war and new twentieth-century disorders. It was in this turmoil we believed that French thought immersed us. All of the plagues I mentioned, and more, are still there, although we seem to have become inured to them and take them for granted. Man's eternal damnation is played out in resignation to what is, as if it has to be.

A generation ago there was no political movement to express feelings of anger, fear, and frustration. We felt alone and, making the best of this loneliness, we romanticized being lost, perhaps taking our cue from *Nausea*, in which Sartre's character Roquentin saw his life as worth very little. If he could only write a song, something as fine as "Some of These Days." Being alone, uprooted, we felt the same way. We thought we could escape the meaninglessness and the resignation we felt so deeply if we could do one thing, write one song or book or have a thought that mattered, that had clarity and effect, that justified our existence—or perhaps our parents' tuition.

We were like the walking stickman on the cover of William Barrett's book *Irrational Man*, the sculpture of Giacometti that haunted us. And while we hoped for that one act that would give our lives meaning, we prepared for the life of sleepwalking assent. As middle-class students (some of us barely in the middle class), we lived through fantasy lives of other people's struggles, sang Spanish Civil War songs and thought about the French Resistance. Of course it was not long before some of us found ourselves—along with a generation ten years younger than us—in a not dissimilar struggle.

In the American civil war of the 1960s, many did not know if they were citizens or guerrillas. But all felt engaged. In the 1950s our engagement with existentialism was a way of avoiding the fact that we were preparing for futures with the meritocratic corporate governmental bureaucracy, which would serve as the social graveyards of so many. We admired Sartre because he had escaped the excellent average of the bourgeois. He was not a crazy saint like Simone Weil nor was he "captured" as Camus was by Henry Luce in his Cold War with the communists.

Sartre lived his life looking for a third way, beyond socialism as it existed in various states, against capitalism and for democracy not only as a process but as an end, with an anarchist's belief in the individual person. No wonder this totally twentieth-century man felt he could only rebel at this century's political creations. As the gifted novelist and philosopher Iris Murdoch put it:

> The deadening civilizations of capitalism and communism are alike rejected and the perfect society where complete stability combines with complete individual awareness, social security with civil liberty, seems less and less possible. So when one is caught between the intolerable and the impossible nothing is justified except a state of rebellion, however vain.

But how to rebel and where are enormously important questions. There was the way of André Malraux, who seemed to be a cross between an intellectual and a gangster. In his youth he had stolen art treasures from another culture (Cambodia) for fame and wealth while proclaiming himself an anti-imperialist. He was a romantic who traveled to other people's struggles while keeping one bag packed for a quick return to established power. So it is not surprising that Malraux ended up an established minister and the mouthpiece of French culture, playing to Charles de Gaulle the role Andrey Zhdanov played for Stalin. Perhaps this is unkind. Malraux did bring expositions to the people, cleaned up the monuments, and set propaganda on a more subtle course.

There was simply no way that Sartre could have been anyone's minister. He ministered to everyone. And like the son of the sailor that he was, he moved from one ideological port to another. In some cases he got the message later than others. Camus's nose for the stench of Soviet concentration camps was more sensitive than Sartre's, who thought that it was important to think in "political" terms, weighing the consequence of attacking the Soviet Union when it was reeling from the Cold War and just recovering from the devastating war with Nazi Germany. Then the Hungarian uprising of 1956 caused Sartre to reexamine his own political assumptions. While he moved closer to the Marxists in philosophic terms, in political terms he moved further away from the Communist party. Often intellectuals seek protection of their ideas by renouncing organizations that ostensibly stand for those ideas. How they handle this internal conflict defines their personal and political integrity.

But what does all this have to do with Sartre? Perhaps it is that each person who decides to become an actor in history seeks a role that fits his definition of integrity. Camus raced to his death, consumed by the problem of integrity and torn by the struggle in Algeria because of his *colon* birthright. Malraux found his life fashioned in honor and pomp. Chatting with Mao Zedong and Zhou Enlai, gossiping with Jackie Kennedy, the intellectual's cultural object, talking the grand talk and sharing ponderous silences with de Gaulle. He sought honor and established power in France in the hope that others would legitimate him and affirm his integrity. But Sartre needed no such external props—neither the Lenin Prize nor the Nobel Prize. He was free enough, secure enough in himself to tell the commissar and the king that prizes were bourgeois affectations. For him, the work of the writer and philosopher could never be constrained or beholden to the official world.

Where did Sartre get the inner strength that enabled him not to fear being humiliated—that had him selling newspapers at the age of seventy in order to protect, and bear witness with, an obscure Maoist sect? He was more aware than anyone that the project of freedom demands an indifference toward one's place in history. To Sartre, the cost-benefit calculations so popular today in America were laughable and demeaning. To care about such matters is to lose integrity and freedom, which to Sartre meant the communal bonds in which each explores the other's possibilities. That is, freedom is linked to the group, the whole, but is a personal act of choice that the person exercises in any particular moment. Where freedom is not linked to the group, it is transformed into a subjective feeling of being alone and lost. Sartre understood the danger that in modern societies freedom can deteriorate into oceanic loneliness.

On another level, he understood the porous relationship between the objective and subjective. Through his books, plays, novels, articles, the magazine he edited, and his political actions, he tied us to ourselves, to others, and to the world. Even though some of his actions were halting, even failures, the left was not above gaining succor from him, whether it was the Russell Tribunal on Vietnam War crimes, or, in my case, his willingness to organize French support for the Boston Five in 1968.

His life taught us how we should be and live in the world. He embodied the profound paradox that to *escape* our existential loneliness we are called to responsibility to the world and to be responsible for what we neither control nor necessarily understand. He taught us that knowing objective responsibility may not help us understand the inside of a situation, that what appears to be a responsible action on the outside is, viewed subjectively, quite the opposite. This truth, in part an existential one, is also psychoanalytic in origin. A hard political truth of our time is that actions and acts double back on each other and assume an opposite meaning. This leads to irony and embitterment for many.

More than any other philosopher in this century, Sartre began from the *situation*—the crisis, the desperation of it. He saw it behind our own doors which we lock, hoping always to find how that door could be opened even though its locking was prefigured. This question, the power of humankind to control its own destiny, dominated Sartre's thought and action throughout his life. At first, in *Being and Nothingness*, it was the person alone who could make his own consciousness. In a way, and here I am oversimplifying his position to the point of caricature, his fundamental assumptions were not that far from the ideas of the American pragmatists, who located the ultimate good in the lives and consciousness of individuals rather than society. The consciousness and good actions of individuals added together could serve as a set of liberating actions for the group. By the time Sartre had written *Critique of Dialectical Reason*, he had come to believe that existentialism was a dependent knowledge system. If it was to have universal meaning, it would have to "be integrated" into Marxism. Subjectivism, he thought, had its limits. For Sartre, there was too much to understand in the world, and this could be done only from the outside, because each of us is on the outside of the Other.

But there was another reason. For all his anarchist leanings, Sartre sought holistic understanding. He believed there is a Truth that could be discovered. This truth emerges in history and action. And while the anarchists and the pragmatists seek many truths, throughout his life Sartre followed the Hegelian-Marxist search for a single, encompassing truth that would unveil itself through history. In his political struggles, which to outsiders looked quixotic, he sought to create a single history that would unveil a universal truth. It did not matter that he would sign everything and picket for anything. When he championed the convicts in prison, or those who lived as convicts in France's ghettos and the *favelas* of the world, when he championed homosexuals, or the Algerians and those philosophers who ran with and for them, he was pursuing truth and being faithful to the same concept of reason that the Enlightenment held. Reason and freedom are known through man's actions and so reason and freedom can be known by everyone, he believed, not merely the Platonic few who leave the cave to peer into the sunlight, but all of us. "I have always considered, and still consider, the truth to be whole," he said.

It makes sense that we continue to search for that truth in our work and lives, breaking out of compartments, linking situations to consequences, hoping that truth will not always stand in conflict with power. But if it does, let us hope that we will have the courage to choose the side that searches for truth, as Sartre did.

Soviet Dissent: In Search of Forgotten Men

Ever since Khrushchev's de-Stalinization campaign, a dedicated segment of the Russian intelligentsia has attempted to establish an opposition to the system of political repression and bureaucratic sadism in the Soviet Union. Their success as a movement is limited, but their bravery is laudable and undeniable, and their purpose worthy of support. Analysts can dwell on political differences between the members of the dissident groups, but the common message is clear: the Soviet Union is a repressive, unfree society that denies its citizens fundamental human rights and makes a mockery of socialist values.

In *Let History Judge*, the historian and educator Roy Medvedev attempted to write an account of Stalinism as the workings of a madman whose intimidated sycophants knew no limits. According to him, the torture and tyranny of Stalin's time had no roots in the Marxist-Leninist tradition. As a communist, Medvedev accepts the fundamental ethos of the Bolshevik revolution, although he is unrelenting in his criticism of Stalin and those who were intimidated by him out of love of party, power, cowardice, or zeal. Although he had encouraged the development of international contacts and worked with Andrei Sakharov and V.F. Turchin in laying out a new program for socialism in the Soviet Union, Medvedev has gently criticized Andrei Sakharov in a *Samizdat* publication. Sakharov, who sees himself as immune from attack and imprisonment because he holds the order of Lenin and is the Father of the Russian Hydrogen Bomb, has sought international support for his movement for human rights in the Soviet Union.

In recent weeks, the audacious struggle for intellectual and political freedom in the Soviet Union has reached new levels. In the highly publicized and overpowering *Gulag Archipelago*, Solzhenitsyn has gone over the grim territory invaded by Medvedev, but from the perspective of the totally disenchanted. Solzhenitsyn uses the Soviet torture and prison system as the lever for reexamining the entire Soviet "experiment" and its assumptions. When *Gulag Archipelago* appeared in the West, the Soviet government attacked it as the work of an enemy of the Russian people, a book that had the possible pernicious consequence of defeating détente between the Western bloc and the Soviet Union. The Soviet officials did not deny the substance of the charges in the book. At this writing, Solzhenitsyn is on the edge of suffering disciplinary action. He is supported by Sakharov and a few other writers and academicians who have called for worldwide support for him as the "pride of Russian culture."

From different political perspectives, both Solzhenitsyn and Medvedev have undertaken a necessary human task: remembering the dead. In his dedication to the *Gulag*, of which only excerpts now appear in English, Solzhenitsyn said:

> This I dedicate
> To all those who did not live
>   to tell of it,
> And may they please forgive me
>   for not having seen it all
>   nor all remembered,
>   for not having divined all of it.

Solzhenitsyn is an authentic embodiment of the gutsy spirit of survival that perseveres despite the horrors of the twentieth century. His writings, basically paranoid, search for another time and another tradition. I do not know if it is the tradition of the benign orthodox Christian Russian landlord, Prince Kropotkin, or of a Kerensky Social Democrat. It does not matter. If all of us cannot follow in his search, we can at least understand that a man whose loneliness and individualism was honed in twentieth-century wars, concentration camps, cancer wards, and police cells would look beyond the catechism of Stalin or the pretension of Western intellectuals for his understanding of what happened in Russia. He survives to continue his literary inquiry.

Naming the Truth

Survivors with such purposes attempt to strike a deal with their audiences. The audience must support the writer to continue writing against the state. In exchange, the writer will teach and be prepared to tell his audience when an urn is an urn, when a pisspot is a pisspot, and how they get used or mixed up in people's habits and consciousness. The exchange that Solzhenitsyn has attempted to make is a good one, for there are lessons that must be constantly taught and remembered if people are to maintain any humanity. The artist, according to Solzhenitsyn, should have no other responsibility demanded of him. But his audience should be assured that the artist will not "surrender the real world into the hands of men who are mercenary, if not worthless, if not insane." Because of the organization of the modern state, people are not ordinarily able to make distinctions of language and action as part of an ingrained value system. The result is that concentration camps become rehabilitation centers, massive bombings are described as surgical strikes, and a concrete neck stock becomes an "exquisite necklace."

This debasement of language and life takes place not only because there are sadistic officials who enjoy and promote institutions that "turn the screw" or who, like the KGB torturer, General Ryazin, are happy at their work; there are also those who act for the Higher Principle. The most honorable bureaucrats, the dogmatists, and those who have a weakness for fashion in politics, believe and hope that by describing their soiled or childish actions in glowing terms, the actions themselves, and the social relations that they create, will clear a path leading everyone back to the Garden of Eden.

Left consciousness and thought have characteristics that can get diverted to such horror and nonsense. The undefined Higher Principle plays on the left's correct practice of attempting to define the interrelationship of things and relations as a whole. By then translating such definitions into liberating ends for people, the Higher Principle can lead to avoidance, to renaming horrible realities to fit ideal intentions.

Questions about reality were not asked because of the Higher Principle. And if they were asked, the inquirer was open to personal attack. Those on the left who talked about Soviet concentration camps were thought of as enemies; raising such questions within a communist nation was viewed as helpful to the capitalist states and therefore a threat to party and state organizations. For men like Andrei Zhdanov, Stalin's culture commissar, the dogma of the party was complete. The question was how the Apparatus and the party could successfully work as "engineers of the human soul."

Following the Khrushchev speeches to the Twentieth Party Congress, a generation of human soul engineering was interrupted. Formerly dogmatic party leaders and specialists in avoidance on the left could no longer evade the issue of the camps and the purges, of cultural and artistic suppression. It became clear that the sinister, corrupt, and sometimes murderous role of the CIA, even capitalist and military encirclement by cold warriors, were not enough to explain away the camps. The issue was the Soviet state—the values of the party and bureaucracy. There was no running away from this crushing weight.

It was Solzhenitsyn, the scientist turned artist, who became the cultural lightning rod for Soviet liberalization. The editors of the Soviet journal of literary criticism, *Novy Mir* (especially Alexander Tvardovsky), stood solidly for Solzhenitsyn because he appeared to be the harbinger of a new honesty.

Initially, Solzhenitsyn and *Novy Mir* were blessed by Khrushchev, but this blessing turned into a curse as Khrushchev lost his hold over the Soviet system because of his failures, so-called, in the Cuban missile crisis and in agriculture. But, in the meantime, Khrushchev had legitimated the feelings of some left intellectuals and made it possible for them to defend Solzhenitsyn without their previous concern that such actions might prove anti-Soviet.

And so Solzhenitsyn was introduced into an informal, worldwide collegium of intellectuals, whose aim is no more than mutual assistance—for survival in the face of imprisonment, possible torture, and oppression. And therefore we know that it is necessary to give our support and lend our names to each other.

By the time the first book of his projected trilogy on the Russian Revolution was published, Solzhenitsyn's views had become a bitter pill to swallow. In *August 1914*, he told his audience that the official explanations of what happened in the First World War had nothing to do with reality. He was not only a novelist, but a revisionist historian as much as Kolko and Williams were revisionists about the American empire. Solzhenitsyn seemed to be saying that while the soldiers "voted with their feet," they did not vote for the Bolshevik revolution.

The Artist and the State

If it were only the wistfulness of a Bourbon emigré for the tsarist restoration, Solzhenitsyn's writings would be as relevant as those of an American loyalist who called for the reunion of the United States with Great Britain in 1850 or 1860. And just as Lincoln feared British moves toward the Confederacy in the American Civil War, proscribing all kinds of writing as treasonous, the present Soviet bureaucracy feels that Solzhenitsyn's writing is a threat to the stability of the Soviet state. Article 70 of the Soviet criminal code forbids "the writing or dissemination of any anti-Soviet works."

But problems of protecting state power are not the concern of either the artist or the people; such are the concerns of the Power Lusters. In the light of détente and prior to the release of *Gulag Archipelago*, the fashionable found ways of dismissing Solzhenitsyn as a crank who would, if he ever left the Soviet Union, become the object of mild contempt and condescending smiles, much like the kind that now surround Svetlana Stalin's name. Such superciliousness misses the historic importance of the political and cultural struggles within the socialist countries.

Solzhenitsyn embodies part of this struggle of art to find transcendent, universal values from particular experiences. Marxists themselves are not ignorant of the importance of this struggle. As George Lukács put it (before Solzhenitsyn questioned the entire Soviet "experiment"):

> When socialist literature uses its own resources to return to its true character, recovering the sense of its artistic responsibility before the great problems of the day, forces now silent can come into action and weigh on the side of renewal. In this process of transformation and regeneration, which signifies a radical change with regard to socialist realism of the Stalinist era, Solzhenitsyn represents a beacon lighting the way to the future.

Bureaucracies may not be able to brook such criticism because they have a large stake in the continuation of hierarchic structures. Yet one would have thought that a socialist society would thrive on criticism, knowing full well that no critique is purely individualistic, but reflects what is in the minds of many about the conditions they live in. Criticism becomes a necessary corrective force in society. It was a right won in the eighteenth-century bourgeois revolution. If socialism is to be a progressive social formation, it must consolidate the gains of past revolutions, not bury them.

Two questions that revolution brings into focus are highlighted in Solzhenitsyn's life. They are relevant to artists and thinkers in the West: what is the continuing effect of class origin on children and the next generation? What is the role of the writer and artist in the socialist country? Once Khrushchev was out of the way, Soviet officialdom explained Solzhenitsyn's work in terms of the Soviet state's theory of original sin—class origin. It had been assumed from previous accounts of Solzhenitsyn's life that he was the son of a petit bourgeois, born into a teacher's family in Kislodovsk, North Caucasus. However, the claim of the *Literaturnaya Gazeta*, after the publication of *August 1914*, was that Solzhenitsyn's mother grew up in a manor house that resembled a castle. "Indeed, old-timers in the village of Sablya still remember the wealthy Solzhenitsyns. The grandfather had up to 5,500 acres of land and about 20,000 head of cattle at the opening of the century. More than 50 hands worked for him."[1]

Solzhenitsyn answered in an underground news journal. He said that his grandfathers were both *muzhiks*. His father's parentage were "ordinary peasants," although on his mother's side the grandfather started as a farmhand who "became a tenant farmer and by the time he was old he actually became quite rich. . . . And he treated his workers in such a way that after the revolution they voluntarily supported the old man for 12 years before he died. Let a state farm director try to ask his workers to do that after he retires." Six months before Solzhenitsyn was born, his father died. The family lived in shacks, rented "from private owners for high payments" because "they could not obtain a room from the state." Solzhenitsyn's mother died at forty-nine from tuberculosis "because of our living conditions" dictated by class origin. "I was at the front at the time and I did not get to see her grave until 12 years later, after prison camp and exile." (Solzhenitsyn had spent eight years in a prison camp as a result of making veiled derogatory remarks about Stalin while a captain in the artillery.)

Solzhenitsyn is an authentic member of the hunted class in the Soviet Union, a membership that for him has spanned fifty years. How many millions of Russians are, in fact, represented by this story—the not-quite-kulak class that is consistently defined through time and offspring as if the badge of class continues to be passed to the children even after the class has disappeared? To coin a word, this *classism* is a central problem for the revolutionary socialist countries. Some have handled it better than others, as in the case of Cuba and China.

As we know, of course, there are other hunted people besides those who are children of the broken class. In Russia, children of old Bolsheviks have become dissenters. But they are not exempt because of their parentage. When we look closely we see that even their parents were victims from the beginning. Why the revolutionary class, the old Bolsheviks, also had to suffer through the concentration camps (worse than others, according to Medvedev) and allow themselves to be brutalized, seems incomprehensible. Some Bolsheviks, Solzhenitsyn thought, did not learn how to withstand punishment because tsarist prisons did not operate to break the prisoner. Other Bolsheviks accepted such torture because they would have used the same methods on their jailers—given the chance. Thus the issue of "standards" had already been resolved. Human feelings were not to get in the way of organizational roles and party assignments.

Practical politics and revolutionary program, the Higher Principle, took the place of natural and decent feelings. And they believed that human relationships were secondary to something else, never understood and never defined. The feelings "of the past," those of honesty and love that they might have had, were to be cast out, thrust down, and repressed as bourgeois, for a "new order" where morality was yet to be defined (against the past) and was to be enforced by the party and police. Not surprisingly, it was the artists who knew what was going on from the beginning. The masters of abstraction and metaphor, the Mayakovskys and the Mandelstams, were never deceived by the false abstraction and metaphor of Soviet politics. And that is why the question of artists and art is so crucial in the development of socialism. They feel the truth of liberation—and know their craft as well.

In a decent society, the questions of writing and surviving are intimately connected. I doubt if any but party-liners would say that Solzhenitsyn's right to speak should or could be contested. The practical question is his right to publish. After the Russian Revolution, Lenin grandly assured the anarchist Kropotkin that his most recent book would be published and distributed in large quantities and cheap editions to barracks, unions, and libraries. Kropotkin objected to having his book published by the state. Instead, he said, it should be published by a cooperative. It was published after his death by a cooperative publishing house that expired soon thereafter, as did all other overground independent cooperative publishers.

The antistate instincts of the anarchists are correct. To survive, the writer must be part of a publishing and distribution network. This is, of course, what the Russian dissidents have attempted with the *Samizdat*—a self-published article or book distributed by one's friends. This form does not come cheap in the Soviet Union. The young Russian poet Yuri Galanskov was imprisoned in 1968 for publishing the *Samizdat* journal *Phoenix*. He recently died in prison.

A Struggle for Human Rights

In daily struggle Solzhenitsyn has thrown down the gauntlet to the world's left. Either stand with him or stand with the KGB. There is no other choice in a society of the oppressed and the oppressors. The argument of dialectics and program that one can and should have with Solzhenitsyn must be suspended until there is recognition that his own struggle is just. It is just exactly to the extent that he acts as an artist who is the custodian of the chain of our inner humanitarian spirit. It does not much matter what theories of aesthetics a writer holds, since no conceptual understanding can be more than a general guide. The relationship of aesthetic theory to ideology within the artist's work is indirect, dialectical; even an "erroneous" theory may nevertheless be a fruitful guiding principle.

Lenin once remarked in a letter to Gorky: "I am of the opinion that there is something in every philosophy which an artist can put to good use—even if that philosophy is idealistic." But where the artist veers from his representation of the fundamental human values he ceases to operate as an artist and becomes something else. Thus when Solzhenitsyn denied the suffering of the blacks in South Africa and those tortured in Brazil and Greece—in an attack on Western liberals and intellectuals—he disputed his own formulation of the special role of art: "impressing upon a bigoted, stubborn human creature the distant joy and grief of others, an understanding of dimensions and deceptions which he himself has never experienced." Solzhenitsyn does not have to deny the suffering of either ourselves or others to get our attention.

Some readers and left activists will wonder about the Solzhenitsyn-like trend in the Soviet Union, a trend that now wants to repeal the Bolshevik revolution. But is it not obvious that its ideals have been long since repealed? Stalin clearly wanted it repealed, with his consistent attempts at *modus vivendi* with capitalist and Nazi leaders, at the expense of local communist and liberation movements. Were the ideals of the Bolshevik revolution, those believed in by poets and workers alike, drowned in the blood purges of the old Bolsheviks and their children? The question now is whether the Russian people have a chance at naming their own revolution.

In March of 1970, Andrei Sakharov, V.F. Turchin, and Roy Medvedev offered a fourteen-point program that would transform the Soviet system into a democratic socialist state. They called for ending the Soviet system of secrecy in which knowledge is merely a function of power; ending work camps for political prisoners (which entails an entirely new attitude toward the definition of crime under Soviet law and practice); developing transnational or cosmopolitan consciousness among its elites, and a "scientific" mechanism for gauging public opinion that was independent of the party structure; allowing free movement within the Soviet Union, leading to an end to the internal passport system; establishing decentralized or bottom-up planning and control of the economy; breaking up the educational system, with less emphasis on elite education; encouraging alternative media (newspapers, journals, and so forth) that would not be operated by either the state or the party; changing the value system of leadership within the Communist party, ostensibly for better "management" purposes; developing a multiparty or two-party system; and cutting back the authority of the Communist party so that the publicly legitimated institutions, the courts, and the Supreme Soviet can operate on their own, free of the charge of puppetry.

By the fall of 1970 Sakharov needed a new mechanism to defend such ideas. The political means that he chose, and the one that Solzhenitsyn has attempted to use, is that of "isolating" the state from the decent opinion of mankind. The Soviet activists founded their argument on the Universal Declaration of Human Rights and formed the Committee on Human Rights (Solzhenitsyn had said that the Human Rights Declaration was the best document of the United Nations in its twenty-five years). They hoped to develop a transnational network of protection that would be free of state involvement and committed to the obligations of human rights, "prepared for effective contacts with public and scientific organizations, and with international non-governmental organizations, if in their activities they proceed from the principles of the United Nations and do not have as their goal the bringing of harm to the Soviet Union."

By November 1973, Andrei Sakharov—the formerly privileged mandarin now reduced to an intellectual worker—had a chance to test the importance of human rights. Sakharov's wife, Yelena Bonner, had been questioned five times in two weeks for involvement in publishing the clandestine journal of the dissidents, the *Chronicle of Current Events*, and for transferring a skyjacker's diary abroad. The KGB demanded that Bonner submit to questioning and Sakharov, after the fifth time, refused to let his wife be questioned. He wrote a letter to the head of the secret police that the transmittal of a prison diary would not "be regarded as a crime by generally accepted juridical standards and in accordance with the Declaration of Human Rights."

During the sixties, antiwar resisters often attempted to introduce international law, the United Nations Charter, and the Nuremberg judgment, with very little success. In other words, the work that Sakharov has begun in his country can be linked to the work that the antiwar movement began within the United States—namely, linking international obligations and respect for human rights as the basis upon which people within states can legally and politically depend. There is legislation now pending before Congress, the Personal Accountability Act, introduced by twenty-four congressmen, which begins to internalize the judgments at Nuremberg so that state lawlessness will not force citizens to become less human.

There are some political historians who deny the importance of internationalizing the struggle for human rights, saying that its effect can only be marginal in the present atmosphere of state sovereignty. But it is through the transnationalization of that struggle through conferences among intellectuals, parliamentarians, and workers, through demonstrations, writing, and analysis, that a standard of decency will be made a minimum for any politics and political programs, whatever the pretension or dogma.

Note

1. *Literaturnaya Gazeta*, January 12, 1972; found in *Solzhenitsyn, A Documentary Record*, ed. by Leopold Labedz (Bloomington: Indiana University Press, 1973).

8

Ideology and the Arms Race

This paper was given in 1985 at a week-long discussion in San Francisco on U.S. and Soviet affairs between leading scholars, writers, and political advisers to high government officials in the Soviet Union and a distinguished American delegation. Gyorgy Arbatov was the chair of the Soviet delegation, and I headed the American delegation. These discussions begun in 1982 had a salutary effect on developments in the Soviet Union in its foreign and domestic policy, notably around glasnost.

The discussions have been carried out from time to time since 1982 and were initiated to review in a fundamental way questions of disarmament, ideology, human rights, relations to the Third World, and international organization. It was clear from the beginning that the Soviet Union's elites were eager to have major trading relations with the United States and were prepared to pay a heavy price for them. In regard to security and defense the attitudes of the Soviets changed significantly over a period of several years. An older generation continued to hold Germany as a major threat and was most concerned about assuring that there would be no invasion of the Soviet Union from the West. The older generation feared nuclear war but believed strongly that the Soviets would have to build up an overwhelming nuclear arsenal for a number of purposes. The Soviets were weakened after purges, civil wars, and repression, and a strong state would not only impress the West but would legitimate the leadership of the Soviet Union in the eyes of the Soviet people. Nevertheless, for the Soviets, disarmament policy was more integrated into their real, rather than propaganda, positions than

U.S. officials believed. The Soviets required a security belt of nuclear and conventional forces in Eastern Europe, or, so they thought, they required disarmament. The United States did not have such real needs. By the mid and late 1980s Eastern Europe was perceived as a liability to the Soviet Union and not much of a security belt.

The United States and the Soviet Union operated on the assumption of a bipolar world. Each side, broadly speaking, used the same forms of weaponry as modes of defense and intimidation. Embedded in each weapon is a social praxis that links capitalism and socialism to state power and imperialism. Adam Smith understood arms and war as unproductive and a waste of human resources. But he must have also seen war and its preparation as a challenge to capitalism. Smith the Scotsman saw markets being linked to civil societies. States to him were relatively unimportant and in fact dangerous because of their imperialist tendencies. But as history unfolded, modern states did not "wither away." They continued to be linked to imperialism and war, with the market dependent on the outcome of imperial thrusts and armed conflict.

Lenin's view of the inevitability of war because of capitalist imperialism was contradicted by Khrushchev at the Twentieth Communist Party Congress on the grounds that the Soviet bloc nations were strong and had a powerful nuclear deterrent that allowed them to cut back conventional forces. The current collapse of the Soviet bloc as a political entity and ideological force now leaves open the question of whether a world path of social reconstruction building on the best of philosophical, religious, ethical, and economic experiences will transform the war system and end the arms race. ☐ ☐

It is a curious aspect of the arms race between the United States and the Soviet Union that both nations are prepared to defend their ideologies—ideologies that both sides claim are liberators and protectors of humanity—by destroying the world. Thus, the Soviets are prepared to risk the world's destruction by the continuation of the arms race and, while Soviet leaders have publicly declared their unwillingness to use nuclear weapons first, they have made clear their need to fall back on massive retaliation (what noted arms theorist Herman Kahn once called a "wargasm") if nuclear weapons were used by the West. I suppose the Soviet position would probably include the use of nuclear weapons against Communist China in an invasion of Soviet territory by the Chinese. Thus, the canons of Marx, Lenin, and the Russian revolutionaries are to be defended by the destruction of the people in whose name the revolution was made.

The American position since the atomic bombs were dropped on Hiroshima and Nagasaki—acts that were meant to impress the Soviets about U.S. will and power—has been remarkably consistent. Any particular American president and his advisers would use nuclear weapons first or second if their perception of the situation so required it. The American assumption has been that the nation's values can be defended by nuclear war or the threat of it. Thus, American leaders continue to see either massive retaliation or first use, including first strike, as viable options, indeed necessities, to defend the American way of life even though they are manifestly war crimes under the Nuremberg standard. It is a tragic situation where the hopes for the American nation of our founding fathers could be played out in the destruction of civilization and humanicide. Both nations are caught, as other nations will also be caught, in the quandary of threatening total destruction—or partial destruction—as the means to defend their respective nations. It may well be that those who made the American Revolution or the revolutionaries who made the Soviet Revolution are rolling over in their graves knowing that the very framework for humanity, its continuation, is being gambled to defend the transitory and subjective interests of both nations or crackpot leaders. Socialism, which was meant to show how collective freedom could be achieved for the individual, becomes its bitter opposite in practice when its proponents encourage a state apparatus that asserts that only that which is permitted is legal. The result of this attitude is an attitude of docility in the population and strong internal police control until there is enough breathing space to upchuck the entire social system. Obviously, a continuous arms race adds to fears, which then result in an internal military establishment and nuclear arsenal that by their nature and presence threaten others. In fairness to the Soviet position on arms control and disarmament, attempts over the Cold War period were made that would have resulted, had the West seriously negotiated them, in the lifting of stringent measures of control over internal Soviet society.

Democracy, which is meant as a means and a system of participation to assure that individuals may collectively decide their fate and that the individual has a right to say "no," also becomes a barely recognizable deformation in the face of the development of a national security state. It places in the hands of a president the right to commit suicide for humanity. And it encourages political leaders to be engaged in continuous conflict throughout the world. Both systems spread state versions of their ideologies through military interventions under the guise of military assistance. Yet it is at least arguable whether intervention is necessary or required for either ideology. Indeed, the experiences of the twentieth century would suggest otherwise—the Soviet intervention in Afghanistan and the similarly questionable exercises of the United States in Central America notwithstanding. Both were dubious ventures according to modern international law as noted, for example, in the International Court of Justice vote against the United States in the *U.S. v. Nicaragua* case. One should not forget that socialist and democratic states sought to end the imperial mode after the Second World War. The ideologies of West and East appeared to recognize the need for new definitions of security that would end the classic imperial position of international politics where the strong thought nothing of acting on their own initiative for their own national or class interests.

The founders and signers of the U.N. Charter sought a new international politics and a new system of international stability and change that would yoke the rule of law to legitimately constituted force. The deaths of over fifty million people in World War II suggested to at least some of the leaders of that time that such a terrifying, all-encompassing event should never happen again. Furthermore—and this is perhaps the most important and relevant fact—there was a sense that all people were entering world history, that narrow nationalism was a central cause for wars and that it was time to set the course of humanity and nation-states in a different direction. While power politics played a critical role in many of the decisions that established the United Nations, one should not forget the more important, central reality. The nation-state was to be tamed through the United Nations and changes in the world and ideological presuppositions about the world that caused the war were to be attacked. As a result of having to live with world law and an international organization, national leaders were to show a bit of humility even to the point of reinvestigating their own stances, and motivations. This was to be "forced" upon them through the process of dialogue and confrontation within the United Nations. It was even thought that nations would be able to come to grips with their own respective histories, by reassessing them through an honest evaluation of their own national history.

It is often the tragic flaw of the powerful that they are reluctant to admit mistakes. They are fearful of opening old wounds, and think that doing so serves no immediate or useful purpose. As a result, most nations and the bureaucracies that govern them are unable to recognize and transcend their past history. This is why profound changes must come from outside the government. No doubt there is a continuous and dialectical struggle often unrecognized in the movement of history and between the social forces that shape them. Governments are either the agents of positive social forces, or their barriers. Some examples come to mind from each nation. But before giving these examples I want to be clear that adversaries often introduce history as a means of masking their real motivations, which are easily discovered in their current behavior. Those who use historical crimes or tragedies as an excuse to eliminate the possibility of finding a way out of the current tragic condition in which humanity finds itself cast themselves as irrelevant to the present and future. Modern national leaders, intellectuals, or for that matter, citizens do not have the luxury of accusatory pyrotechnics. When President Nixon would talk about an action in politics that worked, he would say that one should not hog the credit, "There was enough credit to go around." One might invert Nixon's statement and say that "there is enough blame to go around on all sides." However, at this stage of the twentieth century we should all be able to shake hands and say that we have a joint responsibility for transcending those institutions and ideologies that caused the crimes and tragedies of the past. This may not be as difficult as it appears, for each generation has the luxury of casting a critical eye on the dominant tendencies of its society to ascertain whether they fit with the precepts of justice, security, and freedom.

In the United States we accepted the abhorrent condition of internal segregation until a generation of black and white people said that enough was enough. We were appalled at the effect of segregation on both black and white people and we fought against apartheid American-style using the democratic struggle for justice and freedom that is part of our heritage. We did not allow the powers that be to continue to hide our history from ourselves. We recognized that internal apartheid had to be ended. (We also recognize that in the United States there must be a continuous struggle against those internal tendencies that breed racism.) Almost simultaneous to the civil rights movement was a great antiwar movement which at no little risk to its participants, said "no" to the American intervention in Indochina. One wonders whether within Soviet society there is also the strength for grassroots change, rather than top-down mobilization. The Soviets will find that not only do modern conceptions of freedom require individual and social space for change, but the modern productive system requires such space.

Just as slavery weighs heavily on the American soul, the crimes of the Stalin purges must continue as a weight on the Soviet society. This is not to say that the horrors of the 1930s continue in the same form; it is to say that the tendencies, the structures that gave rise to that behavior persist. It is absurd, for example, that human rights and disarmament advocates who are uncertified by their government should either be declared mad or without value, or imprisoned. If such ideas square with official or state Marxism, it would seem that it is time for quite different ideas about freedom and Marxism.

At the time of the Twentieth Party Congress, Khrushchev pressed for the appointment of sixty-four commissions in the Central Committee to study the Stalin period. Only one commission was appointed and the possibility of dealing forthrightly with a dark period in Russian history was surrendered to expediency.

I am persuaded that nations are required to look at their own history, not as an exercise in masochism, but as an instrument for assuring that future generations can begin to take the "dead hand of the past" off their shoulders. Once this process happens, it becomes possible to reinterpret and reassert enduring values—that is, principles that have everyday effect on the consciousness of people and that define freedom as integral to democracy and socialism. When we examine the question of socialist and democratic values, certain categories come to mind that may be helpful in comprehending our current condition and then moving us toward a direction that begins to make common sense.

A curious aspect of the Cold War is that it developed a logic and dynamic of its own, a geopolitical metaphysics that transcended ideology. There is no question that both sides are tempered by the existence of nuclear weapons even as both sides approach the world as if it is a geopolitical chess game. In this regard we may note two types of convergence. The first may be called a *negative convergence:* both sides end up continuing the arms race, seeking advantage over the other, participating in propaganda battles, spying on one another, distorting their respective internal economies to generate huge defense budgets which in turn distorts technical and scientific advances, postponing necessary repairs of each society's cities and infrastructure. In negative convergence a group of experts seeks to control the direction of the arms race game so that it does not get out of hand. These nuclear guardians think they are controlling the direction of history rather than merely rationalizing a process that is beyond them. While it may be uncomfortable for some to hear this, the arms control process has worked only as a system of bilateral personal courtesies. It has not worked as a means of shaking us from our joint torpor about the arms race itself. Thus, as I have already suggested, attempts at small controlling steps that assume that both sides can basically find a means of security through the arms race have misread badly the lessons of the past generation. We must be brutally honest about these matters.

The longer the arms race continues, the more obvious it is that groups within the military and defense industries entrench themselves against any change, whether incremental or comprehensive. Indeed, in American politics it is just as difficult to obtain an incremental agreement such as SALT II as it would be to obtain an alternative, comprehensive security arrangement. In the United States comprehensive arrangements that set a new framework are more likely to be interesting and supported by grass-roots groups than are technical corrections of the arms race that have as much meaning as the epicycles once added to Ptolemy's theories about the universe. While certain arms controllers have found that they are now able to stand in the same corridors of power, if not the same rooms, with those who control the military apparatus of their respective nations, the fact is that they should have insisted on a far different agenda, one that stuck to the shaping of an alternative global security and disarmament system that related local and regional political interests and needs of nations to economic and social development. We still need a vision of an alternative in the world arena of politics and in the internal politics of both superpowers. In political terms such a vision is not possible unless intellectuals, members of peace movements, and those parts of the scientific academies begin to surrender their notions of "realism" and false pragmatism. This is hard to do, for in the face of thermonuclear war it is usually thought that we are doing enough if we are merely managing our relationships with each other, without trying to set them in an utterly different direction. Thus, we have arms controllers with the best will in the world seeking to manage the unmanageable, lending their support and intellectual sustenance to activities that make no sense.

Both superpowers treat us to arguments of great subtlety about verification, control over one set of weapons as against another, balancing, etc., that make no security sense. Our negative convergence grows out of our military systems and fears. They become reified in our thoughts as things that cannot be changed even though we know that they endanger our freedom and security. The negative convergence of the Soviet and U.S. national security state inhibits our political imaginations so that we find it hard to transcend the frame of reference which ties us to the defense/war dynamic. Negative convergence on an intellectual level causes us to pursue the wrong questions in the wrong way, both in the West and in the East.

There is a possibility of *reconstructive* or *positive convergence*. In both nations, independent groups as well as government officials would begin the task of generating joint ideas and programs in which other nations and independent groups would be encouraged to participate. The tasks would be scientific in the sense that different ideas would be debated in terms that would transcend the usual meanings of power and control. The ideas themselves would serve as a means to link up those who wanted to recenter themselves beyond the arms race, but within their own philosophic traditions. This will require emphasizing several elements in each ideological system, in the realization that there may in fact be lacunae that must be filled. Thus, neither socialist nor democratic theory is complete, merely to be applied in cookbook-style to problems that are far more complex and ambiguous than those faced by the thinkers and the activists of the early part of this and the last century. Intellectual and personal risk are required for us to make progress; historically, this has been how positive changes have occurred. It is a source of concern to me, for example, that I have not received a written critique of the proposal for Common Security and General Disarmament which I put forward at our last meetings.[1] I am aware that the form of discussion within Soviet intellectual life has been stymied by clearances and constraint. But we must be aware that the capacity to test ideas, the space to explore them, and the capacity of groups and governments to attack them if they want to, are the essence of how positive change is made. I would argue that in this area democracy has much to offer socialism, and indeed much to offer the world. This is not to say that ideas do not have consequences and that some are better than others. It is exactly for those reasons that they need public exploration. I am not so naive as to think that all ideas get a hearing in the West, or that institutions, universities, publishing houses, newspapers, and the media do not have their own forms of genteel censorship. Nevertheless, they are unable to stifle debate for very long.

In the socialist system, where so much emphasis is placed on the collectivity, it would seem more important than ever that ideas be explored publicly and differences encouraged just because decisions are made for the groups as a whole. Positive convergence, therefore, is predicated on the coming together of those groups that recognize the transcendent importance of the arms race and who are able and willing to act against it with or without permission. Positive convergence would recognize that a path needs to be set in real time so that human relationships and institutions such as universities, clubs, businesses, and even military groups across national lines can begin to know each other. This path could lead us to set forth a new frame of reference, one that rejects the war system and embraces instead a vision of an alternative. This will not be easy, for any large-scale change in the dynamics and metaphysics of the arms race will require changes in one's own society. They are changes in outlook that would fit with the best in both democratic and socialist ideals. What would gain are those ideas and institutions that would recognize the beginning emergence of a world civilization. Such an alternative vision would ensure practical steps of trade with a sharing of scientific and technical ideas not only in terms of military "know-how" and consumer goods, but more importantly in terms of the future implications of modern science and technology. It would not be inaccurate to say that socialism and capitalism (or democracy) as they are presently practiced by the superpowers are inadequate ideologies for the future, and the arms race metaphysic assures us that there will be no future. Thus, it is surely time for a renaissance and reconstruction of thought and practice so that the hopes of the enlightenment do not turn into an arid desert. Is that too much to ask as a program for our generation? I think not.

Note

1. The Soviets reprinted the proposal in *USA* with a friendly critique by V. Nikitin in April 1988.

9

Dealing with Gorbachev

It is astounding that Mikhail Gorbachev should have emerged from the Soviet system. Gorbachev started out as a reformer who was going to open the window for liberalizing winds to blow across all of the Soviet Union. The members of the aging Brezhnev-Chernenko generation were under attack as they lost their ideological compass and purpose and as internal economic and social problems continued to mount. The isolation the Soviets felt from the standard of living in Europe, the costly war in Afghanistan, and the seemingly endless drain caused by the arms race gave Gorbachev the initial impetus to undertake his reforms. But once a window is opened, it is not only warm breezes that come through. Indeed, for Gorbachev and the world it has been a veritable tornado that has washed out the Communist parties in Eastern Europe and brought to the political surface longstanding rivalries, local nationalism, ethnic strife, anti-Semitism, and other differences that were hidden by the repressive nature of the Cold War and Communist parties, both of which acted as a suffocating blanket on liberalism and unsanctioned fascism alike.

The harsh tonic of "free market" economics will, in the short run, add to the increased immiserization of the poor and working class in Eastern Europe if the wrong lessons are learned from the West. At least in Western Europe there are powerful social democratic restraints to unfettered capitalism, and these serve as a break to personal avarice. The economic question for the Soviet Union is whether entrepreneurialism and innovative thinking plus freedom of personal action can be linked to a set of public needs rather than to motives of personal profit alone.

Over the course of a five-year period Gorbachev has danced and pirouetted like a veritable Nijinsky. As the world watched his virtuoso performance, the "experts" predicted his downfall on a monthly basis. Gorbachev's own style has been that of the statesman who has attempted to garner more power to himself by adopting the presidential system. The Soviet bureaucratic structure that emerged after Stalin's death operated by rough consensus and corruption. But this system, which had long since given up on Marxism as a mode of self-critique except as Sunday school clichés, was in a crisis of stagnation. Gorbachev's attempts to end the stagnation of thought and practice have pushed him into being a combination of Peter the Great and Alexander Herzen. Inside the Marxist tradition he seemed to be more aligned with Luxemburg and Pannekouk than Lenin, favoring workers' councils as the Communist party declines and as the Soviet Union attempts to rationalize its politics through a multi-party system.

While other leaders remain wedded to ideas of a balance of power, like Franklin Roosevelt forty-five years ago, Gorbachev seeks ways to build a different international system. The traditional questions for balance-of-power diplomacy are whether there is a new constellation of forces in the world that will cause the United States and the Soviet Union again to vector towards one another as Germany and Japan increase their strength or whether the United States should increase its commitments to NATO as a way of having influence over Germany, the Soviet Union, and other nations. A different question is whether the United States should break out of these formulas for possibilities in international politics by picking up on the speech Gorbachev made to the United Nations in 1987 when he called for a new international system. Such a notion could be the beginning of a new positive era in international affairs. "Dealing with Gorbachev" was written in 1988 as part of *Winning America*, a book of alternatives for a progressive U.S. administration, which Chester Hartman of the Institute for Policy Studies edited with me.

I met Gorbachev for a moment at a Kremlin reception where he asked me whether the United States and the Soviet Union could ever be friends. I quoted him the remark from George Washington's Farewell Address that the United States should have no "passionate attachments" with any states. He said, "I can assure you, I do not have amorous intentions in mind." ☐ ☐

As a general rule in international affairs, statesmen and diplomats follow the time-honored principle, "If it's not broken, don't fix it." This is sound advice for those who believe it is possible to freeze the future. It is poor advice for the end of the twentieth century, where changes on the international and domestic scene are continuous, necessary, and often tumultuous. Reagan's secretary of state, George Shultz grasped this fact, but his moves to shift U.S. policy toward the Soviet Union merely scratch the surface of what must and can be done.

The extraordinary, energetic leadership of Mikhail Gorbachev may help Americans see the Soviet Union more clearly as a nation that is increasingly desperate economically and eager to adopt new democratic methods so that a suppressed and repressed people can find their individual voices. Nevertheless, even with Gorbachev's presence, and obvious changes in the Soviet Union, Cold War habits will be hard to unlearn. The period ahead requires that the United States and the Soviet Union understand each other and their past relations better. Given the bureaucratic and institutional predilection for backward "geostrategic" thinking, a future administration could easily fall into the rhetoric and blindness of the Cold War, where myths and misunderstandings have been the coin of public discussion. Even though sporadic attempts have been made since 1945 to improve U.S.-Soviet relations, we have understood the Soviet Union in cartoon terms. Rather than approach that country as a sprawling, highly pluralistic, economically underdeveloped and proud nation caught in twentieth-century tragedy and frozen dogma, we have acted as if it were a cross between Satan and Atlas, all-powerful and enormously clever and evil, where everyone marches in lockstep at the command of the Communist party.

It does not take a leap of historical imagination to see that both the United States and the Soviet Union lost the Cold War. Ironically, the vanquished of World War II, Germany and Japan, became the beneficiaries, indeed the victors, in the Cold War. Unfortunately, U.S. foreign-policy makers have not adjusted to this stubborn fact of international politics. Conservatives and their academic supporters continue their Cold War attitudes, hoping to use Gorbachev's "perestroika" as a means to "liberate" the Russian people for very obscure objectives. This group favors a Pressure Strategy.

The Pressure Strategists, like Harvard's Richard Pipes and the Heritage Foundation, believe that the Soviet Union, much like the Ottoman

Empire, is basically weak, that it has little internal regenerative strength, and that a "victory" for the West is possible through a policy of military technological innovation and economic isolation. According to this view, each attempt at liberalization within the Soviet Union should be taken as a sign of Soviet weakness. If necessary, the U.S. response should be military with political probes that would further roll back the Soviet hold on Russia and Eastern Europe. The idea of "rollback," so popular rhetorically with John Foster Dulles during the Eisenhower administration, has continued as a secondary rhetorical theme of American foreign policy since the United States sponsored probes into the Soviet Union and Eastern Europe early in the Cold War. The probes were often undertaken by different exile factions, some of whom were fascist in ideology.

A variation of the Pressure Strategy is espoused in the national security documents of the later Carter and early Reagan eras. Proponents of this view, such as Zbigniew Brzezinski, hold that the Soviet Union can be dismantled through a decapitation and balkanizing strategy that encourages non-Russians within the Soviet sphere of influence to seek independence, autonomy, or legal rights. As Alexander Yanov, a former Soviet historian and now a U.S. professor, put it, "For example, the religion of 55 million Muslims, the nationalism of 50 million Ukrainians and 10 million Balts, not to mention 40 million Poles, are all potential targets for U.S. exploitation of political unrest within the Russian empire."[1] The "dismantling" view will gain currency among conservative groups as non-Russians struggle for greater autonomy in their affairs. Thus, the Latvian, Armenian, and Estonian experiences will become rallying cries within the United States for militant action against the Soviet Union.

According to Yanov, the strategy of balkanization and decapitation is a "godsend" to the Russian new right, which is increasing in size and thrives on the idea of Russian nationalism and purity, Western "corruption," anti-Semitism, and fears that the Russian homeland is going to be invaded by the West. There is no question that Gorbachev and the liberalizers will face difficult political moments as they attempt to restructure the economy at the same time that they must generate a new definition of citizenship for the Soviet Union as a whole.

The third, more official view of the Soviet Union is expressed by those within the universities and the Council on Foreign Relations who have adjusted to the Cold War and who believe in a management strategy. They point to history, saying that there have been some forty years without hot war because nuclear weapons force both sides toward a relationship of competitive management. This attitude assumes that there is very little the United States can do to influence the direction of events within the Soviet Union and that it would be an error to try because the United States would have to change its own commitments and purposes.

What is missing from these established positions are the dynamic possibilities now present in world politics and within the Soviet Union. These possibilities could cause a shift in relationships greater than the U.S. shift toward China in 1971. As the Soviet Union turns to greater democratization in both its economy and political process, European perceptions will change substantially. One result is that changes in the style and thrust of Soviet policy will require the United States to rearrange its alliance relations, reconsider in less ideological and more pragmatic terms its real needs and interests, and adopt an attitude that eschews needless confrontations with the Soviet Union. For example, the United States will need to recognize the obvious: the Soviets want trade and the Americans need markets. Either the United States trades with the Soviets or it will be sacrificing another market to the Japanese, Germans, and Swedes due to our outmoded political assumptions. Trade can become an instrument to end the Cold War.

There need not and should not be any passionate attachment in international affairs to any particular nation or cause except those specifically agreed to, such as the U.N. Charter. In other words, the primary emphasis for a new administration would be on reestablishing the role of international institutions that seek to end the war and Cold War system. Such a goal requires a significant change in attitude and the realization that a number of the steps taken during the Cold War in U.S.-Soviet relations need reconsideration and retracing. It should be noted that by improving relations with the Soviets, we do not have to hinder our relations with other nations. International relations is not a zero sum game, although U.S. policy makers have often been attracted to that metaphor. The position that I hold is called the "New Realism," according to which the U.S. role in the world is in flux and in need of redefinition. The cornerstone of this change will be rebuilding the international system and changing our relationship with the Soviet

Union to one that is in keeping with our national interest rather than based on ideological pretension.

For such an entente to occur it is necessary to be aware of those elements in the past that caused enmity between the two sides. The reasons began early, when the Bolsheviks pulled the Russians out of World War I. This happened a few months after the United States entered the war on the side of the Allies. The Soviet government concluded it had little choice but to sign a separate peace treaty: the Russians had lost 3.7 million men in the war and millions more Russians had died of starvation. Lenin's slogan of "Bread, Land, and Peace" had caught the imagination of the Russian people and there was no turning back from it. Almost immediately, the United States joined with other nations in an ill-fated intervention in Siberia, which amounted to little more than a failed defense of the remnants of the tsar's forces.

But these early incidents were only one side of the story. While the United States did not officially recognize the Soviet government until November 1933, and there was considerable fear of "Bolshevism" in Western governments and media, the fact is that many Americans, including U.S. corporations, helped the development of the Soviet Union during the 1920s. Indeed, some analysts have argued that the Communists learned more from the way Henry Ford set up an assembly line than they did from Karl Marx's theories of capital.

Both nations turned inward during the 1930s: the United States committed to economic and social reconstruction, while Stalin and his henchmen involved themselves in terrifying purges against dissidents, old Bolsheviks, and the so-called Kulak class. They claimed that the purges were the key to industrialization and economic development.

The pressure caused by Hitler's invasion of the Soviet Union and the worldwide struggle against nazism gave life to the idea that an American-Soviet entente was possible. As Henry Trofimenko, a Soviet professor of diplomatic history, pointed out in discussions,

> As to the problems the Allies had to tackle, they were often far more complex than those currently depicted as "insoluble." They concerned the lives of whole nations, the joint elaboration and coordination of military operations on an unprecedented scale, the adoption of a single policy toward the enemies, their attitude to the conquered, the postwar organization of the world, and the principles and forms of

postwar cooperation among states. These problems were resolved quickly and in a businesslike manner. Despite the complexities, difficulties, and even substantial differences in interests, compromises were found that suited all parties concerned.

The abrupt end of lend-lease, disagreement over Poland, the emergence of the United States as the single superpower, with the attendant hubris, the decision of the Soviet government to mask its weakness in bluster and distrust, the omnipresence of U.S. nuclear weapons and bases ringing the Soviet Union, and the arteriosclerotic nature of Soviet life when compared to the West, all helped to reinforce American elite and popular attitudes toward the Soviet Union during the end of the Stalin period. These early conditions blinded us, so that little significance was attached in the United States to positive changes that took place in Soviet life after Stalin's death. Gorbachev's rise to power was not an accident. It came at the end of a long party and bureaucratic struggle to transform the Soviet Union from a benighted and deformed state to one that sought a measure of stability and economic growth in its governance. The ascent has not been an altogether smooth one.

What have been the overriding and deadening political assumptions guiding American policy since 1947? The first was the belief that the United States should relate to the Soviet Union as to a permanent enemy. This was not a simple decision, for it meant two changes in American foreign policy. One was that the United States would alter the legacy left by George Washington that our country should have neither permanent friends nor permanent enemies in its foreign affairs. The second was that the Second World War period of cooperation with the Soviets would be erased from the popular mind. From thence forward our leadership was to assume that what is "bad" for the Soviet Union is "good" for the United States. Thus, throughout the Cold War period we arranged our foreign policy actions along the lines of knee-jerk antagonisms. The result was that our ideological predilection has been in direct conflict with the Soviets in every important sphere of relations. American leaders adopted this view for reasons that are related less to our vital interests than to the bureaucratic illusion that the world is a huge checkerboard where nations are pawns rather than autonomous entities with their own history and needs. Our adversary, the Soviet Union, is to be continuously tested in the game of geopolitics, but curiously never really defeated. (If, for example, the Soviets are having trouble in Estonia, the United States asserts its "right" of free passage in the Baltic Sea to show Estonian dissidents that the United States supports them and will not forget them—a cynical game, since the United States will do even less for the Estonians than it did for the Hungarians in 1956.)

The second assumption is not geopolitical but eschatological. It is that the struggle between the United States and the Soviet Union was religious in character, reminiscent of the Hundred Years War of Catholicism versus Protestantism. The amassing of military force and psychological will must go on because the struggle is really over which ideology is closer to "God" or the ultimate spirit of history. But this view is betrayed in practice by both nations, and even the most militant of Cold Warriors can no longer deny reality. There is a wide variety of communisms and capitalisms and the internal economic character of a nation is not necessarily a guide to whether it threatens the United States. Polycentrism is more than ever the character of international affairs, and all the nuclear missiles in the world, Marxist tracts, and capitalist material goods will not change that reality back to a two-power-bloc system. Since Cold Warriors are notoriously slow at recognizing political, social, and cultural changes in the world, they are enamored of instruments that ostensibly are meant to keep things as they are. Thus, they put their faith in weaponry and technology, not realizing that both these ingredients force even greater change among nations. Except for spasm periods (1949–51, 1961–62, 1979–82), most Cold Warriors have held that military force must not overwhelm the requirement of self-control with the Soviets. But the costs of the U.S.-Soviet Cold War have not been adequately tallied. The United States has spent $6 trillion on the Cold War and its frozen version of the Soviet Union. It has sacrificed 110,000 armed forces personnel and suffered 400,000 wounded for wars that were, in part, an outgrowth of artificial boundaries that stemmed from a failure to resolve differences at the end of World War II.

Change is an imperative because the Cold War has had costs that could be terminal to constitutional democracy. For example, we have been relatively thoughtless in changing the character of our government, increasing secrecy in order to assure the appearance of consensus, and endorsing military adventurism in the name of anti-communism. A new president will have to decide whether to embrace a defense and foreign policy system that allows the institutions and assumptions of the Cold War to continue reproducing themselves like paramecia. A new administration will have to decide whether to embrace a true internationalism based on the U.N. if Gorbachev offers the United States a chance to escape a world view that straps us to the stone of constant threat and fear. That administration will also have to find a moral voice to mount a successful challenge against those within U.S. life who, fearful of modern times, are prepared to risk war for their view of fundamentalist, ethical purity. As I have suggested, this form of reaction is also present in the Soviet Union, where forces of Russian nationalism and fundamentalism hope to destroy the current liberalizing direction. But there are far stronger social forces in the Soviet Union that seek closer, normal relations with the West. The policy of détente was favored by the Soviets through much of the Cold War. For the Soviets this was nothing new. Even at the beginning of the Cold War the Soviets sought to make clear the limits of their grasp. The historian D.F. Fleming pointed out that

> near the end of the Second World War Stalin scoffed at communism in Germany, urged the Italian Reds to make peace with the monarchy, did his best to induce Mao Tse Tung to come to terms with the Kuomintang, and angrily demanded of Tito that he take back the monarchy, thus fulfilling his bargain with Churchill.[2]

The Soviet leadership sought respect from the United States, and in exchange it was prepared to limit its interest and commitments, staying out of the way of the United States. The Soviets played second fiddle to the international symphony led by the United States. They knew that the changes wanted by Third World or Eastern European nations often stemmed from ideas that the United States stimulated either directly or through example. In contrast, U.S. foreign policy has been conservative and restorationist, fearful of international social change. This tendency caused us to generate governmental institutions whose mission was to attack change, especially when it seemed to threaten the status quo ruling elites that were linked to U.S. business and military interests.

The détente of the rascals—that of Nixon, Kissinger, and Brezhnev, men whose reputation in public life was made on the basis of generating fear or corruption—fell apart soon after they left power. The reason for the failure of détente from the Soviet side was the collapse of the shah's government and the emergence of Khomeini in Iran, an unstable situation in Poland, and the inability of President Carter to gain agreement from the Senate for the SALT II treaty. The result for the Soviets was a monumental foreign policy blunder on a scale proportionate to the American intervention in Vietnam. The Soviet-"invited" intervention in Afghanistan destroyed the possibilities of the rascals' détente. The United States, which used trade as a carrot in its relations with the Soviets, turned off the trade enticement. The Soviet managers and planners who had sought liberalization within the Soviet economy through heavy trading and technical assistance were again checkmated by international politics. They had made the mistake of gearing their economic planning to substantially increased trade with the United States as a means of fulfilling their own technological development. The atmosphere between the two sides, from 1979 to 1984, again became poisonous and the respective national security institutions of both nations reinforced each other in their competing weapons claims and needs. Yet sober analysts knew that the Soviet increase in long-range missiles and the Reagan dream of SDI were no answer to the security of both nations. It was obvious that the arms race itself was the single most dangerous dynamic between both nations, which made a mockery of each side's security and of any ideas they had for a nation free of the burden of military institutions and armaments. Sir Solly Zuckerman, the former science adviser to a number of British prime ministers, put it well when he said,

> The arms race can bankrupt the superpowers without adding anything to their respective military strengths. Deterrent systems today cost tens of times more than they did twenty years ago, when the political state of deterrence was just as operative as it is today. From the point of view of political/strategic value nothing has been gained.[3]

It is painful to note that much has been lost in resources through feeding military and defense economic institutions that protect national security in ways that are not dissimilar from protection rackets. Mutual deterrence has become a shared protection racket of the military establishments of both sides. This is hardly a stable way to conduct international affairs or to free up internal energies for domestic needs.

An administration that is committed to closing the Cold War will seek a new system of defense and disarmament, one that transforms the military, bureaucratic systems of both sides and the Third World.

This objective is well within the grasp of creative statecraft. It requires renouncing the technological forces of violence in the world because their value for specific political objectives, from the point of view of the West and the Soviet Union, is minimal. Even non-nuclear, "conventional" warfare and military assistance has its limits. The Soviets learned this in Afghanistan, just as the United States had been treated to the same lesson in Indochina.

The Soviets are no longer convinced that the amount of material and military assistance they provided to the Third World has resulted in very much gain, either for their brand of socialism or their idea of "correct" state-to-state relations. The lesson is that it is possible to obtain good relations in the Third World without much direct investment; less is more in order to assure that superpower confrontations do not occur in the Third World. Conservatives and Democrats nevertheless urge a buildup of conventional forces and small nuclear weapons efforts to avoid conflicts in the Third World. This is a recipe for disaster and flies in the face of the United States' own experience and need for domestic reconstruction.

The evidence is clear. The Soviets want to end the Cold War and, like ourselves, their internal needs require that they do so. The question is whether a debilitating *folie à deux* can be transformed into a more healthy set of bilateral and world relations. This question can be answered operationally, for there are specific steps that can be taken that will enhance world security, and even the U.S. position in the world. These steps, however, must take account of Soviet fears and interests. What are they?

Throughout the Cold War, concern about Germany's long-term intentions has never been far from the Russian mind, whatever the person's age and however far the Russian is from the Kremlin's walls. It is hardly surprising, therefore, that besides the issue of nuclear weapons the direction Germany will take in the next generation is of great importance to the Soviet Union. The détente of the rascals sought to freeze Europe and the German role through NATO and the Warsaw Pact. For at least twenty-five years before Gorbachev, the Soviets were not interested in any plans for military disengagement along the lines either of the Polish Rapacki Plan or the disengagement plans of George Kennan. But mutual military engagement has now become a likelihood. Indeed, both the Soviet and the Polish governments have offered disengagement plans, with the Soviets calling for a cutback of a 1.25

million troops now stationed in Eastern and Western Europe. If a new administration sought such negotiations, in the context of a larger arms and security settlement that precluded a regional arms race in Europe, real gains to world and United States security could be achieved.

Until now neither the Democratic nor Republican leadership has been prepared to consider an alternative security structure to NATO, or to change the alliance substantially into a joint security system with the Warsaw Pact. The harsh economics of increasing trade deficits, a citizenry angry at the decay of the quality of life, and astronomical costs for new weaponry will change this reality. Economic considerations will press the United States toward rapprochement, just as economic concerns are pressing the Soviet government in that direction. The costs of the U.S. presence in Western Europe run in the neighborhood of $160 billion a year. This burden seems anachronistic given the prosperous condition of the Western European nations. Yet there are dangers to U.S. security if France and Germany unite to mount their own nuclear weapons "defense," just as the United States has nothing to gain from Japanese rearmament.

There is no value to further nuclear buildup anywhere in the world. All nations have their antagonists and interests, and each conflict could become a tinderbox for world war if war preparation continues to be the rule of international relations. One wishes that the Bush administration would champion the continuation of a nonproliferation treaty, a treaty originally signed by non-nuclear nations on the promise that nuclear nations would rid themselves of nuclear weapons. The nonproliferation agreement is merely a stopgap measure. It does not speak to the continuing crisis of insecurity caused by the war system.

However, without concrete, cumulative steps in the framework for common security and general disarmament, first by the superpowers and then by other nations, humanity will remain at best trapped in an unaffordable militarism and at worst will find itself involved in terrifying wars. The nations, especially the superpowers, will be trapped in a political version of the second law of thermodynamics. Each step taken forward without changing the framework will not result in significant positive change, because the nations will have no "roadmap" to show them how to proceed. The decline for all nations, and especially for the military superpowers, will continue precipitously. In financial terms, the result will be expenditures of astonishing amounts of money on armaments as the bottom half of humanity sinks further into a swamp of misery.

There are signposts for both the United States and the Soviet Union that, if heeded, will prevent the two from falling backwards. They are found in international law, ethics, the U.N. Charter and covenants, and specific cases of mutual agreements that have worked for both nations in the past, such as the Austrian State Treaty. Thus, for example, multilateral organizations such as the World Bank and GATT should be opened to Soviet participation.

Certain arguments will have to be rejected as casuistical. The tiresome academic debate of whether political tensions cause arms races or arms races cause political tension is irrelevant because both political differences and arms races are utterly intertwined with each other, especially as they relate to U.S.-Soviet relations. The reality of this intertwining relationship can be seen in Third World conflict and local interventions, where military assistance from opposing sides increases tensions to the point of war. This fact requires that the United States and the Soviet Union work through the United Nations in ending the anarchic tendency for "intervention at will" that has gripped many nations. Because the United States and the Soviet Union have played down international law and nonintervention in their activities, other nations have felt unrestrained in their own interventions. A new administration would do much for U.S. national interest by pressing for international legal standards that renounce unilateral interventions and make use of international agencies such as the United Nations.

At the end of the Second World War, the United Nations Relief and Rehabilitation Agency, an allied effort for European rehabilitation, had enormous positive effect. Its successor, the Marshall Plan, was also powerfully effective in helping to restore the Western European economy. The serious flaw of the Marshall Plan was that it became linked with the Truman Doctrine, in which the United States tied itself to the role of world policeman. Nevertheless, the idea of multilateral economic and social responsibility for development is a good one and is especially relevant to twenty-first-century problems around technology, damage to the world's atmosphere, starvation, and world debt.

There is almost no world leader who has not decried the foolish waste of funds for armaments as billions of people live at the edge of starvation. And in the late twentieth century, all political leaders must decry the spoliation of the environment. Problems of starvation, development, and the environment cannot be dealt with unless attention is focused on general disarmament and common security, not increasing economic competitiveness. Hence, the most important activity in diplomacy with the Soviet Union and other nations is developing a common approach to security and disarmament. In 1961, in part as a propaganda exercise but also because the need for it had already been felt, the American and Soviet emissaries, John McCloy and Valerian Zorin, signed an agreement for negotiating general and complete disarmament. This phrase has been referred to in at least a half-dozen treaties between the United States and the Soviet Union. Yet not since 1962 have there been any serious negotiations on general disarmament. Is it now obvious that the United States needs a *comprehensive* disarmament strategy? Its leaders have the choice of continuing the battle of arms control, pursuing the elixir of SDI, or pursuing the path of general disarmament through the Arms Control and Disarmament Agency (ACDA), as well as other agencies of government. It is sad but true that in recent years the ACDA became the justifier of weapons systems and military force rather than being the governmental instrument to come forward with ways and means of bringing about disarmament. A new administration will need a far different set of government advisers, including individuals with greater openness to the peace movement, and that part of the scholarly community that seeks paths and comprehensive answers to replacing the war system. After a generation of arms control, it is obvious that the requirements for limited agreements are as complex and onerous as they would be for a comprehensive disarmament arrangement that encompasses conventional and nuclear forces. Arms control leads nowhere because the war system stays in place.

Judging from past negotiated agreements with the Soviets, and the needs of Soviet society to which Gorbachev is responding, a fifteen-year common security and general disarmament program with the Soviets could be achieved. Even with a strong president, however, the treaty program will require massive citizen support to negotiate and sustain. Is there a greater gift that political leadership and citizen action could offer the twenty-first century than the taming of the dogs of war and the ending of the terrible weight of the arms race? Is it not obvious that the war system and the technologies attendant to it pervert and degrade capitalism and socialism necessitating their transformation as well?

Notes

1. Alexander Yanov, *The Russian Challenge* (Oxford: Basil Blackwell, 1987), p. 269.
2. D.F. Fleming, *The Cold War and Its Origins 1917–1960*, vol. 2 (Garden City, N.J.: Doubleday, 1960).
3. Sir Solly Zukerman, *Nuclear Illusion & Reality* (New York: Random House, 1983), p. 101.

10

Post–Cold War Options: The New Order?

The end of the Cold War is cause for hope and realism. By hope, I mean the practical ways in which humankind, with all its flaws, is able to create a social world and environment that escapes the framework of dominator and dominated. By realism, I mean recognition of the problems that engulf humankind and the earth and the reengagement of our capacity for social invention and imaginations for a common good. Just as there are revolutionary frameworks in science that begin whole new patterns, so it is that uncoordinated mass political activities of people unable to live with the pain of oppression, force new, powerful impulses to the surface that then result in revolutionary change in social systems. The character of that change is never very clear. What is clear is the initial impulse: that "things are wrong" or that the oppression is somehow palpable. It is here where leadership, movements, and ideas based on praxis and political imagination can come together to create a very different reality for humanity.

Many say that revolutionary changes are often metaphors and do not result in the betterment of people's everyday lives. I agree. What we need instead is a social reconstruction that understands that seemingly intractable problems are open to both solution and new ways of refocusing. The romantic pragmatism of social reconstruction is what people are now responding to in various parts of the world. From Asia to Europe, people are looking for new frameworks of legitimacy that they can create with each other and within which they can then live. This is not easy, for the line of historical progress is not a straight ascent.

There are zigs and zags. Great changes have many layers and are deeply textured with different conceptions of time and purpose for different cultures. This makes it even more necessary to ensure that the massive changes that will come at the end of the Cold War will move toward a world civilization that respects vastly different cultures and economies. International institutions, the midwives of world civilization, must be aware of these differences while helping nations comprehend the values and problems that bind humanity together at this stage of history. ☐ ☐

If citizen engagement and political leadership are mobilized for it, the United States can now with other nations, pursue a course of ending the war system. This course requires a strong commitment to international organization, world law, common security, and disarmament, and the recognition of common world problems that transcend borders and cannot be handled by any one nation.

The Bush administration is understandably fearful of dismantling a national security apparatus built by both major political parties, industrial, scientific, and labor managers since the end of the Second World War, and whose members have not been trained to imagine any other set of possibilities than that of a United States tied to the Cold War.

Cold Warriors believed that the United States and the West face an implacable enemy which at a minimum had to be contained, or alternatively, liberated. Adherents of this view preached the importance of a military alliance system that could be managed through a credulous media system, a domestic economy that would grow through Cold War commitments, and an American leadership class secure in itself, its beliefs, and its role in the world.

Our global thinkers have assumed (without proof) that NATO was the cause of peace in Europe. They believe that any changes must build on the security assumptions taken for granted over the past forty-two years, although room should be made for technological changes.

American military strategy is presently wholly infested with hi-tech assumptions linked to forward-attack forces that can strike Eastern Europe quickly and easily. Present NATO planning strategies foster the belief that conventional forces could be reduced if military gadgetry were increased and modernized. It is assumed that "balance" between opposing forces is necessary, although there is no clear understanding of what balance means except in terms of comparing particular weapons that may actually be worlds apart in value and efficiency. Of course there is no longer an enemy, so negotiations on weapons and troop reduction take on the character of a political litmus test that tells the antagonists whether they are able to maintain an atmosphere of calm and stability between themselves. In the past the Soviet and Western discussions stood on common ground.

Discussions between West and East about limiting arms in Europe started from an unarticulated but bedrock agreed assumption, namely control over Germany. The West and the East have lived under an understanding between the United States and the Soviet Union that divided Europe in May 1945. Part of this tacit understanding between Molotov's successor, Gromyko, and successive Western foreign ministers and secretaries of state was the conviction that Germany should not become either independent or a great power. Post–World War II leaders all took cognizance of a tragic fact, namely, that too much blood had been spilled in two wars because of Germany. Consequently they resolved that Germany could not have its own independent status or be a "free floater" in world politics.

Thus, while Western nations, including Germany, have sought ways of containing the Soviets since the Bolshevik Revolution of 1918, Western diplomacy excluding Germany has had another mission since the Second World War: to maintain control over Germany. As Professor Joan Garces of the University of Madrid has pointed out, the recurring Western fear during the Cold War period was that Germany and the Soviet Union would gravitate toward one another in an alliance whose contours were outlined in the 1939 Hitler-Stalin pact. The long-term policies of Soviet diplomacy have been aimed at breaking out of its isolation as a middle kingdom by retaining a security belt around the Soviet Union, while the Western alliance saw NATO as a continuation of the *cordon sanitaire* that was in place against bolshevism after the First World War.

While the 1939 German-Soviet mutual vectoring was a world tragedy fostered by the political miscalculations of two dictators, Hitler and Stalin, each of whom would rather have signed deals with Great Britain and France than with each other, a mutual gravitation between Germany and the Soviet Union in the 1990s could be an extraordinary opportunity for the West and especially the United States. With U.S. participation, the Ostpolitik policies begun by Willy Brandt and pursued by Hans-Dietrich Genscher could lead to a comprehensive disarmament arrangement of conventional and nuclear forces coupled to increased trade, cultural, and human rights guarantees in Eastern Europe.

Such a program, when negotiated in the context of an international general disarmament program, could enhance global security. These goals were exactly what U.S. foreign policy sought at the end of the Second World War, until certain forces and events came together to create the political crash that was the Cold War. The death of Roosevelt and the blind hubris that grew from the atomic bomb along with the United States' economic power gave the United States unparalleled and unchallenged power in the world and caused American policy makers to think it unnecessary to regard the United Nations seriously as an organization for the control of power and the pursuit of shared political goals. Instead the United States opted for a regional alliance system under U.S. hegemony. To some extent, of course, these efforts were successful, and they still play, even in a political and economically revitalized Western Europe.

There is no doubt that the United States can impede and slow an all-Europe settlement. But for how long and to what end? The long-term political direction in Europe appears inevitable because of cultural, technological, and generational changes. The mood among the populace, left-of-center parties, and the youth and business communities in Europe leads one to believe that with proper diplomatic leadership the wars and Cold War that have gripped Europe since 1914 could be at an end, the resurgence of nationalism and fascism among some groups notwithstanding. The Gaullist dream of a European civilization from the Atlantic to the Urals, internally at peace is not out of reach. This should be good news for the United States since it spends approximately $160 billion a year on the present NATO system, and keeps some 300,000 troops in place in Western Europe.

Furthermore, it is no longer intuitively obvious that the United States is a European power. Its trading system is in great flux and more than half its population by the year 2020 will not recognize its roots in Europe. Throughout the Cold War the U.S. interest was mediated through primarily business interests that identified with Western Europe as a trading partner and through long-time financial ties between capital on both sides of the Atlantic. These ties, if not weakening, are changing under the pressure of international competition and the growth of expensive technologies with the capacity to drive political relationships. The Bush administration is committed to buttressing the United States' primary position in NATO by keeping a technological arms race going. Besides nuclear weapons, the conventional war strategies of the West, pressed by the U.S. Department of Defense, are driven by emphases on new military technologies. Such weapons systems as TABAS, long- and short-range Cruise Missiles, ATACM, ballistic missiles, unguided rocket launchers, new types of reconnaissance and strike weapons, as well as basic modernization have been pressed on the NATO allies by the United States through 1989. These weapons schemes and modernization are enormously expensive and add nothing to stability (let alone disarmament), although they provide a *raison d'être* for the U.S. military industrial culture. The Defense Department is calculating that the Western Europeans are unwilling or unable to invest in such weapons. Cold War defense planners believe that because of financial frugality the West Europeans will continue their military dependence on the United States through the 1990s and beyond. They are also banking on another concern that is now gripping the higher reaches of conservative thinking in Western Europe.

Once the Cold War is folded up, the Thatcher government will be at political risk if the British "nuclear deterrent" is bargained away in a multilateral disarmament settlement. The British Labor party—or at least some of its most vocal adherents—will be in a more credible position with the British public because they have long pointed out the disutility of nuclear weapons. The French will also be forced to reassess their own heavy investment in nuclearism—something they may be reluctant to do, given their fixation on *gloire* and a left that gave up interest in disarmament when Mitterand became the French president. It is likely, however, that an American-Soviet agreement that changes the rules of the game away from nuclearism and the arms race would rekindle a movement in France that would link with others in Europe and elsewhere to demand a disarmament policy as part of French security. Such a move would be suggestive of directions a worldwide peace movement will find itself taking in order to press a program of international security and disarmament onto national leaders.

In 1992 the United States will face a West Europe, for which it acted as midwife a generation ago, that will be drawn closer together economically and culturally. With a European Parliament committed to social democratic goals, we may expect a shift in Western Europe's focus away from Thatcherism and the automatic belief that NATO is a bulwark against war rather than a useless cost and provocation. If Europe for the first time in its history moves to a coordinated foreign policy based on economic, political, and cultural interests, the United States will be faced with a wholly new challenge. Western Europe's era of consultative subservience will have come to an end, and will in turn give the United States a chance to throw off its own shackles and begin the arduous task of internal social reconstruction. We need not repeat the litany of statistics that show that our nation faces severe difficulties in its economy, education, and health systems; that increasingly its children are without hope. Polls show that Americans are deeply aware of the need to repair their own nation. This they know far better than either the purpose or reason for NATO, if in 1991 there is one. Americans are further emboldened when they see formerly antagonistic European nations making peace and know that Western Europe is eager to trade with the East and vice versa. With the gross national product of Western Europe greater than that of the United States, it is no wonder that support for NATO among the American people is waning.

In the forty-five years since the end of World War II American popular opinion on foreign policy has passed through four stages. The first was the perception of threat from the East. Parallel to this perception was the feeling that the United States should not be driven off the European continent by the Soviets (1949–62). The second stage was the belief that the United States could not maintain itself as a superpower if it showed any lessening of commitment to Western Europe during the Vietnam War. The third stage was the perception, common among elites, that the United States had real economic interests in Western Europe and that the presence of American troops ensured U.S. investments and the integration of Western Europe under a U.S. nuclear and political umbrella. The present period is one in which members of Congress believe that the Western Europeans are not "burden sharing," that the Western Europeans are getting a free ride off the U.S. taxpayers with no visible benefits to the United States. On the other hand, many Western Europeans are not happy with an American military strategy that turns their nations into a nuclear battlefield or commits them to low intensity war in the Third World. They never look favorably on American plans that hoped to limit any possible war to Europe, giving U.S. planners a pause period to negotiate with the Russians without nuclear weapons being dropped on American soil.

Furthermore, the European irritation with American GIs and U.S. military maneuvers and the high cost of living for Americans in Western Europe has torn the bloom off the NATO rose for American soldiers. The handwriting is on the wall when a distinguished American general who favored NATO, General Andrew Goodpaster, said that the United States should pull back 50 percent of its forces. These changes, when matched to the idea of Robert McNamara that the United States should cut its strategic forces by 50 percent, support the view that something powerful is happening. This is both true and not true. The level of overkill is so great in weaponry that 50 percent cutbacks would still leave both sides sufficient force to destroy the world a number of times over.

Yet, there is a momentum that is clearly different from the past efforts at détente. Without actual combat elected politicians will be hard put to explain heavy expenditures when there is no direct bearing on the regeneration of the society from defense expenditure. These changes will have a ripple effect to other parts of American foreign policy. They have begun in the Middle East where Secretary of State Baker has announced that formerly automatic policies—for example, uncritical American acceptance of Israeli policies that were expansionist in intent and implementation—will not be underwritten by the United States. Such sentiments will apply to Asia as well, where American business is feeling the heavy breath of Japanese and South Korean competitors and where it is unclear that the U.S. military serves as an aid to a U.S. sphere of influence over these areas. Bush's reluctance to support the Congress in its tough policy against China after the massacres in Beijing is related to fear that the United States will lose markets to the Japanese and South Koreans.

A conservative-right coalition tinged with xenophobia might make common cause with a declining labor movement around the coin of nationalism. With foreign products flooding American markets, the American right may be tempted to follow a dangerous course reminiscent of the direction into which nationalists in Japan plunged their nation in the 1930s. At that time the Japanese undertook wars to end their feeling of isolation, protect oil supplies, secure markets, and fulfill their view of destiny.

The American people are not immune to demagogic appeals about foreigners who, it is claimed, destroy our purity and mock our good works abroad. Xenophobes remind Americans that we are surrounded by unfriendly nations who misunderstand the purity of our motives. This political appeal was made with relative success in 1950 after the Communists took power in China. Blame for who lost China gave impetus to the McCarthy purge period in American life. It was the residue of McCarthyism that helped the right's election of Ronald Reagan, and George Bush played the same tunes to gain the presidency in 1988.

The xenophobic are aware that the ostensible reason for the Cold War, the isolation of the Soviet Union, has failed. A scant few years ago conservative and liberal analysts both argued that the Soviet Union was hemmed in, surrounded by socialist and capitalist states that distrusted Soviet leadership and saw the Soviet Union as a basket-case nation in terms of ideas, energy, and the conduct of everyday life. The diplomatically skilled Gorbachev and Shevardnadze have been able through an aggressive foreign policy to turn the Soviets' negative image in the West around. This objective was accomplished by radically reassessing Soviet interests in real rather than rhetorical and ideological terms. Gorbachev transformed prior commitments in Afghanistan, Poland, and East Germany, while accepting American positions on arms control without much hesitation. Furthermore, in another turnaround, it is not unlikely that the Soviets will offer greater autonomy to the Baltic states on the ground that the Hitler-Stalin pact contradicted socialist principles.

The Soviet change in policy is perceived as enormously threatening to those who believe either that real changes are not occurring in the Soviet Union, that the Gorbachev policies are tricks, or that he will fail and there will be return to Stalin-like Cold Warism.

The xenophobic can now add other fears to their original ones concerning the Soviet Union. If the Soviets settle their differences with Japan, China, and Germany, and if their rapprochement toward these nations results in an unwritten alliance, then ironically it is the United States that could be isolated in the world and thus limited in its capacities to maneuver economically and militarily. Indeed, throughout the last decade the United States was often among a minority of four or five in votes in the United Nations General Assembly.

Given that the United States is not performing well against the Japanese economically and that the Japanese are fast replacing the Soviets as the Enemy Other in the popular pantheon of American hates, there will be an increasing belief that the United States must arm to the teeth because of the "enemies" it faces. The long-term interest of the Japanese and the Germans in getting out from under the dictates of the United States is well known in policy circles. The Japanese have, of course, accomplished this feat economically, indeed, offering, and not in a tongue-in-cheek way, economically to develop (read "colonize") part of California. The short-sighted policies of national security managers who urge a greater arms buildup in Japan will soon be seen as a threat by those who formerly called for increased defense expenditures by Japan. Without a clearly defined alternative the American go-it-alone sentiment could increase as Western Europe moves toward confederating linkages on trade and the belief shared among European Social and Christian Democrats alike grows that the assumptions of the Cold War are no longer applicable in changed conditions.

If the Bush administration does not lay out a sufficiently large vision of its purpose—in other words, an alternative to the Cold War anticommunist mentality that has gripped American politics for over forty years—the nationalists who remain inadequately represented by Vice President Quayle would seek to embolden the American military and security apparatus into adventures in order to break out of what they will perceive as American "isolation."

Nationalists know that their sentiment is widely shared in the United States only when blood is spilled. The most likely place for such a local war is, as it has been throughout the post–World War II period, the Third World. Four basic scenarios for such a war come to mind. The first and least likely scenario is one in which the United States claims that one of the industrialized powers is cutting off our supply lines; for example, the Soviets are entering the Middle East through Iraq to deny the United States and Western Europe oil. A second possibility would involve an attempt to confront Muslim fundamentalism where its leadership in a particular state was rhetorically obnoxious and perceived to be funding acts of terrorism; for example, in Iran which from time to time calls for avenging the deaths of Iranian civilians killed by the U.S. Navy. We could also be caught in the aftermath of war between Iran and Iraq. A third dangerous possibility is the Philippines, where a longstanding struggle between revolutionaries and a government rife with factionalism and barely able to govern continues and where the United States would have to choose to give up its long-term military interests to avoid bloodshed. The fourth possibility is a continuous war in various parts of Latin America, especially in

Colombia, Panama, Bolivia, and Argentina, initially entered into ostensibly to stop the drug traffic but in reality to sustain the area as a U.S. sphere of influence. Such interventions would spark cries of Yankee imperialism in Mexico, a nation suffering from a period of corruption and stolen elections and where U.S. intervention, whether for noble or base reasons, would not have a salutary effect.

Wars are often thought to be unifiers by leaders who fear internal strife. But the stratagem of war as a unifier for the United States is both costly and bound to fail: while it would briefly generate a national purpose, it would also increase the level of street demonstrations in the United States and tend to make the nation ungovernable.

Furthermore, an increase of the defense budget in such circumstances would not have the Keynesian effect of adding to general economic well-being unless price and wage controls were placed on goods and services. If this were not done, the right nationalist position would have the effect of increasing the split within the nation between rich and poor, thereby adding to domestic decay and the likely alienation of a labor constituency.

Guns before butter would become the cry of the xenophobes, who would insist that the United States act on a global scale, feeling surrounded and aggrieved. Yet for the United States the chance of such a strategy working is not great, for it would mean that the entire U.S. media system would have to change its internationalist interest and report news in such a manner as to affirm the xenophobic view, namely, that the nation now under siege is truly a "pitiful helpless giant." Such ideas will be rejected by that part of American business that is dependent on international trade.

In the United States, moderate Republican international corporate leaders, who historically have had an allergy to war and the national security state, might conclude that the state is vestigial if a xenophobic position is adopted. They believe that international corporations with their capacity to move literally billions of dollars at the punch of a key reflect a new international social system that seeks at least coequal status with the nation-state. The American business ethos—namely, to penetrate markets and trade with all comers regardless of their ideological stance—will increase tensions between international corporations and those who govern the threat-oriented national security state. In this sense international corporations are riding the wave of global and regional integration, while the national security state thrusts itself full speed backward into the past, hoping that hi-tech military technologies will preserve its relevance to modern conditions.

The long-term underlying thrust toward globalism in the twentieth century will increase in velocity because of communications, television and film, and capital and labor movement. Except in the case of organized labor, it is not the intention of these new forms of communication to sculpt a moral consciousness, yet that may be their consequence. New meanings of human responsibility toward the wretched one-quarter of the world could result from greater communication, even as global economic integration disrupts communities and creates increasingly larger urban centers that are ungovernable.

This complex dialectic between competing forces that intend one thing but bring about another is the basis of twenty-first-century global politics. By retracing its steps back to the end of the Second World War, the United States could fulfill itself as a great civilization. Its leaders and citizens would have to recognize changed conditions, and simultaneously turn inward and pursue a politics of globalism, as well as give up the assumptions of militarism. Conditions are present for a resurgent globalism within American society.

Attempts have been made since the First World War to escape a narrow nationalism and replace it with international institutions, international law, and disarmament, as well as scientific and technological progress that serves humane ends. This impulse has included attempts to rid the world of imperialism, racism, and economic catastrophe. The American attitude toward these attempts has been mixed. The high point of acceptance of such ideas in the U.S. government came at the end of the Second World War under the tutelage of President Franklin Roosevelt. The Rooseveltian assumptions favored an end to spheres of influence and decolonization. And while the British saw the American position as an attempt to take over the colonies of Great Britain, France, and the Netherlands, Roosevelt steadfastly believed that independence for new nations from European domination was the basis upon which a world committed to the U.S.-inspired ideals of the United Nations Charter could be achieved. History is a ragged and jagged story without the abstract straight lines of Euclidian geometry. As a result it is hard to retrace steps and assume that they will come out better "the next time."

Nevertheless, there is a time when there is a chance for humane rationalism. It comes when other international roads that are so obviously dismal necessitate the construction of a different path. The United States' gift to the world—and to itself—would be an alternative vision that will put an end to the Cold War and perhaps the war system.

Certain questions of political tactics should be discussed before we can go forward with the option of resurgent globalism. There will be some who will say, "The policies of the past have been successful. Times have changed. We don't have to look back at the validity of these policies. All we need do is turn the page of history and begin a new chapter."

The other view is that it will be impossible to begin a new period in American history without analyzing and acknowledging the various flawed policies the United States followed throughout the Cold War. The Cold War, according to this view, was not inevitable and at various points it could have ended. One such occasion, for example, was in 1956 when a deal on nuclear weaponry and conventional forces might have been worked out by the United States and the Soviet Union through their respective representatives, Harold Stassen and Valerian Zorin. Perhaps most important of all, because it relates to what a next stage in American diplomacy should be, was the downplaying of the United Nations in favor of building up the military alliance system in specific derogation of the ideas that were most prominent in American diplomatic thought in 1945. While one does not have to mythologize the thinking of that period, it is also true that these ideas held within them an attempt to transcend crude autarkic power politics in favor of world organization and world civilization. To the extent, therefore, that we intend to move beyond the Cold War, its apparatus, and the mind set that we have constructed for that period, historians will have to help us reanalyze specific aspects of the Cold War. Other researchers will be needed to identify the confluence of cultures and values that would promote a shared world civilization.

In the United States the path to democracy and a democratic foreign policy does not have to be invented out of whole cloth. The basis is already present in many of the ideas of our leaders and thinkers, for example, in this century, John Dewey, Jane Addams, Martin Luther King, Jr., Robert La Follette, Albert Einstein, Quincy Wright, Harold Stassen, Franklin Roosevelt, James P. Warburg, George McGovern, Jesse Jackson, Henry Wallace, and Richard Falk. These ideas have been carried on as well by fellows of the Institute for Policy Studies.

This tradition recognizes the inextricable link between internal democratic policies and the foreign policy to be pursued.

This direction for the United States cannot be easily obtained unless there is a strong movement inside and outside the legislative and executive branches setting forth an alternative that is clear, credible, and reachable in a specific period of time. It is an option that will be linked to domestic reconstruction but can stand on its own. That is to say, there is little within a democratic foreign policy that could not be supported by those who hold that we require a critical reexamination of the assumptions and policies that guided us into war and sublimited war between 1945 and 1989.

A beginning in this regard was made in 1975 in various Senate hearings, although they were limited and closed off when they touched too deeply or suggested the need to dismantle various aspects of the national security state apparatus, a task that would begin by repealing the National Security Act of 1947. It is for current political reasons that we need a truer picture of the history of the Cold War, for we will not be able to escape its assumptions and structures without comprehending the negative effects it had on American society. Such historical detective work will enable us to show how the real interests of the nation were undercut by choices made during the Cold War.

National and international law now require a correlation between humankind's permanent interests and the general interests of one's own nation. This may be maddening to the xenophobes. Indeed, the right during the Reagan administration tried its utmost to undo the United Nations, causing the United States to fall behind in its financial obligations to the U.N., ignore U.N. resolutions, as well as decisions of the International Court of Justice. By so doing the United States intended to set itself up as the alternative to the United Nations at a time when its actual economic and political power was in decline. The fact of American (and world) decline was masked by commentators who trumpeted the collapse of Soviet-style socialism. But their analyses did not take into account how weak the American economic and social system is, largely as a result of foolish expenditure and allocation judgments made during much of the Cold War period.

If the United States is not going to be the world policeman, who will be? A policeman of course is only as good as his legitimacy. The political institution of world legitimacy is the United Nations. Thus, it is in that context that nations will have collectively to develop rules of behavior between states as well as how, whether, and when force is to be used.

In that context the United States' mission is to work to secure the peace through mediation, arbitration, and the use of its good offices when requested to do so by parties in dispute. It would seek ways to change political and military disputes into legal disputes that could then be presented to the International Court. And it would lead nations in developing principles of personal accountability for all the world's leaders. It would participate in working on an international security agreement and comprehensive disarmament through the Military Staff committee of the United Nations. It would participate in economic boycotts and other methods short of war if there was agreement to do so by the U.N. Security Council. The United States would reserve a contingent of nonnuclear forces for use under the aegis of the Security Council. These forces could only be used if U.S. constitutional and legal procedures were followed, namely the War Powers Act and a congressional declaration authorizing their use.

In other words U.S. security would be attained through a new international security agreement, comprehensive disarmament (to be described in detail in the next chapter), and strict adherence to the charter of the United Nations. It would refrain from making threats to the peace, and answer threats to the peace collectively under the terms specified in the charter. American leaders have used the United Nations' legitimacy in an inconsistent and often cynical way. Thus, its resolutions for Israeli withdrawal from the occupied territories are vetoed or ignored by the United States. During the Vietnam War, the United States assiduously avoided using the United Nations to resolve that conflict. Instead its good offices were disdained or avoided. The abuse of the United Nations in this way was one factor in splitting the liberal movement in the United States. Although this split had been exacerbated by the Cold War and the national security state, the political divide within American liberalism became a chasm during the Vietnam War.

Like the American Civil War, Vietnam will continue to have powerful cultural and political consequences. Hubert Humphrey was within himself a symbol of the schism. His own supporters turned either right or left as a result of that war, notable examples being Jeane Kirkpatrick, the former ambassador to the United Nations, who went to the right, and the former congressman, Allard Lowenstein, who encouraged Senator Eugene McCarthy to oppose Lyndon Johnson for the presidency. Perhaps the chasm could be transcended by a new liberal and radical appreciation of the United Nations' utility.

Proponents of social reconstruction in their domestic politics should now champion an entire fabric of international rules, from the U.N. Charter to bilateral treaties, that would specifically exclude unilateral military intervention or the evisceration of the U.N. framework. I am not suggesting there be no concern for human rights. Indeed, support by a democracy movement in the United States would begin with assumptions of human rights and the need for the United States to ratify the economic, social, and political covenants and treaty obligations it has so far avoided. There is a domestic logic to such action which of course concerns the right and conservatives. Ratifying these agreements would mean that rights to a job, housing, free speech, and health would become guaranteed collective rights. If such international rules were in fact legitimated by Senate affirmation, the task of Americans attempting social reconstruction would be made somewhat easier.

This very fact has caused the political right to shelve the human rights covenants. While the nation prides itself on human rights, its domestic record leaves much to be desired. There is a curious irony here that should not go unmentioned. While the human rights covenants are seen by conservative forces as an invasion of our national sovereignty, there seems to be no great interest in protecting U.S. sovereignty. Indeed, conservatives are leading the charge in representing foreign clients in the United States who buy land, resources, technology, etc. They operate in ways the indigenous right has operated in the Third World, as a *comprador* class willing to sell out the birthright of its own nation while wrapping itself in the native symbols of patriotism.

This phenomenon has begun to reach alarming proportions. Whereas various nations and foreign corporations have used public relations agents and lawyers to press their case before Congress, the executive, and the public throughout the Cold War, they have now moved to a new stage. They now hire former national security advisers, CIA station chiefs, and other members of the national security apparatus with secret information and privileged access to do their bidding against the broad U.S. interest. This process is congruent with the U.S. multinational corporations and banks that play the international money markets by shifting currencies continuously to escape taxes and, where necessary, to depress the American dollar if their respective firms can show real gains by betting against the dollar in foreign markets. What cries out for attention in these dynamics is a more fundamental definition of obligation, patriotism, and loyalty than the flag-waving type shown by those whose patriotism never gets in the way of their personal finances. Such questions cry out for congressional action, and a movement for democracy should champion it. The scandals attached to the Marcos administration in the Philippines—scandals that brought that nation to its knees financially—are parallel to the gyrations of capitalist operators in the United States, who have used and formulated laws and regulations to assure themselves of the "best deals." There is no reason why U.S. corporations should be permitted to "double-dip" by setting up industrial enterprises in the Third World to escape wage and health requirements for American workers while they seek no tariffs on the goods they import into the United States.

11

Draft Treaty for a Comprehensive Program for Common Security and General Disarmament

The idea that the course of history is predetermined does not take account of the variety of choices that in fact exist at any one moment. Once aware of this obvious point, we are able to call upon our imagination and ingenuity, indeed ourselves, to influence the shape of future history, in terms of both the social structures we wish to bring into being and even the types of accidents we can expect to have as a result of the technologies we choose.

With the following model outline treaty proposal, I am suggesting that there are practical alternatives that can be formulated. These alternatives are not utopian in the sense that the ideas are based on human perfection. Rather they are predicated on need, interest, and historical precedent. While starting from the ideas adumbrated in the United States and Soviet general and complete disarmament texts of the early 1960s, this draft presents a number of major innovations meant to take account of the deep transformations that have occurred since then, especially the dissolution of the Cold War, the increase of mass communications, the astonishing increase in conventional and strategic weaponry, new transnational relations among people, and the emergence of regional military powers.

The underlying conception of the draft is that transition away from the war system cannot be accomplished through the official nation-state alone, although its bureaucracies must be involved in the process. Perhaps the best way to describe the changes I have outlined is to note that they are based on a shifting of the gaze of leaders and people to see new possibilities and new actors. By this shift a new process is begun that allows people to understand that old institutions can act in new ways and that new players on the international scene can be heard from, that technology can be controlled, and that both domestic and international law can be used to protect the integrity of the disarming and peace process.

The treaty proposal is also predicated on the idea that, just as there were hidden movements that needed to find their own consciousness to bring about fundamental change, as the revolutionary changes showed in Eastern Europe and the Soviet Union, and just as there are now environmental movements that have come to grips with the need for a different relationship between human beings and nature, millions of people similarly recognize that we must find ways to transcend the war system. Just as slavery ceased to be the dominant spirit of an age, and therefore ended as a dominant social institution, so it may be that the war system can be retired once we understand that justice and security are obtainable without resort to mass destruction. This hypothesis about our present condition should serve as the filter for settling disputes of power and interest. With such an understanding and hypothesis, we can begin to explore within a practical moral discourse that segment of the human imagination that is given over to political and social invention.

Thus, this treaty outline includes sections concerning the personal responsibility of government officials that are to be internalized in domestic law; a more activist role for the International Court of Justice; recognition of the important role that transnational, private groups of citizens are to play in the assurance, inspection, and verification process; development of an International Disarmament Organization in affiliation with the United Nations; zonal inspection methods; formulation of a new security system; as well as the use of other communications media and physical means of assuring that the disarming and security process is followed. In other words, the replacement of the war system requires a mutually reenforcing institutional system that both builds on existing and creates new customs and laws that will become the dominant spirit of the next period of history. Working with other nations, the United States can be key to the development of such ideas and practices. ☐ ☐

Preface

The purpose of the Treaty on Common Security and General Disarmament is peace, the resolution of conflict through peaceful means, and the creation of conditions that allow justice, economic, social dignity, and human rights to become the basis of human life on earth. The treaty is intended to end the terrifying thrust of the war system and replace it with a peace system. It seeks to follow the terms and spirit of the "Joint Statement of Agreed Principles for Disarmament Negotiations," the McCloy-Zorin Agreement of 1961.

This treaty recognizes that common security and general disarmament require the vision and cumulative willingness to adjust and then reconstruct the international system in light of profound changes in technology, cultural and political attitudes, and the emergence of many independent actors in the international arena. It recognizes that the present course of the arms race is disastrous, and that this course can be changed by people in government and outside of it. This treaty is meant to harmonize national and international interests so that all nations and peoples may have a path to assert the worth of their nation and the dignity of their people and culture.

It has evolved through discussion and negotiation as a project of the Institute for Policy Studies, in Washington, D.C. The commentary to this treaty was written by Marcus Raskin with Jonathan Mercer, as research associate, and should be read in conjunction with the treaty. The commentary follows each article of the treaty. The commentary provides background information, explanation, and comment for the articles in the treaty. Both the treaty and the commentary were recently edited, and reformatted by Matthew Hooberman. Special thanks to Louis Sohn, professor of International Law at the University of Georgia.

Contents

Chapter	Title	Article	Page
I	Basic Commitments	1	232
II	General Principles	2–8	232
III	Initial Declarations	9–13	235
IV	International Disarmament Organization, Its Staff, and the Board of Inquirers	14–23	238
V	Common Security and International Organizations	24–28	242
VI	The Three Stages of Disarmament	29–54	244
VII	Forces, Weapons, and Military Production Facilities to Be Retained at the End of the Disarmament Process	55–60	252
VIII	Verification, Inspection, and Assurance	61–73	254
IX	Industrial Plants and Economic Conversion	74–81	260
X	Miscellaneous	82–83	262
	Commentary on Articles		263

Acronyms

IAEA	International Atomic Energy Agency
ICJ	International Court of Justice
IDO	International Disarmament Organization
ISMA	International Satellite Monitoring Agency
MSC	Military Staff Committee
NGO	Non-Governmental Organization
NPT	Non-Proliferation Treaty
UNU	United Nations University
USACDA	United States Arms Control and Disarmament Agency
WSA	World Security Agreement

Chapter I. Basic Commitments

Article 1

1. Each State Party to this Treaty affirms its commitment to the purposes and principles of the United Nations as set forth in the Charter of the United Nations.
2. Each State Party to this Treaty commits itself to use the machinery of the United Nations for the peaceful resolution of disputes and agrees to the employment of the means provided for in Chapter VII of the United Nations Charter to carry out the purposes of this Treaty.
3. Each State Party to this Treaty agrees not to initiate the use of nuclear weapons, nor to use them against any non-nuclear nation.
4. Each State Party commits itself to a moratorium on testing nuclear weapons pending the conclusion of a comprehensive test ban treaty.

Chapter II. General Principles

Article 2

1. The States Parties to this Treaty intend to achieve common security and general disarmament by the year 2008 by implementing in good faith and in a spirit of cooperation the Program for Common Security and General Disarmament specified in this Treaty. This Program is divided into three stages of five years each, to commence as soon as possible.
2. The purpose of this Program is to secure the peace by eliminating all weapons of mass destruction, including chemical and biological weapons, and all offensive weapons, as well as all military forces that are not required to keep internal order or to participate in a United Nations enforcement action under Chapter VII of the U.N. Charter.
3. All collective self-defense alliances such as NATO and the Warsaw Pact as well as bilateral military cooperation arrangements shall be changed to reflect the objectives of this Treaty and to facilitate the implementation of this Program.
4. Each stage of the disarmament process shall include assurances, inspection, and verification. The disarmament process shall move auto-

matically from stage one to stage two to stage three unless one of the permanent members of the U.N. Security Council and at least one-third of the other states of the other States Parties to this Treaty object thereto.

Article 3

1. This Program for Common Security and General Disarmament shall, in stage one, achieve a reduction of 30 percent of strategic, tactical, and conventional forces. The reductions shall be verified by a zonal system of inspection. Stage two shall achieve a further reduction of 40 percent in the period of five years, on a zonal basis. Stage three shall achieve a further reduction of 30 percent and shall be completed in the remaining time, by the year 2008.

2. While the United States and the Soviet Union will initiate the disarming process, all other States Parties to this Treaty shall enter into the Program in the first stage to the extent that the Program applies to their military forces and to the categories of weapons that they possess. All States Parties to this Treaty that are parties to alliance arrangements such as the Warsaw Pact and NATO shall begin their reduction of forces and weapons in the first stage as a group.

Article 4

1. The States Parties to this Treaty shall establish an International Disarmament Organization (IDO). The IDO shall operate as the world's principal agency for ending the arms race and creating international security for all states, large and small.

2. The IDO shall operate according to the purposes and principles of the U.N. Charter.

3. The IDO shall develop means for assuring that the provisions of this Treaty are carried out fairly, without military advantage being given to any State or group of States.

4. The IDO shall make special efforts to assure that the quantum of armaments and military forces in this world will be continuously reduced to enhance the security of the world's peoples.

5. The IDO will ascertain the effect on the implementation of the Program of any State that declines to participate in the Program provided by this Treaty. It will submit reports on this question to the U.N.

Security Council, the General Assembly of the U.N., and the States Parties to this Treaty.

Article 5

1. Within one month after the entry into force of this treaty, each state party thereto will deposit in gold bullion an amount equal to 5 percent of its military budget for the preceding year into an escrow fund. Any such deposit shall be forfeited by any party to this treaty that decides to withdraw from the program. In cases of violation as determined by the International Court of Justice (See Article 73) or a special tribunal of five persons appointed by the court on request of the IDO, the offending State shall be penalized financially according to a system of fines drawn up by the Board of Inquirers. The fine schedule shall be submitted to the U.N. General Assembly and the Security Council for final acceptance.

2. Revenue from fines—if any—will be used to meet the operational costs of the IDO. Any funds in excess of operational costs shall be made available to the specialized agencies of the United Nations for international aid and development.

Article 6

1. Sanctions for violations of this Treaty may be applied not only to the States Parties to this Treaty but also to States that are not Parties to this Treaty.

2. Such sanctions may be applied by the U.N. Security Council upon recommendation of the IDO or the U.N. General Assembly.

3. The sanctions for violations of this Treaty may include those specified in Articles 41–47 of the U.N. Charter.

Article 7

1. Upon the coming into force of this Treaty, each State Party shall cease all research on new weapons, or the improvement of old weapon systems.

2. The United Nations, first through its specialized agencies and then through the IDO shall establish an international registry of scientists, technologists, and laboratory and industrial workers. The internal

law of each State Party shall be amended to oblige these groups to take an oath by which they will commit themselves not to engage in any research, or developmental or experimental work, on weapons of mass destruction, including strategic delivery vehicles, on other offensive vehicles or weapons, or on military space and laser research. The oath shall either be the following or a variant of it: "I will not use my scientific, educational, or technical training for any purpose that I believe is intended to harm human beings. I shall not work on weapons that, if used, would result in mass destruction. I shall, in my work, strive for peace, justice and the betterment of the human condition."

3. Upon the coming into force of this Treaty, each Party to this Treaty shall cease manufacture, production, or developmental or experimental work on conventional armaments. The manufacture of spare parts may continue for no more than ten years from the date of the Treaty coming into force.

4. Definitions of "research," "experimental," "developmental," "manufacture," and "weapons of mass destructions" shall be determined on the basis of normal uses in international law, scientific inquiry and commercial manufacture.

Article 8

1. The States Parties to this Treaty solemnly undertake to uphold the Treaty and perform its terms in the required time.

2. If a State Party or a group of States Parties is not able to implement a part of the Program in the time allotted for that part in a particular stage, the Board of Inquirers shall be immediately informed so that an alternative technical procedure may be found to accomplish the objectives of the Program.

Chapter III. Initial Declarations

Article 9

The States Parties to this Treaty shall adhere to the following international agreements which shall be considered as integral parts of this Treaty: (a) Protocol for the Prohibition of the Use of Poisonous Gases and Bacteriological Methods of Warfare (1925); (b) Treaty forbidding the military use of Antarctica (1959); (c) Treaty Banning Nuclear Tests in the Atmosphere, in Outer Space, and under Water (1963); (d) Treaty on Principles Governing the Activities of States in the Exploration of Outer Space, Including the Moon and Other Celestial Bodies (1967); (e) Treaty on Non-Proliferation of Nuclear Weapons (1968); (f) Treaty on the Prohibition of the Emplacement of Nuclear Weapons and Other Weapons of Mass Destruction on the Seabed, on the Ocean Floor, and on the Subsoil Thereof (1971); (g) Convention on the Prohibition of the Development, Production, and Stockpiling of Bacteriological (Biological) and Toxic Weapons and their Destruction (1972); (h) Treaty between the USA and the USSR on the Limitation of Anti-ballistic Missile Systems (1972); (i) any other treaties on international security of disarmament that may be agreed upon before the entry into force of this Treaty, unless one of the permanent members of the Security Council or one-third of the Parties to this Treaty object to the addition of a particular treaty to the list.

Article 10

The States Parties to this Treaty are deemed to have waived the right to make reservations to any particular part or article of this Treaty unless both the United States and the Soviet Union accept the reservation and two-thirds of the other States Parties to this Treaty accept the reservation.

Article 11

1. To facilitate inspection and verification each State Party to this Treaty shall deposit an official declaration on the state of its armed forces within a month after entry into force of this Treaty.

2. The United States and the Soviet Union will deposit their lists with the IDO at the same time. These sites shall include personnel strengths, arms and equipment, industrial plants, military bases, establishments and facilities, and all other information that is relevant to the conduct of inspection and verification assignments.

3. Without limiting the generality of the proceeding paragraph, the declaration shall include:

a) the personnel strengths of naval, land, and air forces and auxiliary forces;

b) the number of conscripts and the States Parties' intention with regard to its draft law;

c) the number of reservists that are available for recall to full-time or part-time service;

d) the number, by category, of single atomic and thermonuclear weapons with their yield in kilotons (Kt);

e) the number of multiple warheads, with their yields in kilotons, and the number of individual guidance systems;

f) the number, by category, of delivery vehicles capable of delivering atomic or thermonuclear weapons at a range greater than 100 kilometers;

g) the number of locations of sites for launching these delivery vehicles;

h) the number of rocket-launching sites for peaceful purposes;

i) the number of naval bases;

j) the number of shipyards for building and servicing ships of war;

k) the number of ships of war, by categories and types, including submarines and fleet auxiliary vessels;

l) the number of aircraft by categories and types;

m) the number of airfields and air bases with locations;

n) the number, by category, of plants and facilities producing or servicing various types of military arms and equipment;

o) the number of training establishments;

p) the number of weapons for land forces by categories and types;

q) the number of proving grounds and firing ranges;

r) the number of stockpiles of various categories of weapons;

s) the number, by category, of laboratories engaged in research and development for military purposes;

t) the quantity, by category, of various chemical, biological, and radiological weapons.

Article 12

Any declaration under this Chapter shall indicate with respect to any listed item that is located outside the territory of the State Party making the declaration, in what foreign territory that item is located.

Article 13

Each State Party to this Treaty shall provide the IDO with the locations and times it will discharge members of its armed forces as required by the Disarmament Program. The IDO shall circulate this information to all the States Parties to this Treaty that have notified the IDO of their desire to observe such discharge.

Chapter IV. International Disarmament Organization, Its Staff, and the Board of Inquirers

Article 14

In the initial stages of organizing the IDO, the States Parties to this Treaty, especially the militarily significant States, and the United Nations, shall remain directly responsible, jointly and separately, for carrying out the objective of ending world insecurity caused by the arms race.

Article 15

Each State Party to this Treaty shall be assessed for the expenses of the IDO according to a percentage contribution formula based on that State's share of world defense expenditures averaged over the five years prior to the entry into force of this Treaty.

Article 16

1. A Secretary General of the IDO shall be chosen by the Board of Inquirers for a tenure of seven years.
2. The Secretary General shall be assisted by Under-Secretaries General who will be expert in diplomacy, disarmament, international security, or other fields of endeavor that will facilitate carrying out the objectives of the program.
3. The Secretary General and the Under-Secretaries General, shall be entrusted with the appointment of staff and administration of the IDO.
4. The staff of the IDO shall be supervised by the Secretary General.
5. The IDO shall be staffed by competent individuals from all nations. The IDO shall, as part of the Disarmament Program, conduct training and education activities for its staff, inquirers, and inspectors, and provide them with adequate research facilities.

Article 17

1. Each State Party agrees to appoint a senior national official and give him or her the power of direct communication with the IDO Secretary General on technical matters.
2. The United Nations will appoint an Under-Secretary General who will serve as liaison with the IDO.
3. The IDO shall operate in close association with the specialized agencies of the United Nations and will seek advice, counsel, and staff—where needed—from them and other international agencies.
4. The IDO shall work closely with all nongovernmental organizations (NGOs) in order to obtain nonstate support for carrying out the terms of this treaty.
5. The IDO will negotiate an agreement with, and where necessary, employ the services of, the International Atomic Energy Agency.

Article 18

Each State Party agrees that it will make available to the IDO all information relevant to the obligations of this Treaty and the Disarmament Program. Where the information is not forthcoming by the specified date, the Board of Inquirers may assess fines against the late State Party.

Article 19

1. The staff of the IDO shall owe its primary loyalty to no government. It shall be independent and will, in its conditions of service, hold to the highest standards of integrity and technical skill. It shall specialize in settling disputes or conflicts over technical data or disagreements caused by language or cultural misperception. The staff shall be chosen without regard to race, sex, or age, and shall reflect, to the extent possible, wide geographical composition.
2. The staff shall be instructed in procedures of verification, assurance, and inspection for at least six months prior to acting as independent investigators. Contracts for professional staff shall be for a period of five years.

Article 20

1. The staff of the IDO, including the Secretary General and the Under-Secretaries, shall not receive or seek instructions from any State. All discussions between the Secretary General, the Under-Secretaries, and the staff with government officials are to be considered official discussions when they concern the Disarmament Program and records shall be kept of them.
2. Each State Party to this Treaty solemnly agrees to protect the integrity of the Disarmament Program by respecting the quasi-judicial functions of the Secretary General and the staff of the IDO. On request of the Secretary General, a State Party to this Treaty shall be obligated to facilitate the grant of its citizenship to staff members of the IDO desiring it and to their immediate families.
3. Governments that seek special favor with the IDO through bribery or by suborning its staff may be penalized by the International Court of Justice, or the special tribunal appointed in accordance with Article 5, Section 2 of this Treaty, in ways proportionate to the transgression. Military force or the interruption of the Disarmament Program may not be used as a penalty for subornation.
4. Where possible, the IDO shall seek to determine what inadequacies in the procedures for implementing the Disarmament Program might have caused a State Party to this Treaty to act irresponsibly or to seek undue influence.

Article 21

1. The IDO shall have the power to hire consultants, call on research institutes, award contracts for specific work, and seek advice and counsel from nongovernment organizations.
2. All such discussions are to be considered official and records shall be kept of them.
3. No individual, institute, or other organizational body shall interfere with the Disarmament Program or seek to corrupt the staff of the IDO.
4. Where such improper acts occur, the IDO shall inform the authorities of the State of which the alleged guilty party is a citizen or resident so that it may take appropriate legal action in accordance with its laws, including those laws enacted by that State to implement this treaty.

Article 22

1. The Board of Inquirers shall have the following functions:
a) to appoint the Secretary General of the IDO;
b) to appoint regional Under-Secretaries General of the IDO;
c) to recommend to the U.N. Security Council and General Assembly the fines to be imposed on States violating this Treaty and the punishments that ought to be meted by States Parties to other violators, in accordance with any regulations that may be adopted pursuant to this treaty or the United Nations Charter. Direct use of force shall only be allowed where there is a grave threat to international peace and security;
d) to fix the assessments and contributions of the Parties to this Treaty;
e) to initiate, formulate, and approve all agreements with States Members of the United Nations, specialized agencies of the United Nations, and other international institutions, that may be required for carrying out the objectives and terms of this Treaty;
f) to adopt the same rules for the Chair of the Board as are followed for the Presidency of the Security Council;
g) to meet in places other than where it is permanently located if the Disarmament Program would be facilitated thereby;
h) to establish committees comprising consultants, specialists, and members of NGOs to facilitate the implementation of the Program;
i) to supply interim reports on the implementation of the Program to State Parties, the U.N. Security Council and the General Assembly. It shall issue also special reports on technical aspects of verification, inspection and assurance;
j) to regularly use satellite television, film, radio, and other means of communication to report to the world's people on the progress in the implementation of the Disarmament Program;
k) to report on current research relevant to the implementation of the Program to the States Parties to this Treaty, the United Nations, and the international public at large.

Article 23

1. The Board of Inquirers shall consist of the permanent members of the U.N. Security Council, and thirteen other members elected by

the General Assembly from among those States that are Parties to this Treaty. Five of them shall be elected from a list of major powers, other than the permanent members. The list shall be prepared by the General Assembly upon the coming into force of this Treaty, and shall be revised at twelve-year intervals.

2. Each member of the Board shall be elected for a term of four years. Terms shall be staggered. Each State member of the Board shall appoint a specially qualified person as its representative on the Board. The Board may prescribe the qualifications of these representatives.

3. The Board shall be responsible for the implementation of the Disarmament Program.

4. The Board of Inquirers shall involve nongovernmental groups, such as scientists, technologists, peace disarmament groups, organizations of former military officers and personnel, women's groups, labor unions, and political parties, to secure their participation in the disarming process. In preparing its reports, the Board will take into consideration reports prepared and testimony presented by these groups.

Chapter V. Common Security and International Organizations

Article 24

1. The Military Staff Committee of the U.N. Security Council shall meet on a continuous basis with the special representatives of the States Parties to this Treaty and of the IDO to fulfill its obligations of preparing a World Security Agreement (WSA). Once that Agreement comes into force, its implementation shall parallel the process of implementing this Disarmament Program.

2. At the end of each stage of the Disarmament Program, the consecutive parts of the World Security Agreement shall be presented to the U.N. Security Council and the General Assembly for debate, approval, and implementation.

3. The Military Staff Committee shall be responsible for the implementation of the World Security Agreement, and shall exercise for this purpose functions similar to those performed by the Board of Inquirers with respect to the Disarmament Program.

Article 25

1. Each State Party to this Treaty shall contribute contingents of armed forces to a United Nations Force that shall supplement the standing United Nations Peace Force specified in Article 26, Section 1.

2. The primary military emphasis of the U.N. Force shall be highly technological and nonlethal. It shall explore the efficacy of various sublethal methods of maintaining the peace. The U.N. Force may also be used for aid in handling natural disasters, on request of the State concerned. It may be used to secure human rights and other humanitarian purposes only pursuant to orders of the U.N. Security Council.

3. All uses of the U.N. Force shall be in conformity with regulations adopted by the U.N. Security Council, and shall be subject to decisions of the Military Staff Committee of that Council.

Article 26

1. The Military Staff Committee under Article 43 of the U.N. Charter shall organize a modest Peace Force not dependent on contingents from States Members of the United Nations.

2. Over the course of the three stages of the Disarmament Program all weapons, vehicles, and armaments shall be destroyed to the extent provided for in the Disarmament Program. In the last stage of the Program, a State Party to this Treaty may deduct from the percentage to be destroyed those weapons, vehicles, and armaments that are needed for its contribution to the U.N. Force, to the extent provided for by the regulations prepared by the Military Staff Committee and approved by the U.N. Security Council.

3. No international organization or peacekeeping force shall retain, develop, or contract to be developed, weapons of mass destruction and terror weapons, nor shall it be allowed to try and secure the peace through plans and programs of terror, mass bombing, or other means that would violate the principles for the protection of noncombatants embodied in the Red Cross Conventions of 1949 and the Protocols of 1977, or the principles specified in Section 1, Article 32.

Article 27

1. The Military Staff Committee in cooperation with the staff of the IDO shall prepare for inclusion in the World Security Agreement rules

governing ways to handle border incidents and plans for securing armed forces upon short notice from States Members of the United Nations, whenever necessary for the maintenance of international peace and security.

2. The World Security Agreement may authorize the Military Staff Committee of the U.N. Security Council and the IDO to make arrangements for border patrols in, including but not limited to, the Middle East, between China and Vietnam, the Soviet Union and China, North and South Korea, Cambodia and Vietnam, the Republic of South Africa and its neighboring states. The Military Staff Committee shall make prompt arrangements for the withdrawal of troops that have crossed another State's borders.

Article 28

1. From time to time, but at least every five years after the end of the third stage, the States Parties to this Treaty shall meet to discuss whether further reductions in forces retained may be made. They shall also discuss the further implementation of the World Security Agreement as a primary way of keeping the peace.

Chapter VI. The Three Stages of Disarmament

Article 29

The States Parties to this Treaty agree that the armed forces and armaments of each of them that may remain after each stage shall be determined precisely in accordance with the provisions of this Treaty.

Article 30

1. The State Parties to this Treaty shall encourage independent measures of disarmament announced and executed by any State able to do so.

2. Any State Party to this Treaty may act, either individually or together with other State Parties, to reduce its armed forces and armaments in advance of the stages of the Disarmament Program. It shall not, however, be subject to inspection and on-the-ground verification until the time and period called for in the Disarmament Program.

Article 31

Within each stage, the reductions shall proceed on the basis of quantitative measures, unless otherwise agreed by all the States Parties concerned. The categories for the disarming process shall be: (a) space delivery vehicles and space objects, including lasers; (b) ballistic delivery vehicles under twenty-mile range; (c) ballistic delivery vehicles greater than twenty-mile range; (d) airplanes with speed above 1,000 mph; (e) airplanes with speed less than 1,000 mph; (f) nuclear warheads under 20 Kt; (g) nuclear warheads over 30 Kt; (h) naval vessels; (i) artillery, including rockets; (j) tanks; (k) armored vehicles; (l) chemical, biological, and radiological weapons; (m) munitions; (n) uniformed full-time military personnel.

Article 32

1. At the beginning of stage one of the disarmament process, the States Parties to this Treaty shall take the necessary legislative or other measures to give effect in their domestic laws to the principles of international law recognized in the U.N. Charter and judgment of the Nuremburg Tribunal and by the Tokyo Tribunal, so that the destruction of innocent populations, the preparation for aggressive war, the use of terror weapons, or the use of force in international relations in a manner inconsistent with the U.N. Charter shall qualify as a crime not only against international law but also against domestic law.
2. Such criminal provisions shall be in force as part of the domestic law of each State Party to this Treaty by the end of the third stage of the disarming process.
3. Each State Party to this Treaty shall embody in its criminal legislation a nonsurrender clause that will make it a domestic crime to surrender to an aggressor state. Legislation to this end shall be in force by the end of the first stage of this Program.
4. The military codes of each State Party shall make clear the duty of its military forces to observe scrupulously the principles specified in Section 1 of this Article.
5. As States Parties to this Treaty disarm, the IDO and the Military Staff Committee shall, upon request, instruct national military forces and others on the use of nonviolent techniques as a primary way of encouraging noncompliance with any aggressor state.

6. The United Nations and the IDO will encourage universities, law schools, institutes, and governments to prepare teaching, informational, and research materials to facilitate the implementation of this Article.

Article 33

1. In accordance with Article 11 of this Treaty, the States Parties shall within a month after the coming into force of this Treaty, file the declarations containing the interim but comprehensive official inventories of all military equipment, a list of all industrial plants that engage in the making of military equipment in substantial amounts, the contract and requisition data, and military personnel lists. The inventories and lists shall not include the location of these weapons, plants, and forces. Such disclosure shall be made later only to the extent required by the zonal disarmament procedure.

2. All States Parties to this Treaty may amend the inventory and personnel lists throughout the first state. In the second stage the inventory and personnel lists may be amended twice. In the third stage the inventory and personnel lists, which in that stage should include not only members of regular armed forces but also paramilitary and intelligence personnel (as specified in Section 2, Article 44), may be amended once.

Article 34

States Parties to this Treaty shall have a choice of two methods of zonal disarmament. They may choose: (a) complete disarmament of a zone without any prior disclosure of the forces, military equipment, and industrial plants in that zone, followed by a verification of the fact of such disarmament; or (b) presenting an inventory of the forces, military equipment, and industrial plant, followed by the verification of this inventory, and by disarmament of such a percentage of these forces, military equipment, and industrial plants as is required to fulfill the Disarmament Program for a particular stage or part of a stage. A State Party to this Treaty may not change methods without the express consent of two-thirds of States Parties including the consent of either the United States or the Soviet Union.

Article 35

In the first stage of the Program, the States Parties to this Treaty shall withdraw their forces, including their artillery, rockets, airplanes, and ground forces from areas where there is a danger of direct engagement with an adversary, because of either individual or alliance policy. Wherever direct engagement exists between opposing sides, a process of "back-off" shall be completed in the first fifteen months of the first stage.

Article 36

The States Parties to this Treaty shall designate depots at which weapons and war materials will be destroyed before inspectors of the IDO and invited nations. Citizen monitoring through NGOs and citizen groups shall be encouraged.

Article 37

Nuclear weapons shall be destroyed according to the following procedures:
 1) Each nuclear weapon shall be detached from its mode of delivery.
 2) Its guidance system shall be destroyed.
 3) The fissile material shall be removed from the weapon and deposited.
 4) The weapon shall be physically destroyed.
 5) IDO inspectors shall be present at the destruction of the weapon.
 6) States Parties to this Treaty shall be invited to witness the process of physical destruction.

Article 38

 1. The fissile material shall be:
    a) denatured as quickly as possible.
    b) placed under the custody of the IDO.
 2. The IDO, through the Secretary General and Board of Inquirers, shall make public on an annual basis the progress it was able to make with regard to denaturing the fissile material.

Article 39

Thermonuclear weapons shall be destroyed in the following manner:

1) The atomic trigger shall be denatured as quickly as possible after being removed from the weapon.
2) The weapon shall be detached from its mode of delivery.
3) Its guidance system shall be physically destroyed.
4) Tritium shall be disposed of, with maximum safety precautions, through burying in a geologically stable area of the deep seabed.
5) The remainder of the weapon shall be physically destroyed.

Article 40

Ballistic missiles shall be destroyed according to the following procedures:

1) The guidance system shall be physically destroyed.
2) Fuel shall be removed.
3) Toxic fuel shall be encapsulated by vitrification, concretization, or other means and disposed of by the disarming State with full concern for the environment and human safety.
4) Where there is any scientific doubt about the harmful effects of any fuel related to the delivery vehicle, it shall be destroyed or buried in a geologically stable area of the deep seabed.
5) The remainder of the vehicle shall be physically destroyed.

Article 41

1. A limited number of missiles may be maintained by States Parties for satellite surveillance during the implementation of the Program. At the end of the third stage of the Program, the States Parties to this Treaty shall ascertain whether independent satellite inspection should be continued in order to reinforce the satellite and on-site inspection system of the IDO.

2. These missiles shall not be used without prior notification and examination by the IDO. Their launchings shall be public, and journalists and representatives of citizen groups shall be entitled to witness them.

Article 42

1. All launching pads, silos, underground depots and platforms, and mobile and fixed launching systems that can be used for storage or blast-off and are capable of delivering nuclear weapons or other weapons of mass destruction shall be monitored continuously or demolished.
2. Launching and guidance systems for controlling such vehicles, including their equipment, shall also be monitored or demolished.

Article 43

Launching for peaceful purposes of satellites shall occur only after prior notification to the IDO. Such launchings shall be public and journalists and representatives of citizen groups shall be entitled to witness them. Launchings shall be limited to no more than two sites in any State Party.

Article 44

The States Parties to this Treaty agree that they will destroy all anti-satellite weapons, and will cease all research, development, manufacture, or deployment of space satellites capable of destroying other space satellites.

Article 45

1. The States Parties to this Treaty agree to reduce the personnel of their armed forces according to the terms of this Disarmament Program.
2. The States Parties to this Treaty agree that for the purpose of the Program, "military personnel" shall mean the armed forces of a State including civilian employees with the armed forces who serve a military purpose. Paramilitary and police forces, border and custom guards, who have been issued machine guns or other heavy weapons are also to be considered as "military personnel."
3. The full-time cadre for the training and absorption of reserve forces shall be counted as part of the armed forces. Each Party agrees that it will reduce substantially its organized reserve forces by the end of the third stage of the Program.

Article 46

1. The States Parties to this Treaty shall reduce and eliminate all naval ships, except those specifically allowed for defensive purposes under the terms of this Treaty. Naval ships shall be divided into two categories, those that are: (A) in storage at the time of the entry into force of this Treaty; and (B) those that are part of deployable battle forces.
2. Each State Party to this Treaty agrees that all ships other than those specifically allowed at the end of stage three shall be destroyed under the supervision of the IDO. The Board of Inquirers may allow the acquisition for peaceful commercial use of individual ships where military equipment has been removed from the vessel and destroyed, provided that the Secretary General of the IDO has certified that the ship is no longer capable of military attack use.
3. Nuclear units shall be removed from military nuclear-powered ships. They shall either be destroyed or placed in safe custody of the IDO. The Board of Inquirers may require that IDO inspectors be stationed on board nonmilitary, nuclear-powered ships.
4. A State Party to this Treaty may invite the IDO, other States Parties, or others to witness the destruction and dismantling of its ships and hulks.

Article 47

1. During the implementation of the Program, States Parties to this Treaty shall refrain from activities at sea that may lead to incidents that may start a war and shall refrain from engaging in forward strategies beyond sea lanes ordinarily used for international navigation.
2. To prevent naval incidents, inspectors from the IDO shall be authorized to board any naval ship of a State Party to this Treaty and may cruise on it for a limited period, as determined by the Board of Inquirers.
3. In the third stage of the Program, the IDO shall be entitled to appoint one or more inspectors per vessel, but no more than six per vessel. On board, the inspector shall have inspection rights, diplomatic immunity, and access at appointed times to the ship's crew and officers, and to the principal documents on board, to the extent to be specified by regulations adopted by the Board of Inquirers.

Article 48

1. The States Parties to this Treaty agree that they will reduce during all three stages of the Disarmament Program, military aircraft in all categories: in the first stage by 30 percent of the inventory declared in accordance with Article 11; in the second stage by 40 percent; and in the third stage by 30 percent.
2. Airplanes, guidance and navigational systems, and other military instruments attendant to air warfare, shall be destroyed physically at depots assigned for that purpose. Such destruction shall be witnessed in accordance with Article 36.

Article 49

Destruction of chemical, biological, and radiological weapons shall be carried out by means to be determined by a panel of scientists and technologists chosen by the IDO or by the States Parties to this Treaty.

Article 50

1. Inhumane weapons such as enhanced radiation weapons, maiming weapons such as napalm, and other weapons that cause adverse long-term toxic effects to persons or land are prohibited.
2. The States Parties to this Treaty note with grave concern that the use of herbicides and defoliants may lead to ecocide. Weapons deliberately designed to produce adverse changes in the environment are prohibited.

Article 51

1. Research, development (including testing), production, use, and military planning for or in connection with possible use, are prohibited in relation to unnatural and inhumane weapons.
2. This prohibition applies to:
   a) herbicides and defoliants;
   b) enhanced radiation weapons, whether involving a nuclear explosive device or the spreading of pulverized nuclear waste by air or any means whatsoever;
   c) weather modification of any kind whether it be rain, fog, hail, lightning, or severe storms;

d) climate modification;
e) electromagnetic radiation;
f) electrical behavior of the atmosphere;
g) interference with the ozone layer;
h) wide-arms fragmentation munitions;
i) fuel-air explosives;
j) napalm-follow-on controlled fireballs;
k) viral and bacteriological poisoning of food, water, or the atmosphere;
l) genetic modifications of viruses and bacteria for military purposes.

Article 52

Installations needed for the purposes of maintenance, repair, and manufacture of armaments shall be abolished in the last stage of the Program. An exception is to be made for the repair, maintenance, and manufacture of weapons that may be retained under this Treaty for the purposes of maintaining internal order and for the forces to be contributed to the U.N. Force, to the extent provided for by the regulations prepared by the Military Staff Committee and approved of by the U.N. Security Council.

Article 53

Industrial training and educational activities that are part of the maintenance, testing, and development of a prohibited weapon are prohibited.

Article 54

Leaders of militarily significant States shall report to their own nations at least twice a year on the importance of continuing the Disarmament Program. This report shall have maximum media coverage.

Chapter VII. Forces, Weapons, and Military Production Facilities to be Retained at the End of the Disarmament Process

Article 55

1. By the end of stage three the States Parties to this Treaty shall

retain only those weapons, forces, and industrial capacity for military purposes that may be viewed as necessary for the maintenance of internal order and for supplying contingents for the enforcements measures under Article 25.

2. The States Parties to this Treaty agree that the remaining forces needed for the maintenance of internal order and the maintenance of international peace, as specified in Section 1 of this Article, shall be stationed in particular zones designated by the IDO at the beginning of each stage of the Program.

Article 56

The Board of Inquirers shall report to the U.N. Security Council any threat to, or breach of the peace, and shall recommend to it what action under Chapter VII of the U.N. Charter should be taken by the Council.

Article 57

The States Parties to this Treaty may, after the third stage, retain short-range fighter planes with a maximum speed of 2.1 Mach per hour, helicopters with a maximum speed of 250 mph, and naval aircraft with a maximum speed of 3 Mach per hour. All such aircraft shall be deducted from the initial total that is subject to reductions under Article 48. No aircraft may be fitted with air-to-surface missiles, even if they have only limited range.

Article 58

1. The States Parties to this Treaty shall, in cooperation with the IDO, or the United Nations, undertake regional and international arms discussions to end the export and import of armaments and war materials one year after this Treaty enters into force. Replacement parts may be bought and sold throughout the first stage of the Disarmament Program. At the end of the first stage an international arms trade conference shall be called under the joint aegis of the United Nations and the IDO to ascertain the means needed to assure that the arms assistance and arms replacement trade system will end at an early date.

2. Each State Party to this Treaty shall inform the IDO about all arms and material that it has exported in the ten years prior to the entry

into force of this Treaty, or that were in transit at that date, and the destination of those exports.

3. Each State Party to this Treaty undertakes to inform the IDO also of all arms imported in the ten years prior to the entry into force of this Treaty, or that were in transit to it at that date, and the sources of export.

4. The IDO shall encourage scientists, workers, journalists, and scholars to report their information and finding on all aspects of the arms race and military assistance.

Article 59

The information to be furnished by States Parties to this Treaty to the IDO shall include information as to licenses for the local manufacture of armaments from designs provided by an exporting country, whether the original designer or not, and the extent to which such license makes an importing country self-sufficient in the manufacture of any particular armament. It shall also include the names of the persons, natural or juridical, involved in the licensing or manufacturing process.

Article 60

Each State Party to this Treaty undertakes to amend its domestic law so as to ensure that the operation of this Chapter shall give no right to obtain in its courts, damages or other remedy for international breach of contract.

Chapter VIII. Verification, Inspection, and Assurance

Article 61

1. The States Parties to this Treaty recognize that the Program for Common Security and General Disarmament provides an overall framework for ending the arms race and depends on building up common institutions and social relations of trust.

2. Each State Party to this Treaty agrees that effective verification of this Treaty is important to achieve common security and general disarmament and undertakes to cooperate for this purpose with the IDO.

3. The IDO and the States Parties to this Treaty shall, to the extent possible, rely on technical means of verification by satellites and other nonintrusive monitoring devices.

4. The States Parties to this Treaty shall develop a system of assurance by challenge and response, to be followed, if disagreement persists, by verification. Joint or international projects of verification, assurance, and inspection, and of research related thereto, are encouraged between the States Parties to this Treaty.

5. Any failure to comply with the obligations of the agreed-upon Program for Common Security and General Disarmament shall be presented to the Board of Inquirers and reported by it to the U.N. Security Council for required action.

Article 62

1. On a twice-yearly basis, through the media, and by means of official proclamations, leaders of all States Parties to this Treaty shall encourage the citizenry to cooperate in the inspection, verification, and assurance process.

2. The IDO shall make arrangements for NGOs such as research institutes and universities, and for international professional organizations that have networks of scientists and technical personnel throughout the world, to join in a public system of assurance, inspection, and verification. Such arrangements shall confirm their right and duty to make public their data on the implementation of the Program by presenting them to the IDO, the States Parties to this Treaty, and the media.

3. The States Parties to this Treaty shall encourage universities, research institutes, and others to carry out studies, discussions, and transnational contacts to assure that the inspection and verification process is effective and does not lead to a verification system that is either too unwieldy, ineffective, or intrusive.

Article 63

1. In the first two stages of the Program the State Party under inspection shall have the choice of deciding whether it is to be inspected by the IDO or those State Parties commonly thought to be its adversaries. In the third stage the inspection shall be conducted by the IDO.

2. In the first stage of the Program, assurance, inspection, and verification shall be arranged in three ways:

a) by checking against inventory and personnel lists and ascertaining that what was to be dismantled and destroyed or disbanded has in fact been destroyed or disbanded (for instance, through direct on-site inspection at specified depots);

b) through an independent satellite capacity under the control of the IDO which shall be able to ascertain, through photography and sensor technology, the character and location of the forces of each State Party (see Article 64, section 1);

c) through testimony of NGOs, scientists, and other means of public testimony likely to provide information on the extent of the implementation by each State Party of its duties under this Treaty (see Article 62).

Article 64

1. The IDO shall encourage joint and multilateral satellite inspection systems among adversaries. Information gathered through such means or through unilateral satellite inspection shall be made available to the IDO for examination, unless the States concerned agree otherwise (see Article 63, section 2, b).

2. In the presence of representatives of the United Nations, the IDO will inspect the destruction and dismantling of weapons of mass destruction, strategic delivery vehicles, and other offensive weapons.

Article 65

The Secretary General of the IDO, in consultation with States Parties to this Treaty, shall establish Committees of Verification to assist the Board of Inquirers, in relation to all questions relating to verification of disarmament and in particular to deal with:

a) the procedures to be used for verification in each category of weapons and military forces;

b) the technical means of making these procedures effective and credible and facilitating their application;

c) the areas and subjects of research necessary for ensuring that verification procedures are both effective and credible; and

d) the perfecting of verification by challenge and response.

Article 66

For the purposes of assurance, inspection, and verification, the IDO shall have the following rights and responsibilities:

a) to require the maintenance and production of operating records concerning matters relevant to the Program;

b) to call for and receive progress reports from States Parties to this Treaty, and until technical inspection and verification satellite systems are perfected, it shall have the power to send inspectors into any area.

Article 67

1. The IDO shall be able to send inspectors into, or station inspectors in, the territory of any State Party, as directed by the Board of Inquirers. They shall have access at all times to all places within designated zones, according to the particular stage of the Program. They will have continuous and permanent access to the seat of government. They shall have data and access to any person who, by reason of his or her occupation or special knowledge, works with material, equipment, facilities, personnel, financial expenditures, or any other matter bearing on the successful outcome of the Disarmament Program.

2. Each State Party to this Treaty shall direct its government officials to cooperate fully with the inspectors. These officials shall identify and indicate the exact location of all materials, equipment, facilities, records, and data that are subject to inspection during the stage of the Disarmament Program then in progress.

Article 68

1. The Secretary General of the IDO shall inform, in writing, the State Party to this Treaty that is to be inspected, of the name, nationality, and background of each inspector proposed and shall transmit a written certification of his or her relevant qualifications. The State Party concerned shall inform the Secretary General within ten days of receipt of such a proposal whether it accepts the designation of the inspector. If so, the inspector is then designated as one of the IDO's inspectors for that State Party and the Secretary General shall notify the State Party concerned of such a designation.

2. If a State Party at any time objects to the designation of an inspector

for that State Party, it shall inform the Secretary General of its objection. In that event, the Secretary General shall propose to the State Party an alternative designation or designations. The Secretary General shall immediately report to the Board of Inquirers, for its appropriate action, any repeated refusal to accept the designations of an inspector where such refusal would impede the inspection and verification process, and where technical satellite inspection is deemed insufficient.

Article 69

1. The visits and activities of inspectors shall be so arranged as to ensure the effective discharge of their functions with the minimum possible inconvenience to the host and disturbance to the facilities inspected.
2. Transportation, lodging, and other services shall be provided by the State Party under inspection.
3. The States Parties to this Treaty agree that the IDO shall have full rights to install sensing and recording devices and communications instruments in zones that have become subject to inspection. These devices may be installed—where necessary—inside plants, and will be standardized types for all States Parties to this Treaty.
4. To the extent consistent with the effective discharge of their functions, the inspectors shall conduct their activities in harmony with the laws and regulations existing in the State under inspection.
5. No inspector or other staff member of the IDO shall disclose to any person whatsoever any industrial secret or other similar confidential information coming to his or her knowledge by virtue of his or her official duties.
6. Inspectors shall be granted the privileges and immunities necessary for the performance of their duties.

Article 70

1. The Secretary General of the IDO shall determine upon the basis of the reports of IDO inspectors whether:

    a) the State Party under inspection has performed all its current obligations under this Treaty;

    b) the State Party has seriously failed or omitted to perform those obligations; or

c) the State Party while in arrears in the performance of those obligations is seriously and sincerely striving to fulfill these obligations.

2. The Secretary General shall present a report to the Board of Inquirers that may contain recommendations, whenever necessary, with respect to the remedial steps to be taken to carry out the terms of the Disarmament Program.

Article 71

1. Any State Party to this Treaty that suspects that an activity in contravention of this Treaty has been carried out or is about to be carried out, may lodge a formal objection with the Board of Inquirers. The State Party to this Treaty against whom an objection has been lodged may respond and offer an explanation.

2. Nongovernmental organizations and other groups may file with the Secretary General information that shows noncompliance with the terms of the Treaty. The State Party against whom an objection is raised may respond and offer an explanation.

Article 72

1. Objections raised under either of the Sections of the preceding Article shall immediately be investigated by a special committee of Inquiry comprising five persons chosen by the Secretary General of the IDO from a list prepared by the president of the International Court of Justice.

2. The committee's report shall be presented to the Board of Inquirers for special remedial action, unless the investigation has disproved the complaint.

Article 73

1. The International Court of Justice may give advisory opinions on any legal question arising under this Treaty that is brought to its attention by the IDO. Its advisory opinions shall be delivered within three months of filing the request, and shall be made public.

2. Any dispute concerning the interpretation or application of this Treaty may be referred to the International Court of Justice by any

State Party to this Treaty that is a party to the dispute in conformity with the Statute of the Court, unless the Parties concerned agree to another mode of settlement. The time limit for the decision by the International Court of Justice shall be no more than six months from the date of the filing of the application that brought the dispute before the Court.

3. Each State Party to this Treaty undertakes to propose to its legislative authorities during stage three of the Program that it should be authorized to accept the compulsory jurisdiction of the International Court of Justice in any legal dispute to which it is a party.

Chapter IX. Industrial Plants and Economic Conversion

Article 74

1. For the purposes of inspection and verification, detailed information about industrial plants that produce armaments, and transportation centers (whether by rail, land, air, or sea), shall be submitted by each State Party to this Treaty to the IDO and to the other States Parties to this Treaty within one month after the entry into force of this Treaty.

2. The plant facilities include those that are:
a) devoted to the production of armaments;
b) plants and installations wholly or partly engaged in their repair and maintenance;
c) plants, arsenals, laboratories, or installations engaged in the testing or experimental operation of armaments.

3. These provisions apply to both privately and publicly owned facilities.

Article 75

The manager, owner, members of the board of directors, and local labor union president of any plant belonging to a category specified in Article 74 shall sign an affidavit stating that military production, testing, experimentation, and shipping have ended in that plant in accordance with the terms of this Treaty. These affidavits shall be filed with the national government and the IDO and shall be accessible to the public.

Article 76

1. IDO inspectors shall be entitled to investigate, on a spot-check basis, the condition of the various plants in order to verify that development, production, experimentation, storing, and testing of weapons have ended in accordance with the terms of this Treaty and that such activities have not been restarted.

2. Journalists and others are encouraged to write about the implementation of the provisions of this Treaty relating to the prohibited plants or prohibited military facilities.

Article 77

1. The internal laws of the States Parties to this Treaty shall be revised in order to impose on each industry wholly or in part involved in military contracts the obligation to file an economic conversion program.

2. The States Parties to this Treaty are aware that dislocations may occur as a result of the disarming process, and therefore each of the States shall make arrangements consonant with its own economic system to develop national, industrial, community, and worker conversion programs.

3. Both the IDO and the United Nations shall establish special units that shall conduct studies on economic conversion and shall assist States in economic conversion by providing any State requesting such assistance with economic data, information about available international assistance, and other advice.

Article 78

1. The States Parties agree that all plants wholly or partially involved in military construction shall be subject to the terms and stages of the Disarmament Program.

2. Machine tools and equipment designed for the production and maintenance of armaments shall be destroyed by the end of the third stage, except when they are needed for the limited purposes specified in Section 1 of Article 55 of this Treaty.

Article 79

Military academies may be maintained for the purposes specified in Section 1 of Article 55 of this Treaty. Their respective course of study shall include training and participation in nonmilitary techniques, in the maintenance of internal order, and in cooperation with the United Nations Force.

Article 80

1. Each State Party to this Treaty shall furnish full details of its military and paramilitary budget and appropriations to the IDO. It shall give the IDO inspectors, specifically trained in financial verification, access to financial and budgetary records.
2. The States Parties to this Treaty agree to reduce their military budgets and appropriations for military and paramilitary purposes simultaneously with, and in proportion to, the reductions in their armed forces and armaments.

Article 81

1. The Board of Inquirers shall submit an annual report to both the U.N. Security Council and the U.N. General Assembly on the reductions of national expenditures that have been achieved by the States Parties to this Treaty as well as the expenses of dismantling, destroying, or converting to civilian use, arms, armaments, industrial plants, and other military items.
2. The States Parties to this Treaty shall submit to the IDO the information required for the preparation of the reports to be made under Section 1 of this Article, as well as documents relating to defense budgetary planning, military procurement, weapon acquisition, and personnel projections.
3. The IDO report shall prepare studies and make recommendations as to the use to which the savings resulting from disarmament might be put in aiding national economies, providing economic and technical aid to the developing countries, and stimulating world trade.

Chapter X. Miscellaneous

Article 82

This Treaty shall be subject to ratification by the signatory States in accordance with their respective constitutional processes. Instruments of ratification shall be deposited with the U.N. Secretary General who shall notify each ratification to all U.N. Members and to nonmembers who have signed the Treaty. It shall enter into force when ratified by all the permanent members of the U.N. Security Council, by all the members of the NATO and Warsaw Pact alliances, and by two-thirds of the other States Members of the United Nations.

Article 83

Where a conflict exists between this Treaty and other treaties, this Treaty shall take precedence, except in the case of a conflict between this Treaty and the Charter of the United Nations, the Charter shall prevail.

Commentary

Article 1

1. We the peoples of the United Nations determined to save succeeding generations from the scourge of war, which twice in our lifetime has brought untold sorrow to mankind, and to reaffirm faith in fundamental human rights, in the dignity and worth of the human person, in the equal rights of men and women and of nations large and small. (Preface to the United Nations Charter)

The purposes of the United Nations are: 1. To maintain international peace and security, and to that end: to take effective collective measures for the prevention and removal of threats to the peace, and for the suppression of acts of aggression. . . . 2. To develop friendly relations among nations based on respect for the principle of equal rights and self-determination of peoples. . . . 3. to achieve international cooperation in solving problems of an economic, social, cultural, or humanitarian character. . . . 4. To be a center for harmonizing the actions of nations in the attainment of these common ends.

(Purposes and Principles. Chapter 1, Article 1 of the U.N. Charter)

2. Articles 41–47 of the U.N. Charter read as follows:

Article 41 of the U.N. Charter

The Security Council may decide what measures not involving the use of armed force are to be employed to give effect to its decisions, and it may call upon the Members of the United Nations to apply such measures. These may include complete or partial interruption of economic relations and of rail, sea, air, postal, telegraphic, radio, and other means of communications, and the severance of diplomatic relations.

Article 42 of the U.N. Charter

Should the Security Council consider that measures provided for in Article 41 would be inadequate or have proved to be inadequate, it may take such action by air, sea or land forces as may be necessary to maintain or restore international peace and security. Such action may include demonstrations, blockade, and other operations by air, sea, or land forces of Members of the United Nations.

Article 43 of the U.N. Charter

1. All Members of the United Nations, in order to contribute to the maintenance of international peace and security, undertake to make available to the Security Council, on its call in accordance with a special agreement or agreements, armed forces, assistance, and facilities, including rights of passage, necessary for the purpose of maintaining international peace and security.
2. Such agreement or agreements shall govern the numbers and types of forces, their degree of readiness and general location, and the nature of the facilities and assistance to be provided.
3. The agreement or agreements shall be negotiated as soon as possible on the initiative of the Security Council. They shall be concluded between the Security Council and Members or between the Security Council and groups of Members and shall be subject to ratification by the signatory states in accordance with their respective constitutional processes.

Article 44 of the U.N. Charter

When the Security Council has decided to use force it shall, before calling on a Member not represented on it to provide armed forces in fulfillment of the obligations assumed under Article 43, invite that Member, if the Member so desires, to participate in the decisions of the Security Council concerning the employment of contingents of that Member's armed forces.

Article 45 of the U.N. Charter

In order to enable the United Nations to take urgent military measures, Members shall hold immediately available national air-force contingent for combined international enforcement action. The strength and degree of readiness of these contingent or plans for their combined action shall be determined, within the limits laid down in the special agreement or agreements referred to in Article 43, by the Security Council with the assistance of the Military Staff Committee (MSC).

Article 46 of the U.N. Charter

Plans for the application of armed force shall be made by the Security Council with the assistance of the Military Staff Committee.

Article 47 of the U.N. Charter

1. There shall be established a Military Staff Committee to advise and assist the Security Council on all questions relating to the Security Council's military requirements for the maintenance of international peace and security, the employment and command of forces placed at its disposal, the regulation of armaments, and possible disarmament.

2. The MSC shall consist of Chiefs of Staff of the permanent Members of the Security Council or their representatives. Any Member of the United Nations not permanently represented on the Committee shall be invited by the Committee to be associated with it when the efficient discharge of the Committee's responsibilities requires the participation of that member in its work.
  3. The MSC shall be responsible under the Security Council for the Strategic direction of any armed forces placed at the disposal of the Security Council. Questions relating to the command of such forces shall be worked out subsequently.
  4. The MSC, with the authorization of the Security Council and after consultation with appropriate regional agencies, may establish regional sub-committees.
  (U.N. Charter, Chapter VII, Articles 41–47)
  3. In February 1982 the Reagan administration reaffirmed the Carter administration's position on no-first use which was presented by Secretary of State Cyrus Vance at the 1978 U.N. Special Session on Disarmament. Vance said:

> The United States will not use nuclear weapons against a non-nuclear weapon state party to the non-proliferation treaty or any comparable internationally binding commitment not to acquire nuclear explosive devices, except in the case of an attack on the U.S., its territory or armed forces, or its allies, by such a state allied to a nuclear weapons state or associated with a nuclear weapons state in carrying out or sustaining the attack.

The Soviet foreign minister Andrei Gromyko stated to the U.N. Conference on Disarmament that the Soviet Union would assume "an obligation not to be the first to use nuclear weapons" (June 15, 1982). A no-first-use pledge should not, however, be used as an excuse to build conventional forces.

For all the discussion of inspection and verification in the arms control and disarmament literature, very little discussion is dedicated to assurance or what process is created that satisfies the participants in the disarming and security dynamic. There is also very little written on what constitutes the epistemology of verification. Is this an empirical or inductive-statistical conception? Is it related merely to weapons and weapons counting or other indicia to account for good faith? The guiding principle of this document is that there is an overall commitment to a new security and disarmament program. It does not start from the assumption of a pause between stages of disarmament. Instead, the presumption is the reverse; namely, that the process moves on from each stage unless it is clear that there is a flaw in the process.
  4. Negotiations on the Comprehensive Test Ban (CTB), which broke down in 1980, were resumed in July 1986, but proved to be fruitless. The Reagan administration made it clear, however, that the talks were to probe the verification aspects of the unratified test treaties, and not to sign a Comprehensive Test Ban treaty. The Soviets were urging the signing of a CTB.

Article 2

  1. The year 2000 would be more desirable but 2008 is more realistic. The year 2000 is a millennial year, and thus a year of hope and goodwill. It is also an

important year psychologically, for people will be thinking about the massive changes that have occurred and will occur. It is likely, however, that the disarmament process will not be completed by this date. Hence the date 2008 is inserted. Nevertheless, the process will be into the second stage by the year 2000 and with enough momentum by then to be in place.

The three-stage approach to disarmament is borrowed from the McCloy-Zorin principles. The Soviet plan scheduled disarmament within five years, the U.S. in a minimum of nine years. This treaty plans for three stages of five years each. Virtually all nations, including the United States, are on five-year planning cycles. It is my hope that the world will be into the third and final stage of disarmament by the year 2005.

2. Exactly how large a military force is needed to maintain internal order may require clarification and greater definition. Internal order refers only to a disarming nation's domestic order. It does not include the domestic order of nations absorbed by fraud as in the cases of Latvia, Estonia, and Lithuania. Thus, if violent change occurs in a neighboring state that threatens peace, only an international force through the United Nations can intervene. Weapons of mass destruction or chemical, biological and radiological weapons are not instruments to maintain internal order.

3. All states parties to this treaty will incorporate the treaty into their security arrangements. It is possible that a security arrangement would be initiated prior to the Disarmament Program.

4. By moving to the next stage automatically, the disarmament process will be able to get past the first stage and build a momentum of its own. The nature of the disarming process as a means to change international relationships has not been sufficiently explored. There is evidence to suggest that if disarming becomes a continuous and cumulative process it will alter international enmities.

Article 3

1. Disarmament includes tactical, strategic and conventional weapons. Zonal inspection is discussed in Article 34.

2. Because approximately 98 percent of all the nuclear weapons in the world are owned by either the Soviet Union or the United States, it is these two powers that must initiate the disarming process. NATO and the Warsaw Pact must also take a leading role in disarmament, for these two alliances combined account for 75.4 percent of world military expenditures in 1980 (World Military Expenditures and Arms Transfers 1971–80). (The reduction of weaponry and forces refers to those resources assigned to the alliance systems.) Of course, a new question is raised if the Warsaw Alliance unilaterally dissolves.

Article 4

The McCloy-Zorin principles state, as in this treaty, that the International Disarmament Organization (IDO) will "implement control over and inspection of disarmament." However, whereas the IDO for McCloy-Zorin was to be "created within the framework of the United Nations," the IDO in this treaty will work closely with (rather than being an agency of) the United Nations. There is no doubt that a number of difficult—but not insoluble—organizational questions will present themselves between the IDO, the Board of Inquirers, and the U.N. Security Council (see Commentary, Article 6).

1., 2. The IDO will not preempt the role of the United Nations. For the United Nations, in contrast to the IDO, was not founded exclusively for the purpose of achieving arms control or disarmament (see Commentary, Article 1, section 1).

3. The IDO's execution of the treaty's terms shall be founded as much as possible on quantitative and technical rather than political decisions. When the IDO's decisions are disputed, they shall be resolved by the International Court of Justice (ICJ) (see Article 73). So long as the disarming process is continuous and cumulative, temporary advantage by one nation over another because of disparity between particular weapon systems will not be fatal. Each side must feel secure in knowing that any temporary disadvantage will be quickly corrected through the cumulative process.

4. The reduction of arms is not the sole instrument for an increase of world security. Thus, the United Nations (with the IDO in an advisory role) will consider various ways to enhance world security. This will be done without reliance on weapons or new alliances but through the World Security Agreement (see Chapter V of treaty), activities such as cultural and scientific exchanges and world development and environment programs.

5. There is no way to determine in advance what effect nonsignatories will have on the treaty. There can be a problem with "free riders," or those that benefit from a certain arrangement without bearing any of the costs. Minor powers and Third World countries will be more prone to sign the treaty once they believe that the major powers really want disarmament and are not just looking for a way to prevent the minor powers from acquiring nuclear and high-technology weapons.

Article 5

This article seeks to find a means for assuming the seriousness of the endeavor without stopping the process of disarming, since violation of the treaty does not (necessarily) mean abrogation or alteration of the treaty.

1. A possible alternative to placing X billion dollars into an escrow fund is basing contributions on a certain percentage of GNP. All signatories would contribute an equivalent (rather than equal) amount toward a security bond. (There is no legal precedent for using security bonds in this way.) The treaty seeks a mode of social indemnification for small states parties.

2. If fines cannot be successfully applied to payment of costs for the disarming process, or there are funds "left over," they might be supplied to economic development. First priority remains that of applying fines to the IDO costs.

Article 6

1. A revision of the U.N. Charter may not be necessary if a nonsignatory (state nonparty) to this treaty is a U.N. member pledged to its purposes.

2. A tension may appear to exist between the U.N. and the IDO. Article 39 of the U.N. Charter states: "The Security Council shall determine the existence of any threat to peace . . . and shall make recommendations, or decide what measures

need to be taken." In contrast, the IDO's function is to help fulfill the objectives of Article 39, by eliminating any threat to peace.

Article 7

1. Because the qualitative arms race begins in weapons research, the weapon laboratories must be shut down. This will be difficult to verify.
2. The international registry will be composed of various national academies (such as the academies of science and engineering) whose members will take a form of the Hippocratic Oath made applicable to scientists and other technical workers. As part of this process, labor unions would be asked to have their members also take the "Hippocratic Oath."
3. This will be verified by on-site inspections, which are discussed in Chapter VIII. One might conceive of a program of "on-site" inspections in which the host nation, beyond a certain number of guaranteed inspections, can charge doubting nations for a "peek."

Article 8

1. Prompt completion of treaty obligations is important to avoid military imbalances that can create political instability.
2. This exception clause allows for adjustments in the technical procedures of disarmament.

Article 9

(a) This agreement, signed on June 17, 1925, in Geneva, was a reaffirmation of the Versailles Treaty (1919), which prohibited use of poisonous gases, was imposed by the World War I victors on Germany, Austria, Bulgaria, and Hungary. The ratified treaty was deposited in France by the Soviet Union on April 5, 1928, and by the United States on April 10, 1975. (The United States ratified the Geneva Protocol only after public outrage over the U.S. use of chemical weapons in Indochina.) This is the "last formal agreement under international law dealing with the use of specified weapons." (Alva Myrdal, *The Game of Disarmament*, Pantheon, 1982, p. 233) This agreement bans use of asphyxiating, poisonous, or other gases, and of bacteriological methods of warfare.

(b) The ratified treaty was deposited in Washington on November 2, 1960, by the Soviet Union and on August 19, 1960, by the United States. The treaty states, in part, that "it is in the interests of all mankind that Antarctica shall continue forever to be used exclusively for peaceful purposes and shall not become the scene of international discord." (*Arms Control and Disarmament Agreements*, USACDA, p. 22)

(c) Although official efforts to achieve a test ban treaty began in May 1955, the seemingly insurmountable problem of verification (or at least a system of verification agreeable to all parties) prevented acceptance of a comprehensive test ban (CTB). Premier Khrushchev proposed (July 2, 1963) banning nuclear tests in areas where verification was not disputed, namely, in the atmosphere, outer space, and under water. The ratified treaty was deposited in Washington, London, and Moscow by the Soviet Union and the United States on October 10, 1963. Article 1 of this treaty is reprinted below:

> Each of the Parties to this Treaty undertakes to prohibit, to prevent and not to carry out any nuclear weapon test explosion, or any other nuclear explosion, at any place under its jurisdiction or control:
> (1) in the atmosphere; beyond its limits, including outer space; or under water, including territorial waters or high seas; or
> (2) in any other environment if such explosion causes radioactive debris to be present outside the territorial limits of the State under whose jurisdiction or control such explosion is conducted.
> (Ibid., p. 41)

It should be noted as well that the test ban treaty calls for security and general disarmament as the stated policies of the signatories.

(d) This "nonarmament" treaty is modeled somewhat on the Antarctica Treaty. The ratified treaty was deposited in Washington, London, and Moscow by both the United States and the Soviet Union on October 10, 1967. The treaty declared that "The exploration and use of outer space . . . shall be carried out for the benefit and in the interests of all countries irrespective of their degree of economic or scientific development and shall be the province of all mankind." Part of Article 4 is reprinted below:

> State Parties to this Treaty undertake not to place in orbit around the Earth any objects carrying nuclear weapons or any other kinds of weapons of mass destruction, install such weapons on celestial bodies, or station such weapons in outer space or in any other manner.

(e) The ratified treaty was deposited in London, Washington, and Moscow, by both the United States and the Soviet Union on March 5, 1970. As summarized in *Arms Control and Disarmament Agreements,* the Non-Proliferation Treaty is aimed to:

> prevent the spread of nuclear weapons; provide assurance, through international safeguards, that the peaceful nuclear activities of stages which have not already developed nuclear weapons will not be diverted to making such weapons; promote, to the maximum extent consistent with the other purposes of the treaty, the peaceful uses of nuclear energy through full cooperation—with the potential benefits of any peaceful application of nuclear explosion technology being made available to non-nuclear parties under appropriate international observation; express the determination of the parties that the treaty should lead to further progress in comprehensive arms control and disarmament measures.
> (USACDA, p. 88)

(f) The ratified treaty was deposited in Moscow, London, and Washington by both the Soviet Union and the United States on May 18, 1972. Parties to the treaty agreed:

not to emplant or emplace on the seabed and the ocean floor and in the subsoil thereof beyond the outer limit of a seabed zone . . . any nuclear weapons or any other types of weapons of mass destruction as well as structures, launching installations or any other facilities specifically designed for storing, testing or using such weapons.
(Article 1)

(g) This treaty eliminates the entire class of chemical and biological weapons, unlike the Geneva Protocol of 1925 ([a] above) which prohibited the use, but not the production and stockpiling, of biological and chemical weapons. The ratified treaty was deposited in London, Washington, and Moscow by both the United States and the Soviet Union on March 26, 1975. Article 1 is reprinted below:

Each State Party to this Convention undertakes never in any circumstances to develop, produce, stockpile or otherwise acquire or retain: (1) Microbial or other biological agents, or toxins whatever their origin or method of production, of types and in quantities that have no justification for prophylactic, protective or other peaceful purposes; (2) Weapons, equipment or means of delivery designed to use such agents or toxins for hostile purposes or in arms conflict.

(h) This treaty aimed to prevent the development or deployment of an antiballistic missile (ABM) system that would defend against a missile strike. One chosen site for each country was excluded from the agreement, i.e., it could be defended. The treaty was signed in Moscow on May 26, 1972, by the United States and the Soviet Union.

Article 10

As a general rule in international law a nation has the right of reservation to any particular segment of a treaty it finds distasteful. However, the type of Treaty outlined here would not favor such sovereign flexibility because of the interrelated nature of the Treaty to arms and national security.

Article 11

1., 2. Should the IDO exist before declarations on the state of armed forces is made? The problem in formal terms is that the IDO is created by this Treaty. The IDO in its skeleton form could accept the declarations and then within six months verify through off-site means the accuracy of each declaration (see also Commentary, Article 33, section 1).

3. This list is meant to detail the universe of personnel, weaponry, and systems that need to be disarmed or demilitarized.

Article 12

This clause is intended to guarantee that no country will benefit by sending its military hardware out of its country (perhaps to a militarily insignificant country) to prevent detection.

Article 13

The demobilization of forces will be accomplished in an orderly and systematic way. This article concerns only active (or uniformed) military personnel (see Article 45 and commentary).

Article 14

The criteria for defining "militarily significant" will be established by negotiation through the U.N. Security Council with the advice of the General Assembly. This article also involves changing the alliance system, unilateral and bilateral cutbacks, and changing the atmosphere by deemphasizing or eliminating propaganda.

Article 15

The nations that have invested most heavily in their defense system will be expected to make the largest contribution for carrying out the terms of the treaty and for paying the costs of the IDO.

Article 16

1. The seven-year term is chosen because it is approximately midway through the fifteen-year disarming process. An alternative possibility is to make the term ten years. This would give the Secretary General time to work through two stages of the disarmament process.

2., 3. Top advisers should come from many fields of endeavor and understanding, since the problem of disarmament is primarily one of relationships between nations and groups.

4. The secretary general has primary responsibility for the operations of the staff under the Board of Inquirers.

5. Staffing of the IDO should be diverse. However, this may prove to be difficult because of the necessity of staffing the IDO with highly skilled technicians. Grants for training should be given by nations and foundations now. These should be granted to the U.N. University and other universities. The United States and the Soviet Union should establish a common fund for training inspectors and other staff from Third World countries. The Board of Inquirers is encouraged to seek information and staff from NGOs (see Article 22, section 1, h, i).

Article 17

1. In the United States the person appointed would most likely be the director of the Arms Control and Disarmament Agency since the director is charged with the responsibility of being the president's chief adviser on arms control and disarmament questions.

2. There is a U.N. under-secretary general for Disarmament; the presently small secretariat will have to be substantially expanded.

3., 4. See commentary, Article 62.

5. The International Atomic Energy Agency (IAEA) came into force in 1957 with the objective, according to its charter, of accelerating and enlarging the use of atomic energy for "peace, health, and prosperity throughout the world. It shall ensure, so far as it is able, that assistance provided by it or at its request or under its supervision or control is not used in such a way as to further any military purpose." (IAEA Charter, A XII, S.6.) The IDO will work closely with the IAEA.

Article 18

Obligations under this treaty include being sure that information relevant to the terms of the treaty is in fact forthcoming. The Board of Inquirers in conjunction with the signatories will work through the ways and means information shall be forthcoming. The purpose of the penalty system is to keep the disarmament process going by acting as a deterrent. Under the terms of the treaty, nations shall not be able to decide whether a fine should be levied. This is the responsibility of the board alone, or there should be rigid, nondiscretionary rules about when fines are to be levied.

Article 19

1. The development of a staff whose loyalty is to the United Nations and the IDO and not to a particular state will be largely the responsibility of the United Nations University (UNU). According to its charter, the UNU is to be "an international community of scholars, engaged in research, post-graduate training and dissemination of knowledge in furtherance of the purposes and principles of the Charter of the United Nations."
2. The staff shall be broad-based and will serve for one stage (five years) of the disarmament process.

Article 20

1. This is to help ensure the independence and integrity of the IDO. The staff and the under-secretaries will take orders only from the secretary general of the IDO. This article is meant to guard against a situation in which members of the IDO become instruments of individual states.
2. States Parties to this treaty will not try to influence the IDO in any way. The granting of citizenship to any state may be considered as a way of bribing an IDO inspector. Protection mechanisms are necessary to ensure the independence of those in the IDO.
3. The treaty will not be abrogated because of violations to it. However, penalties commensurate with the transgression will be determined by the International Court of Justice (see Article 73). Article 94 of the U.N. Charter follows:

> A) Each Member of the United Nations undertakes to comply with the decision of the International Court of Justice in any case to which it is a party.
> B) If any party to a case fails to perform the obligations incumbent upon it

under a judgment rendered by the Court, the other party may have recourse to the Security Council, which may, if it deems necessary, make recommendations or decide upon measures to be taken to give effect to the judgment.

4. This clause allows for correction or modification of the technical procedures that might cause a nation to cheat.

Article 21

1. Because so much of the expertise and interest will be in the nongovernmental community, the IDO will need the help of that community to do its work.
2. Its discussions, however, should always be considered on the record so that there will be no chance of any nation concluding that one group is conspiring against another nation.
3. It is important for the IDO to protect the integrity of the process; a major way to do so is for the IDO to make clear the types of relationships it will have with the NGOs. A problem that may occur here is where a citizen or group of a host nation tells the IDO in confidence of a violation. All "whistle blowers" should be protected against punishment.

Article 22

a) The secretary general of the IDO will work closely with the U.N. secretary general.
b) These are to be people with technical and diplomatic skills.
c) The Board of Inquirers has recommending or advisory power. Historically, except in mixed-claim commissions, fines have not been used, although reparations are rewarded after a war. The fine system is found in Western nations' municipal law. The "direct use of force" is a decision of the U.N. Security Council and not the IDO.
d) Assessment will be made according to standard U.N. procedures.
e) The IDO is the central body for carrying out a multilateral program of disarmament. It should be reiterated that unilateral initiatives in disarmament do not require inspection, only notification (see Article 30 and commentary).
f) The purpose of rotation geographically is to assure that no nation "owns" the IDO's infrastructure, and that the disarmament and security process is a continuous one.
g) This will not only facilitate the board's work, but also will allow it to show an international presence.
h) To make the disarmament process work, and for the IDO to be internationally credible and have the support among movements and established institutions, it must relate to them by hearing the advice of outside experts and disarmament groups as well.
i) The reporting process emphasizes the IDO's ties to the U.N. structure.
j) Parties to this treaty will report to their citizens at least twice a year at equivalent times. Public relations are important to maintaining public support.
k) The board shall both initiate and consider reports on the problems of disarmament.

Article 23

1. Although the Board of Inquirers is distinct from the United Nations, it stays within the U.N. framework as much as possible. The thirteen other members chosen by the General Assembly are to be "militarily significant" or population significant countries. At the 1962 Disarmament Conference, eighteen countries were considered "militarily significant." The criteria used to define "militarily significant" will be established by negotiation through the Security Council with advice from the General Assembly.
2. Staggered terms are introduced for continuity of the disarming process.
3. There will be a secretariat responsible to the secretary general under the aegis of the IDO's Board of Inquirers.
4. If the Disarmament Program is to be successful, all states parties to this treaty must agree to involve these groups. Special researchers, experts, and consultants will not only add to the intellectual quality and diversity of opinion, but will also reduce costs. More important, this will actively involve the citizenry in the Disarmament Program.

Article 24

1. The Military Staff Committee's (MSC) first and only task was to examine from a military standpoint Article 43 of the U.N. Charter (reprinted in Article 1, section 2, para. 3, of this Commentary). The MSC presented to the Security Council a forty-one-article draft outlining the general principles that would govern the organization and the use of the U.N. forces, as well as a report specifying the exact composition of this force. Neither report had the unanimous support of the five delegations to the MSC. When presented to the Security Council, the reports again were not unanimously supported.

Although the MSC still meets every other week, except for the Iraqi crisis of 1990, it has done little of substance since the 1948 deadlock over Article 43. The most significant and stubborn disagreement concerning the principles governing the U.N. forces concerned Article 11, the "Contribution of Armed Forces by Member Nations." The Chinese, French, British, and U.S. delegations agreed:

> Each of the five Permanent Members of the Security Council will make a comparable initial overall contribution to the armed forces . . . these contributions may differ widely as to the strength of the separate components, land, sea and air.

In contrast, the Soviet Union argued:

> Permanent Members of the Security Council shall make available armed forces (land, sea and air) on the Principle of Equality . . . deviations from this principle are permitted by special decisions of the Security Council.

The MSC, like the treaty itself, will only work if there is a modicum of trust between the major powers. The end of the Cold War between the superpowers gives hope that such trust may exist.

2. Here it is recognized that a World Security Agreement is not static but dynamic; thus, such an agreement must be flexible to respond to changing conditions.

Article 25

1. A nation that does not have a military of sufficient size to allow it to contribute to the U.N. Force is excused from this article.
2., 3. The U.N. force should not be armed with weapons of mass destruction. The U.N. force will, whenever possible, employ nonviolent means and use nonlethal weapons. The U.N. force will not have a monopoly on violence and will not be able to use force in and of itself to stop the aggression of states. The question of whether it should have a substantial standing armed force and its character should be debated in the MSC. The answer to this question depends on the constitutional processes of nations contributing defense forces and signatory nations to the agreement.

Article 26

1. Article 43 of the U.N. Charter is reprinted in the commentary on Article 1, section 2.
2. The weapons turned over to the United Nations shall not be weapons of mass destruction. Their use or threatened use would defeat the purpose of building a security system not predicated on weapons of mass destruction.
3. International organizations will observe international law. It gains humanity nothing if our international organizations use or have nuclear weapons in their arsenal.

Article 27

1. The paramount reason the MSC was unable to establish a World Security Agreement was because neither the United States nor the Soviet Union wanted Article 43 of the U.N. Charter implemented. The Soviets feared that the West would rig the enforcement mechanism to favor the West. The Americans feared the introduction of Soviet troops into troubled areas. Inis Claude writes in *International Conciliation* of the "official mythology of the Western bloc," which credits the Soviets with the failure to establish a U.N. enforcement mechanism. Claude contends that the negotiations "revealed a complex pattern of disagreements," which "involved largely but not exclusively a Western-Soviet cleavage."
2. The purpose of the MSC's recommendations is to ensure reductions in national forces according to the terms of the treaty. The IDO will work and then absorb the functions of national patrols. The absorption does not have to happen during the fifteen-year disarmament process and is not necessary for the successful operation of this Program.

Article 28

This will allow for a periodic reassessment of the Disarmament Program. It will also ascertain whether residual forces after the third stage shall be further cut back.

Article 29

If at the end of a stage of disarmament a country has more arms and forces than agreed to in the treaty, then that country will be required to independently disarm to the agreed level of arms. The nation that is behind in the disarmament race will move more quickly while the nation in compliance might slow its pace. Inspection by the IDO shall continue.

This article does not contradict the idea that the disarmament process is continuous and does not stop at the end of a stage. The approximate numbers of what each side should have left at each stage can be determined at the onset of negotiations.

Article 30

The disarming process does not require bilateral or multilateral steps. Indeed, some critics have argued that disarmament negotiations are a delusion. Since the arms buildup is a subjective and unilateral process, there is sense to the argument that independent steps will be needed to initiate the disarmament process. To have an independent disarmament process work, it will be necessary for nations to surrender their ideas of forward defense. This doctrine, in effect, sanctions the fighting of wars on another's territory. The willingness to scrap this view is related to the development of an alternative international system of security and a multilateral or bilateral disarming process. It should also be noted that the internal bureaucratic dynamics of nations are affected by international processes that then legitimize various actions of groups.

Article 31

These weapons are disarmed first for they are most clearly perceived as offensive or terror weapons.

Article 32

1. Extracts from the charter of the International Military Tribunal at Nuremberg are reprinted below:

> Article 6: The Tribunal established by the agreement referred to in Article 1 hereof for the trial and punishment of the major war criminals of the European Axis countries shall have the power to try and punish persons who, acting in the interests of the European Axis countries whether as individuals or as members of organizations, committed any of the following crimes:
> The following acts, or any of them, are crimes coming within the jurisdiction of the Tribunal for which there shall be individual responsibility:
> (a) Crimes against Peace: Namely, planning, preparation, initiation of waging of a war of aggression, or a war in violation of international treaties, agreements or conspiracy for the accomplishment of any of the foregoing:
> (b) War Crimes: Namely, violations of the laws or customs of war. Such violations shall include, but not be limited to, murder, ill-treatment or deporta-

tion to slave labor camps or for any other purposes of civilian populations of or in occupied territory, murder or ill treatment of prisoners of war or persons on the seas, killing of hostages, plunder of public or private property, wanton destruction of cities, towns, or villages, or devastation not justified by military necessity;

(c) Crimes against Humanity: Namely, murder, extermination, enslavement, deportation, and other inhumane acts committed against any civilian population, before or during the war, or persecution on political, racial or religious grounds in execution of or in connection with any crimes within the jurisdiction of the Tribunal, whether or not in violation of the domestic law of the country where perpetrated.

Leaders, organizers, instigators and accomplices participating in the formulation or execution of a common plan or conspiracy to commit any of the foregoing crimes are responsible for all acts performed by any persons in execution of such plan.

2. The Nuremburg Judgments are central ideas for the control of government officials and the military. They have yet to be confronted by statesmen who must now be persuaded to see their utility and moral worth in securing a disarmament arrangement.

3. An example of a no-surrender clause is found in Articles 237 and 238 of the Constitution of the Socialist Federal Republic of Yugoslavia (SFRY):

A 237: It shall be the inviolable and inalienable right and duty of the nations and nationalities of Yugoslavia, working people and citizens to protect and defend the independence, sovereignty, territorial integrity, and the social system of the SFRY, established by the Constitution of the SFRY.

A 238: No one shall have the right to acknowledge or sign an act of capitulation nor accept or recognize the occupation of SFRY or any of its individual parts. No one shall have the right to prevent citizens of the SFRY from fighting against an enemy who has attacked the country. Such acts shall be unconstitutional and punishable as high treason. High treason is the gravest crime against the people and shall be punished as a serious criminal offense.

Article 33

1. Study groups of defense industrial managers in the militarily significant states either separately or under the aegis of the United Nations would meet to talk through ways of inventorying their equipment and material. Defense officials of each nation would also begin such joint discussions. A common inventorying and notation system would be useful although not critical. Separate discussions could go forward between designated military on how to compile the inventories and military lists. The process of exchange of information between U.S. and Soviet scholars on military conversion began in earnest in 1988 on a nongovernmental basis.

2. The assumption of this section is that there will inevitably be statistical

error or a sheer inability to account for all weapons at any one time. The approximation theory of science is applicable. As each side moves from statistical or abstract reporting to empirical reporting, the inventory lists will become more refined.

Article 34

The two methods of zonal disarmament offered here present two ways to achieve the same objective. The second is preferable but more time-consuming; the first allows for more secretive societies to do their own disarming, with verification following the disarming to ensure that the whole zone has been disarmed, thereby not involving the three-stage percentage cut back. (See Louis B. Sohn "Progressive Zonal Inspection: Basic Issues," in S. Melman, ed., *Disarmament: Its Politics and Economics* [Boston: American Academy of Arts and Sciences, 1962], pp. 121–33.)

Article 35

By withdrawing forces from areas of conflict or potential conflict (such as the border between North and South Korea, in Central Europe, or Lebanon) or by setting up military zones of distance, the chances of regional conflict disrupting the disarming process will be diminished.

Article 36

Inventory maps at the proper time would be made publicly available through the United Nations or IDO. Citizen inspection is an important element of this treaty. The question to consider, however, is the relationship of on-site inspection by an adversary or the IDO to citizen inspection. Some nations may prefer international inspection to citizen inspection (see Chapter VIII).

Articles 37–40

These articles could be combined into one article that is much more general. It might read as follows:

> Nuclear weapons and their launchers (e.g., missiles) should be destroyed with IDO inspectors and citizens as witnesses in such a manner that:
> (a) no vital component could be reassembled for use;
> (b) dangerous materials would be placed under the safeguard of the IDO, which would find environmentally safe ways to guard or dispose of them;
> (c) this disposal would have to meet with the approval of the States Parties to this Treaty.

There are several difficulties with the specifics of Articles 37–40 as they currently stand:

Article 37

The trigger must be disarmed prior to removing the fissile material. What sort of container the fissile material should be deposited in, and where, needs to be established.

Article 38

A bureaucratic question emerges as to whether the IAEA should receive the fissile material rather than the IDO. It may be enough to have the IDO contract with the IAEA for its services, using its expertise, experience, and organization.

Article 39

Unless the treaty bans nuclear energy, Uranium–235 and plutonium will continue to be produced; thus, taking fissionable material from weapons and disposing of it will not prevent the acquisition of fissionable material.

One last point: because we do not know exactly how the Chinese or Soviets build their nuclear weapons, it may be risky to delineate the exact steps for dismantling weapons.

Article 41

The purpose of this article is to assure continued satellite production for peaceful and security purposes. This article assures the involvement of the IDO in satellite surveillance.

Article 42

This article is problematic. For commercial, communications, and many other reasons, we cannot expect people to give up the use of space. However, any launching pad, silo, etc., can be used for either peaceful or military purposes, and there is no way of determining (without on-site inspection prior to and during blast-off) exactly what is being launched. Some comprehensive system of inspection must be set up, since a space shuttle or Boeing 747 is as capable of carrying nuclear weapons as a B–52. Spot inspections and prior notification may be part of the policing of launching sites, as well as designating specific sites for launches.

Article 43

Satellites will be launched only after prior inspection by the IDO. Only through such inspection will it be possible to verify the peaceful use of the object to be launched. Limiting the number of launching sites will make inspection easier.

Article 44

Because all satellites must be inspected prior to and during launch, it will be possible to verify that no ASATs are deployed.

Article 45

1. The command staffs of each nation will invariably be the last to be dismantled. Thus, the likelihood is that each nation will hold onto its general officers and skeletal military organizations to the end of the disarmament process.
2. This section, which is aimed at militarized civilians, will be difficult to administer. For example, what happens to GS-15 computer analysts at the Defense Department? The answer to this question involves economic and personnel conversion (see Chapter IX). Those forces mentioned in the second sentence may be retained (pursuant to the treaty) for domestic policy and/or they may be retained until the end of the last stage.
3. Here the principal concern is reduction of the cadres, who are responsible for organizing the reservists, by the end of the third stage. It should be noted that a strong argument remains for continuing the reservists as a defensive force.

Article 46

1. The intention is not to restrict but to enhance freedom to travel on the seas by reducing and eventually eliminating the offensive power of navies. Coast Guard ships are not to be eliminated. A method can be agreed upon based on tonnage and size to determine (1) how many ships a state may retain, and (2) the number of inspectors per ship, e.g., six inspectors on an aircraft carrier, four on a battleship, two on a cruiser, etc.
2. Ships that are transformed completely and irreversibly for peaceful purposes need not be destroyed. The transformation should be witnessed and the resultant nonoffensive ships would be inspected by the IDO. On the U.S. side, attention should be paid to the Washington Naval Conference to ascertain what lessons may be learned.
3. Nuclear units refer to the nuclear weapons systems or bombs on a ship.
4. The destruction of these ships should be accompanied by at least as much fanfare as their creation and should be witnessed by representatives of as many nations as possible.

Article 47

During the Cold War, the United States and the Soviet Union played games of "chicken" with their navies. Such games are dangerous. Rules were worked out in 1970 to eliminate this dangerous behavior.

Article 48

1. Aircraft should be divided into three categories: strategic, tactical, and defensive with limited range. Planes that are defensive with limited range may be retained.
2. One possible way to implement this section is for each state publicly to propose a method of destroying their weapons, and the proposed method would be implemented barring objections from other states parties to this treaty.

Article 49

The destruction of chemical, biological, and radiological weapons must be environmentally safe, even though this is a difficult process. The convention on the Prohibition of the Development, Production and Stockpiling of Bacteriological (Biological) and Toxin Weapons (1975) does not specify how these weapons would be destroyed. The only article that directly addresses the destruction of these weapons, Article II, is reprinted below:

> Each State Party to this Convention undertakes to destroy or to divert to peaceful purposes, as soon as possible but not later than nine months after the entry into force of the Convention, all agents, toxins, weapons, equipment and means of delivery specified in Article 1 of the Convention, which are in its possession or under its jurisdiction or control. In implementing the provisions of this Article all necessary safety precautions shall be observed to protect people and the environment.

Article 50

1. Although all weapons may be considered inhumane, some are more cruel and inhumane than others. Weapons that cause unnecessary suffering and can only be used indiscriminately, affecting civilian populations of this and future generations genetically, are militarily excessive and illegal. Maiming weapons include: incendiary weapons, such as napalm and white phosphorus, cause unnecessary suffering and are generally used indiscriminately (as in terror bombing); dum dum bullets and high-velocity on-impact rifles, such as the M-16, are unnecessarily cruel. Weapons that have a long-term toxic effect, such as Agent Orange, are discussed in detail in Article 51 of the commentary. It is time to inventory non-nuclear weapons to ascertain their effects on noncombatants. A start in this direction was made in the 1977 Protocol for the Protection of Non-Combatants.

2. Defoliants and herbicides, when used on a mass scale, as in Vietnam, destroy crops (denying food to humans and domestic animals) and forests (denying food and shelter to wildlife). The delicate ecosystem of South Vietnam will probably take at least 100 years to repair. (Prototype of Ecocide, "Air, Water, Earth, Fire: The Impact of the Military on World Environmental Order," International Series no. 2, Sierra Club, May 1974, pp. 19–21.) Weapons that have a long-lasting and negative effect on the environment are prohibited.

Article 51

1. This article is aimed at transforming research and development away from the weapons laboratory and toward useful and humane purposes. Those involved in any aspect of research and development—scientists, skilled labor, etc.—will be expected to take an oath whereby they swear or affirm that they will abstain from any activities that lead to the creation or completion of weapons of mass destruction (see Article 7, section 2).

2. a) This is somewhat problematic since herbicides and defoliants are usually used for peaceful purposes. Again, the IDO should develop international standards and then decide on a case by case basis.

b) The "enhanced radiation (ER) weapon for battlefield use is characterized by officials as a 'crude forerunner' of a third generation ER weapon." According to Edward Teller, the ER warhead now in use is "at the beginning of the defensive use of nuclear weapons." Another third-generation weapon being developed is "An x-ray laser pumped by x-rays from a nuclear explosion for use as a defense against incoming ballistic missiles above the earth's atmosphere, or as an anti-satellite weapon." (*Nuclear Weapons Data Book*, vol. 1, p. 29. Ballinger, 1984)

c) In the 1950s and later in the 1960s scientists sought ways of modifying weather. As an instrument of national policy such tactics could be disastrous for large areas of the world.

d) Climate modification is a variant of Article 51, section 2, c).

e) According to the *Nuclear Weapons Data Book*, electromagnetic pulse (EMP) weapons are part of the new "third generation" of nuclear weapons:

> EMP weapons specially designed to create a large electro-magnetic pulse to burn out enemy communication, utilizing directed or non-directed EMP created by a nuclear explosion above the atmosphere. The realm of advanced technologies now includes a directed form of EMP using a "high power microwave coherent beam of immense peak power." The Department of Defense Directed Energy Program (under DARPA) includes "radio frequency weapons" as one of its three major programs. (p. 29)

f) See Article 46, section 2, e) (above).

g) Interference with the ozone layer could cause, among other things, blindness and skin cancer.

h) The various "cluster bomb units" (CBUs) developed during the Vietnam War have been improved to blanket much larger areas. CBUs normally comprise a dispensing system, which can be attached to the underside of an aircraft or packed into a missile warhead, and a multitude of bomblets. The earlier cluster systems used unguided "dumb" submunitions that were scattered in a random pattern over the battlefield; future systems will dispense "smart" submunitions, capable of seeking out enemy targets and exploding when they are within firing range. Advanced cluster-dispensing systems now in development include the West German MW–1, the U.S. LADS (Low Altitude Dispensing System), the French Durnadel runway cratering system (which the U.S. Air Force plans to purchase) and the British JP–233 dispensing system. (Michael Klare, "The Conventional Weapons Fallacy," *The Nation*, April 9, 1983)

i) These munitions dispense a cloud of highly volatile fuel (ethylene oxide, propylene oxide, or propane) that, when ignited, produces a powerful blast capable of leveling entire city blocks. An FAE (fuel air explosive) of this type used in Vietnam, the BLU–82/B "Daisy Cutter," has been described by observers as the "closest thing to a nuclear bomb." The Pentagon is now developing an advanced fuel-air munitions, FAE–2, and other explosives. (Ibid.)

j) Experimentation of this kind has gone forward unhindered as a weapon of use in so-called brushfire wars.

k) Recent discussions within the United States about the need for defense against viral bacteriological poisoning has also opened the door to an arms race in this field. There is no doubt that defensive weapons research is integrally related to offensive activity.

l) Advances in genetic modification techniques for military purposes must be controlled and directed to peaceful and humane purposes or else the research must be banned altogether.

Article 52

Where the installation is integral to the operation of the weapons that are being disarmed, the alternative is to close the installation at the same time that the weapons are destroyed.

Article 53

The purpose of this article is to disband the infrastructure that supports weapons systems. This article could have First Amendment problems in the United States. The treaty intention, however, is only to interrupt government-sponsored activities and contracts.

Article 54

The purpose of this article is to assure a continuous reporting and participatory system with each nation's respective public.

Article 55

1., 2. The U.N. Charter does not specify what kind of weapons or how many may be considered necessary to maintain internal order. This is further complicated by states facing a "rebellious" or "revolutionary" populace. Whatever one's political theory of the state, there is no need for any nation to retain weapons of mass destruction so that internal order might be maintained. Where new states are "born," recognition by other states should be predicated on the acceptance of a common security and global disarmament treaty in exchange for a U.N. collective security arrangement.

Article 56

An important consideration in this article is whether the recommendation of the board will in fact become a political bloc to override the concerns of other nations. This is now likely even if the U.N. veto is kept intact.

Article 57

The test of what is a defensive weapon aircraft is its (a) range, (b) speed, and (c) capacity to carry nuclear devices and cruise missiles.

Article 58

1. Prohibiting the import and export of arms will have a variety of significant consequences. For example, the economies of countries will suffer varying de-

grees of dislocation unless a careful policy of conversion is followed (see Chapter IX). Conversely, those countries that spend large sums on weapons will liberate those monies for peaceful purposes. A new approach to foreign policy will be required for those countries that attempt to use arms and military assistance as a political lever. This has wide implications for revolutionary movements; the state will have less firepower to stop them and yet movements themselves will have a harder time getting weapons. The consequences of this are unpredictable.

2. The purpose of this section is to set up a database and provide an accounting of the quantity and quality of arms around the world. Some of these numbers are already available through nongovernment research institutes such as the London-based Institute for Strategic Studies, the International Peace Research Institute in Norway, and the Arms Race and Nuclear Weapons Project in Washington, D.C.

3. As in Article 58, section 2, this section provides an accounting of weapons in the world. This is to be done in good faith, but could be checked with independent methods such as input/output analysis.

4. This section again, builds up transnational activities to control and monitor national actions.

Article 59

By recording who imports, licenses, sells, and creates weapons by keeping a paper or computer train, it will be easier to assure compliance with the treaty. Further measures to prevent the illicit arms trade are necessary and these should be worked out in the framework of the Disarmament Program.

Article 60

This refers specifically, but not exclusively, to arms contracts that are ended by a state or any other party, by signing this treaty. In other words, there can be no domestic or international breaches by weapons contracts once the treaty is signed.

Article 61

1., 2. This treaty aims to construct a new frame of reference whereby people and states recognize the contradiction between arming and security covenants. Verification, inspection, and assurance are central to this treaty and are taken very seriously.

3. A variety of agreed-upon technical methods of verification, such as independent satellite monitoring (see Article 63, section 2.b and Article 65, section 1) and seismic stations, will provide a cross-reference for disarmament assurance; such cross-reference is essential since verification is, unavoidably, an inferential exercise. However, technical forms of verification—regardless of their sophistication and accuracy—can offer only probabilities, not certainties. Thus, verification will never prove satisfactory unless there is a modicum of trust and integrity in the process of disarmament. Trust is built up through common projects and activities that are systematic, not regulative. For example, civilization is predicated on a fundamental or constitutive set of social relationships that assures the continuation of the species. It is in the constitutive context that conflict is regulated.

It is for the latter reason that all parties enter the treaty in good faith and recognize that it is in their interest to cooperate with the IDO's verification process. Again, the end of the Cold War makes this a realistic objective.

There are nonintrusive technical means to verify a party's compliance with the treaty; for example, seismic stations, reconnaissance aircraft, space-based electronic and photographic reconnaissance, surveillance vessels, horizon backscatter radar, and air sampling, to name a few.

Unfortunately, weapons technology is increasingly going in directions that surveillance technology cannot follow. For example, weapons are becoming more versatile, dual-capable, and mission-flexible. The tremendous advancement in miniaturization and micro-miniaturization makes it easier to conceal weapons. Rapid progress in the field of sensor deception is making it possible to disguise the characteristics of weapons. Weapons are also becoming increasingly mobile and diverse, which will further frustrate the intelligence analyst. Furthermore, the work on defensive weapon systems speeded up under the Reagan Strategic Defense Initiative (SDI) has thrown up more problems for surveillance. In short, surveillance technology simply will find it increasingly difficult to provide accurate intelligence in a growing number of areas. Even the seemingly simple questions of whether a warhead is nuclear or conventional, and if nuclear, what yield is difficult to ascertain. (William Kincade, "Challenges to Verification: Old and New" *Arms Control*, December 1982)

4. In addition to the limited technological or nonintrusive methods of verification, there is a process of verification through challenge and response. A party suspected of a treaty violation would be expected "voluntarily to offer clarifying information to allay suspicion, the assumption being that the suspected Party would itself be vitally interested in establishing its innocence. An 'invitation of inspection' might be forthcoming spontaneously in some instances and under pressure in some severe cases of doubt." (Alva Myrdal, *The Game of Disarmament*, p. 301) Thus, where doubt exists there is a process of explanation for the alleged violator. Whether such on-site inspections after a challenge are to be obligatory will be decided by codicils to the treaty.

Assurance is a means to secure nonphysical proof of good faith adherence to the treaty.

5. The IDO aims to deter states from violating the treaty. Its fundamental purpose is not to catch violators "red-handed" or after the fact. The treaty will not be terminated or necessarily structurally altered because of a party's violation. In other words, the violation of the treaty is not grounds for scrapping the entire treaty, although it may require changes in implementing the treaty.

Article 62

1. This article attests to the need to "humanize and socialize" the disarming process and to include nongovernmental groups as part of it. Because of the treaty's far-reaching implications, the long-term success must include citizen participation.

2., 3. Throughout the treaty the assumption is that networks of scholars and technical people will work together transnationally to implement this treaty. Alva Myrdal in *The Game of Disarmament* outlines how this system could work.

Article 63

1. The attempt in this article is to take account of the suspicion and distrust between adversaries. If the adversarial method is used, then certification should be required by the IDO.
2. No single system makes up the definition of verification; it is only through different modes of examination that reasonable people can find a working or commonsense definition of verification.
    a) The IDO will have access to citizens of signatory nations on matters relevant solely to the disarmament process.
    b) The French proposed an international satellite-monitoring agency (ISMA) at the 1978 U.N. Special Session on Disarmament. The United States contended that an ISMA might become politicized, would cost more than it was worth, and would release sensing technologies and thus raise American security concerns. The Soviets offered no response to the French plan.
    A June 10, 1981 report by the Group of Governmental Experts appointed to study the implications of establishing an ISMA suggested that an ISMA would have to evolve slowly over time. According to this group, ISMA would be able to "identify gross environmental changes on the surface of the Earth and in the atmosphere," photograph "preparatory activities on the ground for nuclear tests," and measure the tests' "nuclear and electromagnetic radiation." In addition, an ISMA could "detect and describe military measures prohibited by the Treaty." (*The Implications of Establishing an ISMA* [New York: United Nations, 1983], pp. 23–27)
    An ISMA could also monitor international conflicts and potential conflicts. For example, an ISMA could provide the following services:

    > early-warning of attacks through observation of build-up of military and paramilitary forces; evidence of border violations; cease-fire monitoring; assistance to United Nations observers and peace-keeping missions; strengthening of international confidence-building measures and observation of the use of, or threat to use, force. (Ibid., p. 55)

    c) Article 62, sections 1–3.

Article 64

1. In the era of détente various proposals for joint satellite activity were worked out and agreed to by the United States and the Soviet Union. These programs could serve as the basis for establishing joint satellite inspection teams (see Article 63, section 2, b).
2. The official presence of the IDO or United Nations is necessary to record for the world the actual destruction and dismantling processes of nuclear weapons. U.N. representatives will also be present when the adversary is the inspector.

Article 65

These committees will be set up as soon as possible to start work on the perfecting of the verification process.

Article 66

a) As states with nuclear power plants (who are also members of the NPT) are required to keep records of the quantity, location, and type of fissionable materials for the IAEA, similar records on armaments, troops, etc., will be available to the IDO. The shroud of secrecy—forever the bane of disarmers—will slowly be removed.

b) The IDO retains the authority even after assurance systems are perfected to inspect any area according to the time schedule of the treaty.

Article 67

1. To better understand how these inspections would be carried out, it is helpful to examine the IAEA, which was created to verify compliance of the NPT and has no authority to discipline violators (see the commentary on Article 17, section 5). The IAEA is a less ambitious attempt at control of atoms than the Baruch Plan of 1946, which called for the international ownership and control of nuclear energy. All signers of the NPT agree, in brief, that non-nuclear weapons states will not acquire nuclear weapons and that nuclear weapons states will not transfer nuclear weapons to non-nuclear weapons states.

Although technical/nonintrusive means of verification are used as much as possible, on-site inspections by IAEA inspectors "enhance the credibility of the safeguard system by introducing an element of human judgment and dedication to the principles of effective international verification." (Mark Imber, "Arms Control Verification: The Special Case of IAEA-NPT 'Special Inspections', " *Arms Control*, December 1982, p. 56)

According to Imber, there are three kinds of IAEA inspections:

(a) ad hoc inspections used [1] to verify the information in a state's initial report on its nuclear facility, and [2] whenever there is to be a transfer of nuclear material across national boundaries;

(b) routine inspections to guarantee the accuracy of a state's reports and records (the number and intensity of these inspections are greatly limited); and

(c) special inspections undertaken when the IAEA feels the information supplied by a state is inadequate.

2. The IDO, like the IAEA, will have some flexibility in determining the frequency and intensity of inspections. Thus, states that are the most cooperative, prompt, and accurate in their records will probably receive the fewest inspections of the least intensity.

Article 68

1. The purpose of this section is to present a "full faith" picture of inspectors so that the host nation will know who will be on its territory. The host nation will become part of the process.

2. A state's objection to an inspector is not necessarily a sign of wrong doing. The state may fear commercial espionage by an inspector, or distrust an inspector because of his or her nationality, or be seeking to hide an accident or some inefficiency. However, repeated refusals would slow down the process and would be considered against the host nation, and should be dealt with promptly.

Article 69

1. Obviously, administrative guidebooks of "dos and don'ts" will have to be prepared by the IDO and the host nations.
2. There is no other way for an inspector to travel except by relying on the services of the host nation. It is in the host nation's interests to provide these services.
3. This section again raises the question of intrusion, patent rights, and property rights. The standardized sensing and recording devices should be manufactured under the auspices of the IDO so that there is no possibility of abuse. This is important since the installation of these devices will be very contentious.
4. When the laws of a state conflict or prohibit the "effective discharge" of the IDO inspection, the national laws of the state shall yield to the treaty provisions. It is in the state's interest to cooperate; however, there should be some appeal procedure. Obviously, the task of the inspectors will be limited to specific activities from which inspectors will not deviate. If there is to be a disarming process, difficulties arising from this inspection process have to be worked out swiftly and cordially.
5. Inspectors' tasks do not include the acquisition and use of information for the purpose of selling or reporting to other nations. The question of confidentiality is critical in this regard. It will be especially important in Western nations where there are great concerns that industrial secrets, patents, etc., not be made public. However, repeated obstruction on these grounds will be duly noted. Information passed on to the IDO and its inspectors is received in confidence, although carrying out the treaty is paramount.
6. Inspectors will be given the same privileges that diplomats are accorded. However, violations will result in the replacement of the inspector after appeal. The job is too important to overlook violations of duty.

Article 70

1. To the extent possible, determining whether the host nation is in compliance should be a straightforward factual task of assessment. Thus, the secretary general of the IDO would have the task of ascertaining compliance or failure. The secretary general also has the more discretionary task under this article of determining substantial compliance and ways that the host nation will seek to comply. These considerations are atmospheric and subjective and may have to be changed because of their seemingly subjective character.
2. The secretary general does not have powers of punishment although he or she can recommend remedial steps to the Board of Inquirers.

Article 71

1. The purpose of this section is for the objector to put forward evidence of suspected violation, and the task of the IDO and Board of Inquirers is to set forth measures to allay fears of the states or objectors, by dealing fairly with them.
2. This section is meant to include NGOs as an important element of the disarming process; their opinions and objections will be taken seriously and addressed fairly.

Article 72

1. This section deals with serious substantive activities that cannot be handled through a compliance and confidence-building system that would satisfy the complaining party.
2. As a general rule no nation will turn over its sovereign power of decision making to a nonnational body. However, where a nation has agreed to a general means of mediation and dispute settlement in the context of the treaty, it is in the nation's interest to comply with the mediation.

Article 73

1. The ICJ may give advisory opinions to the United Nations. This authority can be broadened to include questions directed to it by the IDO. Because of the nature of the disarmament process and fears around security questions where there may be interruptions or unacceptable ambiguities, and because political matters often deal with events that appear central and ominous at the time but transitory and trivial in the light of history, the question of timely decision is important. Hence, the three month time limit. International public pressure will urge that this time limit be observed.
2. This section refers to questions of legal interpretation. To the extent possible, the process should be seen as a legal one, outside the realm of decisions predicated on raw power. The purpose of this section, therefore, is to turn questions that are thought of primarily in power terms into issues of law. Again, the time limit should be observed.
3. This section should be read in the context of the treaty. Where jurisdiction of the ICJ is not accepted, differences may still be resolved by mediation or arbitration.

Article 74

The question of access to industrial facilities is a ticklish one. Access to private property is an important legal question which, in the United States, will no doubt be resolved in the courts. The Soviet government (and tsarist regimes in the past) allows only restricted travel (requiring their citizens to carry residency cards), and may find it difficult to grant access and travel rights to their own citizen inspection teams. If these teams are to be genuine, they cannot be handpicked by any government. The political will must be present to allow looser travel and access rights in restrictive societies. Assurance, inspection, and verification (see Chapter VIII) in terms of examining these facilities can be done on a limited or zonal basis.

Note the initiative of a private group, the Natural Resources Defense Council (NRDC), in setting up seismic monitors in the Soviet Union in July 1986 and the agreement to allow the Soviets to set up similar equipment on private property in the United States.

Article 75

This article seeks to involve the economy in assuming that military production has terminated. The way to keep wide-ranging arms agreements is through the involvement of wide-ranging sectors of society.

Article 76

1. The host country will ask IDO inspectors to check from time to time in disarmed zones plants to assure the IDO that disarmament has occurred. If no invitation is forthcoming or if suspicions are raised, spot-checks can be carried out by the IDO (see Chapter VIII).
2. Media attention should be directed to the disarming process, whether critically or supportively, as a means of informing the respective nations on the status of the disarmament process. This section is also meant to assure that attention is paid to the rights of journalists.

Article 77

The conversion of the weapons industries to peaceful and useful industries should be looked at not as a problem but as an opportunity. Successful conversion plans will not only help those who work in the weapons industries, but will also help to eliminate the political and institutional base for the arms race and war. An international conference, sponsored as a Special Session of the U.N. General Assembly, should be held on worldwide economic conversion of military to peaceful industries. Military expenditures have caused a new form of dependency that is a drag on economic development and revitalization the world over, but particularly in the Third World.

Article 78

1. Suggested guidelines might emanate from continuing world conferences as to how corporations involved in military production as well as civilian production will carry out the disarmament process and conversion plan. If not, they should be worked out by the IDO.
2. Tools used only for the production of weapons will be destroyed. Nations will no doubt attempt to keep their "blueprints" and "mockups." It is not likely that these will be discovered. Throughout the disarmament process they will probably be kept as a secret national security deposit.

Article 79

Military academies must be decoupled from the arms system. They could continue in the context of defense rather than wars outside of their own nation. They would work closely with other military academies in sustaining a world security system. Students at the academies would be expected to become familiar with and comply with the terms of this treaty.

Article 80

1. Although it is expected that this reporting—as with the treaty as a whole—will be carried out in good faith, there are a number of aids, such as input/output

analysis, that will be used to verify the accuracy of a party's reported budget.

2. Cutbacks in a nation's military should begin to be reflected in the nation's budget allocation system.

Article 81

1. There will be an international accounting of the resources saved and spent on the process of worldwide disarmament. The purpose of this accounting is for nations to assure each other that disarmament is in fact happening. It will also create a climate for international and domestic economic and social development.

2. An important concern here is the cutback, and elimination of appropriations for covert operations that are either destabilizing of regional security or a prologue to larger military actions.

3. This section is meant to act as one more assurance that the disarmament process is in fact taking place.

Article 82

In the context of domestic American law, the treaty would, of course, have to be approved by the Senate, because of its far-reaching implications. The purpose of depositing the treaty with the U.N. Secretary General is to make clear the integral relationship the implementation of the treaty has with the United Nations. Furthermore, it is to make clear that major treaties have a fundamental bearing on the fate of nations beyond those that might be most immediately involved in their observance and implementation.

Article 83

The treaty is meant to be a fundamental document in international law and international relations. That is to say, while no nation will surrender sovereignty to another nation, it is also clear that an international security system is needed to protect against the erosion of security and sovereignty which occurs through a continuation of the arms race or wars of mass destruction. Thus, the treaty may be seen as the protection of fundamental sovereignty of nations, which can only be protected within the community of nations and where the most fearful institutions and means are transformed.

12

Fulfilling the Ideals of the French Revolution

In March 1989 I gave a lecture in Paris sponsored by UNESCO on the occasion of the two hundredth anniversary of the French Revolution. The current fashion of some historians to question the validity and goals of the French Revolution is a reflection of the Reagan period. It should not be surprising that historians, like Supreme Court justices, live in the reality of their present existence. They are not immune to dominant fashions, and where necessary they are not averse to joining the latest one, until, of course, a newer one comes along. Historical research is often instrumental in that the historian puts the politics of the present into events of the past.

The French Revolution created tendencies of liberation that had not previously coalesced in Europe. There is no doubt that seeing both groups, the strivers and unseen, and giving them rights was and is a phenomenal gift that the French Revolution gave to the future. These are rights that are remade in every generation, deepened and strengthened to the point where people at large have rights as well as power. The French Revolution's fundamental message was the continuing struggle of people against Authority—right, left, or center—whenever that Authority constitutes itself against the people. □ □

It is no mystery that there is a strong relationship between the Anglo-American conception of human rights and those ideas that inhered in the Declaration of the Rights of Man and the Citizen. By the end of the eighteenth century, people had made a discovery. In the West they invented themselves as *individuals* who could have relations with others to control their destiny outside of kingly or godly authority. This was a powerful new realization that no mere ocean could limit. This social invention built on the early seventeenth-century work of Locke and then on the thought of Montesquieu. Both believed that the basis of liberty and democracy (even if limited to one particular economic class) was grounded on divided government and the consent of the governed. Later, the American philosopher John Dewey put this point rather quaintly. He said that those whose feet are squeezed are in the best position to know whether their shoes are too tight.

Dewey, who eschewed greed in all its forms, did not contemplate the world problem of whether we all should wear shoes, and if so, how they are to be distributed and who gets them. This problem is not an abstract one as Imelda Marcos, the Marie Antoinette of the Philippines, learned when the populace found that she had over three thousand pairs of shoes while most of her countrymen and women had one or none. Although the reality may be different, the spirit of modern revolutions does not hold with such inequality. The American Revolutionary War against the United Kingdom started as a series of economic complaints about taxation and the unwillingness of the British to support the colonies in border skirmishes with the Indians. The Declaration of Independence and later the Bill of Rights also seemed to be grounded on certain givens, namely the absence of external physical constraint, the right of the person to think freely, to go where he cared to, and later to organize and associate with others. Obviously, each one of these liberties was curbed in different sections of the United States according to custom and the power of churches. But such ideas became the framing ideas for white, especially Anglo-Saxon, men who came with or aspired to have their own property.

The genius of the French revolutionary process was that it recognized the existence of the wretched and sought ways to bring them into history. The *sans culottes* were to have a historical presence. Never mind that this presence would later be downgraded. Once stated, the poor would have standing as part of the political process. Bringing the wretched, the poverty stricken—that is, those who were part of a working class or who had no work—into the political process represented the beginnings of a stunning change in world history. It meant that through politics, poverty—by which I mean the condition of abject and continuous dependence that puts a person under the control and whim of others—was no longer to be considered a natural condition.

This eighteenth-century impulse retains its power. It is not seen as natural today that a person should be the object of others, whether the "others" are market forces, personal torturers, political parties, commanders of state economies, or wielders of nuclear weapons. In the latter case those in control of an economy have the power to decide whether a person can work or not work depending on what his or her political views might be, whether they are currently fashionable and in line with ruling party dictates.

Freedom therefore cannot be separated from the question of how a person's dependence is to be broken, just as even contingent freedom can really begin only when a person can live beyond economic necessity. In other words, to attain freedom, needs must be answered but never according to the types of economic pathology such as conspicuous waste and conspicuous consumption which the American economic thinker Thorstein Veblen warned against. When Robespierre stated, "Everything which is necessary to maintain life must be in the common good and only the surplus can be recognized as private property," he was not wrong. His problem was that he had no way of bringing this objective into practice without destroying the common good itself.

In the twentieth century, the Soviet Union foundered on exactly the same rocky shore. Both the French and the Bolshevik revolutions caught themselves in the vise of insisting that the so-called new man could be created. For both revolutions the new man was a blank slate to be written on. He would be given virtue. The authority of the Committee of Public Safety or the Communist party would use its power to define the unvirtuous, deceitful, or wrong-headed. And Authority would have the power to destroy and root out the miscreant. Such an authority was not invented by modern revolutions. Indeed, one may find such ideas in Plato's Republic and Statesman. In practice, such an authority was there, in the Catholic church, especially during the Inquisition. Democracy seemed to be a way to escape an Authority that rested on the power and rights of a vanguard party or God.

Contrary to Hannah Arendt's brilliant formulations in *On Revolution,* democracy was a feared conception in the eighteenth century in England, France, and the United States, just because its proponents accepted the conservative formulation that to make disinterested judgments for the common good, a person must have property. This meant that property and access to it were a sine qua non for citizenship. Of course, it was obvious then as it is now that some people and organizations have enormous economic and social appetites. They arrange the public space for their enormous needs, including social privileges and increased economic holdings for themselves and their heirs, thereby both creating and sustaining enormous inequality.

In recent times there have been those who have argued against the idea of equality because it creates a leveling effect and does not reward merit. It is true, as John Dewey has pointed out, that democracy poses the problem of liberty and equality. It does not resolve the tension between them. It is for this reason that *egalitarian interdependence* is the principle way of resolving the conflict between liberty and equality. In egalitarian interdependence we recognize that there are many tasks that some can perform and others cannot. However, there is an assumption that capacities and needs vary and that all may contribute where judgment matters, and that judgment is itself a capacity that is not necessarily found among those with the greatest intellectual or financial capacity. In any case, equality and judgment are neither static nor individual. They are conceptions that are to be applied in the context of social interaction and interdependence. They begin from the premise that each person has inalienable rights, that which defines the person as a person and cannot be taken away. Simultaneously, each person is equal according to being able to fulfill his or her needs and capacities and gives back to the body politic accordingly. It is not an overstatement to claim that those who question the value of equality and refuse to adapt its meaning to modern needs would no doubt have seen ample reason to stay with King George III, Great Britain, or the *ancien regime* in the eighteenth century.

But I am getting ahead of my story. What I want to consider are two sets of questions. First, what is the relevance of the Declaration of the Rights of Man and its meaning for the world generally and in the present and future context? And second, what might we consider as a definition of rights in relation to the common good and democracy at the end of the twenty-first century? Each of these terms demands elucidation. But each term is surely predicated on the idea of *inclusivity,* that is, that everyone is part of history and not an object of others. Obviously, that is the way things are in abstract idealism. In reality, our institutions—our schools, jails, hospitals, armed forces, mental asylums—create voluntary and involuntary conditions that reduce people to objects, as, I might add, does our military technology when it is coupled with political authority that operates from whim, self-aggrandizement, or mistake. Humanity can be destroyed without notice.

Perhaps the first thing to notice about the French Declaration and the American Constitution is that France and the United States are mentioned only in the preambles. From this we may deduce that the French and the American documents were meant to be universal. That is to say, both peoples were acting as agents of humanity. There is of course a certain hubris attached to this attitude, for it assumes that where these universal characteristics are not found, then it is all right, to use Robespierre's terms, to force people to be free. This Jacobin danger must be constantly attended to in laws and institutions, for it is an attitude that can lead to horrendous consequences. That is why I believe firmly that democracy is both a means and an end requiring that limits be constantly exercised over power. Justice is not found by enforcing virtue.

The first question that the Declaration of the Rights of Man and the American Constitution force on us is whether the powerful or the powerless need rights. One view popular among some at the time of writing of the American Constitution was that a Bill of Rights was superfluous because the people were all-powerful and could act as they wished. It was only the weak who needed rights because they had no power, and they were outside the political nation. That is, they were not among those people who supposed, proposed, and opposed.

One must remember that at the time of the American Constitution's drafting, the new nation, was made up of three categories: citizens, associates, and slaves. Those who needed rights were the associates who had no power, the landless, the unemployed, women. Those who already had power—the landed, the employers, and the rich—had rights that inhered in them as human beings. Slaves were, of course, property without rights or power. The idea of rights as part of the biological need of men, and women, that which describes man and woman as something more than a beast, does not begin to take hold until after our century's concentration camps, when it became clear that no one can or should be seen as a blank slate where human dignity may be systematically destroyed and then rebuilt, a process used in some armed forces and religious orders as well as totalitarian political groups. Thus, the idea of the person as more than a social construction gives rise to a modern meaning of how people are to be treated. It also gives rise to the conception of the common good. The declaration, responding to the conditions of prerevolutionary France in which social distinctions destroyed the conception of the common good, did not end privilege or social distinctions but made them dependent on the fulfillment of the common good. Of course, the bourgeoisie in 1789 were not about to give up either distinctions or privileges. They were just getting enough of them to become a self-conscious class. The fact is that no society can operate for very long without social privilege. The question is how those with privilege serve the common good.

Once people say that there should be a common good, and when we say that everyone is, "endowed . . . with certain inalienable rights, that among these rights are life, liberty, and the pursuit of happiness," we have curious but altogether felicitous results.

Every institution of the society, whether public or private, is constantly challenged to live up to that pursuit. And the power of government when used for this purpose becomes an actor and is acted upon. Each group is to have the common good in mind. Power is shared and free-floating (flowing) within a (competing) forcefield of federal and local governments, institutions, and people. Government is challenged to secure the common good as institutions become aware of their shortcomings and as individuals and other groups press claims against each other and the government for new rights or for broader interpretations and applications of old ones.

This point of view fits with Rousseau's conception of the general will. The solution to the problem of how to determine the general will, who determines it, and whether that will has the right to ride roughshod over individual rights is not clear from the practice of the French Revolution. Indeed, how the general will is to be determined (is it just public opinion in its rawest, unconsidered form?) is still not known.

There are clues given in Article 2 of the declaration, which asserts that the aim of every political association is to serve the natural rights of man, enumerated as liberty, property, safety, and resistance to oppression. Of course, these terms can only be generally understood as one lives them. One person's liberty may be another's oppression. Property for the few may be no property for many and therefore end as oppression in practice. Perhaps this was understood by Jefferson who believed the common good came from the pursuit of happiness rather than property. (Of course in practice he doubled the size of the United States with his purchase of Louisiana from Napoleon.)

Throughout the struggle between the society and the state runs the issue of the economic underpinnings for all citizens. The common good begins from the principle of a common social product to be equitably shared. How this is to be accomplished reflects a continuous, sometimes dialectical relationship between the institutions of society and state as they come together in new shapes and forms, with each element of society challenging the other to make good, to find a common ground for every one to pursue happiness. This includes the challenge of direct action. The modern world has chosen democracy as the means to obtain good ends and to get those who previously had no voice to find their voices.

Finding their voices and staking out a claim is different under the U.S. Constitution and American Declaration of Independence than under the 1789 French Declaration of the Rights of Man. The Constitution evades the question of sovereignty, whereas the French document claims that sovereignty inheres in Nationhood, defined as the people and its institutions. The American Constitution is less explicit and more mechanistic, concerned with the question of when does a bill become a law and who has power to act in certain cases. Under the Ninth and Tenth Amendments those rights and powers not expressly mentioned are reserved to the people and states. It should be noted that in American law—that is, through decisions of our Supreme Court—those rights have been interpreted as privacy rights. Such an interpretation, in my view, is narrow and incorrect because it does not build on the new elements Americans sought for themselves after the revolution from Britain, namely, the right of participation in controlling their public destiny.

In this sense, modern liberty and rights as they relate to the thought of the eighteenth century are more in keeping with the French Declaration's Fourth Article, which states that the rights of liberty have no bounds "other than those that ensure to the other members of society the enjoyment of these same rights." The bounds, determined by law, then become the frame for participatory rights; conversely, participatory rights are determined by struggle over the meaning of law. While one may praise the majesty of the law, it is important to be aware that laws are the struggles between different groups that are then codified. Law is the politics of the past frozen into ice blocks, which must be melted from time to time. Otherwise, law is the dead weight of the past on the present. Article 5, which states that only those actions are forbidden where there is a specific law to forbid them, is also an underpinning of Anglo-Saxon law. Indeed, we may find this again in the Ninth and Tenth Amendments.

It should be noted that freedom of political, social, and economic expression must be predicated on this understanding of the individual's relationship to the society. Otherwise he or she is forever waiting for the police knock on the door, for detention and imprisonment or worse. Without stealing the thunder of my distinguished Soviet colleague, Sukharev, it is heartening to see the Soviets reversing what appeared to us to be the Soviet law, namely, that the "revolutionary" state was beyond the reach of laws.

I have already adverted to the question of the general will. Article 6 of the French Declaration claims that "the law" is the expression of the general will. But we are aware that there is nothing called "the law." There are laws and they are man-made. They may be contradictory and beg for differing interpretations, often as a result of struggle. It is this very clash that then decides the general will—or in my terms, the common good. In time perhaps international law will be integrated into local laws and will be at the top of the hierarchy of laws.

Since any citizen, according to Article 6, may become a government official—without distinction other than that of talent and virtue—it is assumed that there will be many different sorts of people who comprise the government, including minorities and women. This is not an easy condition to fulfill because of class and social biases that are difficult to escape. In the U.S. Senate there are, for example, no blacks and only two women, although over 80 of the 100 senators are multi-millionaires. There is one other question that Article 6 raises: the meaning of virtue. If virtue means skill, that is one thing; if virtue means that one can have no vices, that is quite another. The latter would open the door to a kind of fundamentalism, religious and political in the case of a Khomeini or a Stalin, or Robespierre that would wreak havoc on ordinary mortals. For evil and vice are found all over, and the virtuous should not use that fact as a means to destroy and render antiseptically clean what by nature humanity is not.

Article 7 makes clear that no one can be "accused, arrested or detained except in the cases determined by the law." Here Anglo-American law makes a clear advance. The Fifth Amendment in the American Constitution's Bill of Rights gives the individual the right against self-incrimination, whereas the Declaration on the Rights of Man states that the citizen must give "instant obedience" to the law:

"Resistance makes him guilty." In the French Declaration the burden shifts to the accused. And if it is the case that only the "virtuous" can get into positions of power in the first place, the accused may be, in practice, quickly damned. Article 7 could be a hunting license for state terror.

Article 9 is a protection against cruel and unusual punishment, a protection also found in the American Constitution. The question is not only whether there are means to curb beatings and inhuman treatment. Perhaps in the future prisons themselves will be seen as forms of punishment that are cruel and silly for purposes of rehabilitation. (I say this at a time when the U.S. Supreme Court has backtracked on capital punishment, assuring us that killing, if done by the state is all right but if done by the individual is not.)

Article 10 seems to guarantee free expression, even of religious belief: "No one may be disturbed on account of his opinion. . . ." However, what is first given is then taken away, for the document then says so long as the opinion "does not interfere with the established Law and Order." Yet, Article 11 makes clear that a person "may speak, write and publish freely," again with the exception of when this is an abuse of "liberty," which is to be determined by law. The First Amendment of the U.S. Constitution has no limiting clause, and no notion of "Order" is presented that would limit political opinion and speech. Thus, the unvirtuous and the vicious are thought to be protected in American constitutional law. However, there are hundreds of local U.S. statutes that attempt to curb free expression in the public and the private space and allow the state to move against a person for opinions expressed privately, for obscenity, pornography, and the maintenance of order.

In continental as well as in Anglo-Saxon law exceptions that may appear reasonable in fact are openings for state authority to curb expression and speech. This question becomes even more complicated in modern times. Should advertising be seen as protected speech? Art works? Pornography? And so on. And what happens with regard to subliminal messages when the listener or consumer does not even know he or she is being manipulated? Or poisonous speech against particular groups? In any case, more expression at this stage of history is needed from the body politic as a whole to guide its direction and social development.

Article 12 establishes a "public force" to be operated for the benefit of all and not for any particular group. The concern about any public force is that it should operate according to law. But this article, ironically, is silent on whether the force has to operate according to law. For the lawyer Robespierre, the idea of public force became the practice of terror as the means to assure virtue. In the American experience it was not until 1903 that ideas of a national public or police force emerged—specifically after the murder of a federal judge. After the Civil War, national guards were formed in various states to protect property. When the National Guard was insufficient, federal troops were called out to keep order, often as not to break workers' strikes. Today the United States has many national police forces and yet no single national police force. It also tacitly protects civil disobedience, a system of citizen action that should be seen as a mode of protected speech when it is in defense of fundamental human rights. It is in the realm of fundamental human rights and world law that a new architectonic of law can be developed and in turn integrated into local law and diverse cultures.

Note that according to Article 13 of the French Declaration, taxes are to be equally distributed, "in proportion to the citizen's ability to pay." This question of proportionate or instead progressive taxation is still debated. In the United States it was taken for granted until 1913 that there should not be a general income tax. This view has, of course, now changed, although the American debate around proportionate and progressive taxation remains.

Article 14 claims that the citizens themselves, or through their representatives, may consent to a proportionate tax and its method of collection. In the United States as a matter of public policy it has been thought useful to close the gap between rich and poor through taxation under the theory that too great a gap creates economic and social inequity that can yield grave social dislocations. This modern liberal point of view has been rejected recently by the Congress, a grievous error from the standpoint of the common good. The opposing assumption that providing incentives for greater personal wealth will yield greater investment has not been borne out recently in the United States.

Article 15 calls for a right of accounting from a public official. This concept has only recently found its way into American law in a manner that makes sense. While Congress has the power of the purse under the Constitution and maintains oversight power, it remains especially difficult to hold bureaucracies accountable for their actions. There is now a so-called Whistle Blower's Act to protect those in government who are aware of wrongdoing and call the miscreant to account, and from time to time efforts have been made to hold government officials to account for military adventures. In the latter case not much has come of such attempts. During the Vietnam War, a group of congressmen sought to internalize the principles of the Nuremberg trials into domestic law. That effort failed. On the other hand, at the end of the Vietnam War, Congress forced on an unwilling president a law obliging him to inform Congress that he is about to use troops abroad in combat. He receives a sixty-day "free hit," so to speak, at which point he must come back to Congress for support. Ironically, the law, called the War Powers Act, takes away constitutional powers from Congress. Since its passage all American presidents have refused to abide by its *legal* terms. I am told by Soviet colleagues that in the aftermath of the Afghanistan war the Supreme Soviet is seeking means to control its executive in order to prevent similar frolics from happening again. It should be noted that both wars grew out of an internal deficiency: namely, the refusal to follow the principles of open debate and separation of powers.

Under the French Declaration's Article 16, an "empirical" statement is made asserting that there can be no guarantee of rights and no separation of powers without a constitution and where these do not exist there is no constitution. What is being dealt with here, as in the U.S. Constitution, is the assurance that the usurpation of power without authority is easiest in a system lacking a principle of separation of powers—a principle that automatically leads to checks and balances between groups and therefore, perhaps, greater wisdom. In the American political system, separation of powers results in deadlock on economic and social rights issues.

Article 17 concerns the sacred and inviolable nature of property, which cannot be taken without just compensation. As I have suggested, property and liberty were coextensive in the eighteenth century.

This point of view surely undergirded the American Constitution. The question now to be raised is whether the French, American, and Russian revolutions implied that because that eighteenth-century conception was correct, a system in which everyone held property first as individuals and then as part of the body politic would have to come into being if freedom is to exist for the many. All three revolutions opened the door to such ideas as opportunity, equity, and sharing, all of which were thought to be the sine qua non for freedom.

While these questions do not go away, new ones are added. I want to at least touch on a few of them to show why we must go beyond the eighteenth century in our conceptions of freedom, rights, and citizenship. We can no longer live, intellectually speaking, off the capital of that time.

A twenty-first-century spirit can build on the eighteenth-century bourgeois liberal sentiments that spoke for generosity and openness, tolerance of differing ideas, and belief in science and technology so as to serve the end of public happiness and, finally, the rule of law. The twenty-first-century declarations of rights, however, must incorporate the project of social reconstruction that will *exclude* certain institutional patterns of behavior such as the preparations for genocide (foolishly calling that preparation "defense") and the perpetuation of those forces of production that transform the environment so that our constructed social environment becomes the enemy of all living things as a result of choices made by humanly controlled and guided institutions and forces; and *include* the realization of collective and individual worth that guarantees that quantum of decency in society by which the principle of caring may be exercised, a sentiment that is natural and necessary for the continuation of all species especially the human species and of course a forum for participation that offers the capacity to say yes and no to the polity without fear of retribution.

It is through an understanding of these terms that humankind will be able to cope with current and likely future realities such as the capacity of humanity to commit suicide either through war, foolish consumerism, or environmental plundering; a population explosion that cannot be contained in earlier political forms constructed for city-states or small nations; the profound power of elites to engineer consent against the opinion or interests of human civilization as a whole; and the extraordinary project of science and technology that fits into undemocratic political and social relationships.

Where, one might ask, is the political and intellectual underpinning for the solution of these questions, or if not their solution, then at least the paths to their solution? Several considerations enter into these calculations. The first is that humankind is the root and guide of itself, of its physical and animal environment. But it is the individual person who within him or herself comprises the possibilities of a common good. This formulation means that the root of social existence—no matter how many billions of persons there are in the world is—the person. The person, especially as citizen, is both a social construct and a palpable living being with needs and desires that are shaped by his or her own choice and by social interaction. Since, "no man is an island unto himself," and yet is the root of social existence, certain judgments must constantly be considered in the light of each new problematic situation in which human beings find themselves. By this I do not mean a free-floating existentialism in which the person can choose anything. Instead, I mean a reconsideration of fundamental political questions such as what are the limits of what under no circumstances I will turn over to the nation or the sovereign, thereby limiting its power; what *am* I prepared to turn over to the group or the sovereign, and, finally, what is a dialogue between the group and myself.

In modern times, we have turned over the right, really the power, to commit suicide to the sovereign, especially in those nations that have nuclear weapons. This genocidal power must and can be taken away from sovereigns or groups of individuals operating with state authority. No person gave or can give the state the power or right to commit suicide for the whole. In other words, a wholly different mode of defense is required: one that comprehends humanity or world civilization as a whole—but that starts from the person as the root. Once we begin with the person, we must immediately stretch and see what the empathic roots are between people, for those roots if nurtured will assure the continuation of the human species. In the twentieth century we have—and God knows there is an abundance of evidence—fixed on inhumanity, torture, treachery, and fear as the standard qualities in international politics. But there remains underneath all we have seen and known a principle of caring and empathy that can guide world civilization. I doubt if world civilization can come into being without a principle of caring and empathy undergirding it. According to the empirical studies of the social scientist Carol Gilligan, women may hold the key to the caring sense as it includes rights and responsibilities:

> For women, the integration of rights and responsibilities takes place through an understanding of the psychological logic of relationships. This understanding tempers the self-destructive potential of self-critical morality by asserting the need of all persons for care.

Unless we find a means of making active the empathic sensibility, the survival of the basest will govern social and political relationships.

You will recall that one of the charges against revolutionaries was their naive attempts to perfect an inherently deformed creature—man. But modern critical and reconstructive thought shows us that within human civilization there is an internal spirit that emanates from caring and an egalitarian interdependence that is denied at humanity's peril. Human beings do not require perfectibility. They require respect, dignity and attention to material needs.

The interdependence, to come into being would be laced with a science and technology grounded in a continuing dialogue on its ethical implications and a principle of renunciation—that is, knowing what we will not collectively do to each other under any circumstances. Such interdependence includes raising up individual, collective, and cooperative enterprises to what is not meanspirited or repressive or stupid, thus allowing, indeed encouraging, people to want to work as their untrammeled selves and for the common good. Finally, it assures us that humanity will recognize all "races" as equal in civilization, with women and men beginning as complementary equals in the project of regeneration and development of a world civilization. This is the beginning of our declaration for the twenty-first century. It builds on our past, knowing that the greatest compliment to our forebears is to build on what they paid dearly for—but then to transcend it. It will take what the eighteenth century offered as rights and see them now on the eve of the twenty-first century as components of being human.

Note

1. *In a Different Voice* (Cambridge, MA: Harvard University Press), p. 100.

Afterword

So, one Cold War is over. Its end may be considered symbolized by the marriage of President Eisenhower's granddaughter to the leading scientist of the Soviet Union, who happens to be a member of the Supreme Soviet. Soon it will be hard to remember what the Cold War was about. But one should not forget that in much of the world the Cold War was a continuous slow motion hot war in which millions of people died. It may still be played out between the have and have not nations.

The United States was a very active participant in titanic conflicts throughout the period of the Cold War, notably in Indochina, Korea, Latin America, the Middle East, and Africa. Nationalist liberation movements were seen as tools of the Darth Vader of the East. Soviet regimes, on the other hand, adopted a reactive posture to the United States, fearing that the United States would intervene in its sphere. Until Gorbachev, Soviet governments preferred to make war on their own people through the Gulag, demanding lock-step allegiance in their quest for utopia. Earlier Soviet governments also used military intervention as their means of assuring allegiance in their sphere in Czechoslovakia in 1968, Hungary in 1956, and Afghanistan in 1979. In 1990 Soviet leaders still seek to create quiet through repression by dampening rational, ethnic, and tribal divisions in their sphere of influence and imperial domain.

During the Cold War, empires collapsed, civil wars, revolutions, and counterrevolutions occurred, and the superpowers were there as military trash dispensers and geopolitical pyromaniacs. But was the Cold

War between the United States and the Soviet Union necessary? It did not seem so when American troops met Soviet troops at the Elbe in 1945 and there was great rejoicing between the two. That moment, like a wedding ceremony, seemed much more than a photo opportunity. But the Cold War gave people and institutions a way of understanding the world without having to look at it too closely. And the national security state played an important part in this skewed understanding.

For the United States, the national security state played a double role in the Cold War. It was its instrument and perpetuator. It provided the words and structure for U.S. involvement in worldwide conflict. This state formation will neither wither nor fade away. The national security state will be with us as long as no major structural ideas to transform the war system are put into practice by citizens and far-seeing leaders. For the conventional-minded, the modern national security state has become a tolerable instrument that fights wars and manages unruly populations at home and abroad. It can produce large armed forces at a few day's notice as Bush did in the Middle East in 1990. This state formation grounds itself on the belief that human survival demands paranoia concerning the intentions of others, as well as secrecy, spying and counterspying, overwhelming military power, imperial pretension, narrowness of public debate, and all the other social elements attendant to manipulation and control. Thus, it is also a mechanism intended to secure stability, quiet, and passivity among the populace. Yet the capacity of the modern state to provide this service is not very great. And, even if the CIA and the KGB were to join hands as one conglomerate, they would not be able to command passivity in a world where consciousness is turning against such enterprises. Perhaps this world consciousness can be set against the war system. It is neither romantic nor utopian to believe that the mass of humanity will not put up with gulags and prisons, torture and genocide, as the way governments should conduct business. But such a belief is only made real when movements and institutions work to make it real. In the United States this means dismantling the apparatus of the national security state, a task that will be gladly embraced by citizens imbued with the spirit of freedom and dignity.

The nagging question remains. Was the Cold War necessary from the side of the United States? With the death of Stalin, it was certainly not necessary. And it may be that more subtle diplomacy by the West could have avoided the Cold War even when Stalin was in control. The

Cold War's origins, of course, began with the success of the Bolshevik Revolution, which because of its class struggle, propaganda, and false promises of future economic and social justice, scared governments and capitalists. (It was hardly the regime's violent character that scared hard-headed leaders from the West. It was rather its pretensions of justice and equality that frightened Western leaders.)

There were more immediate reasons for concern on the Soviet side, for by the Second World War American leaders seemed to accept the Bolshevik regime as necessary to the survival of the West. The origins of the Cold War stemmed more directly from the character of the Second World War and how it was fought. The Soviets did most of the fighting in Europe during the war and lost 27 million people in the process. The Soviets believed that their allies, the United States and Great Britain, were cavalier with Russian lives in the fight against Germany. Before the Normandy invasion in June 1944, Stalin repeatedly called for a second front to relieve pressure on the Soviet Union. His call was rejected by the West at the insistence of Churchill, who was concerned about the numbers of British soldiers that would be lost in a direct early attack on the European continent. Had the West attacked Hitler's armies in Europe earlier than June 1944, the Western allies would most likely have advanced either to the Oder or the Vistula, not the Elbe, as Charles Yost, former American Ambassador to the United Nations, has pointed out. The Soviet armies would never have reached Berlin.

There were other judgments made by the West that were debatable if the fundamental purpose had been to avoid conflict with the Soviets. But "conflict avoidance" was not the fundamental policy objective of the United States during the Cold War or at its inception. This was to be the American century, as leaders from Henry Luce to Henry Wallace and Walter Lippmann had so stated. It was no wonder, therefore, that American leaders concluded it was of secondary concern whether there would be Cold War with the Soviets. For if a Cold War meant the mobilization of our own people and "Western civilization," then Cold War was a good thing.

Many historians consider the U.S. cutoff of lend-lease immediately after the Second World War and its refusal to act on the Soviet request of $6 billion in aid in January 1945 as evidence that the United States was not going to help the Soviets in its postwar recovery. Perhaps it would have been possible at that stage to work out multilateral conditions that would have encouraged the Soviets to undertake a very different mode of economic development than they embraced once they decided that they would have to rehabilitate themselves without help from the outside.

These are iffy but important questions to consider at the end of the twentieth century, for leaders, whatever their ideological hue, find themselves in a situation similar to their counterparts in the 1945–50 period. The question is whether the United States will act with a closed-hand policy. The first point to be made is that Gorbachev is no Stalin; any reluctance that Americans might have had at the end of the Second World War to support a Stalin government on the grounds that he was a totalitarian tyrant is not relevant in 1990.

The forces Gorbachev has brought into play, by and large, are liberal ones that seek to balance freedom, nationhood, and social responsibility. This fact is undeniable, and the Bush administration showed glimmerings of understanding these enormous changes. Yet the Cold War habit of mind and apparatus that predicates national security policies on the principle of antagonism continues. NATO as a military alliance and the modernization of genocidal weapons are two examples of incredibly large expenditures of resources that feed antagonism between nations. These policies, like the Cold War itself, continue to have a boomerang effect on the United States, hastening its own decline because our leaders are unable to put on the political table a new agenda of activity for the society that does not depend on Americans as the world's warriors.

It is an irony of our time that the so-called American decline can be avoided if we throw the premises and the institutions of the Cold War into the dustbin of history and concentrate on internal and international reconstruction. Reconstruction is not an impossible task compared to what other generations have had to face or what future generations will face if we do not begin. Now.

Index

Abourezk, James, xii
Accountability system, joint, 135
ACDA. *See* Arms Control and Disarmament Agency
Acheson, Dean, 48, 75, 122
Adler, Selig, 26
Afghanistan
  as foreign policy blunder for Soviets, 204
  military intervention in, 85, 134, 188, 303, 307
Alger, Bruce, 69
Allende, Salvadore, 16, 17, 21, 86–88
Alperovitz, Gar, 110
American Revolution, 294, 303
Anderson, Robert, 63
Antarctica Treaty (1959), 235, 269
Antibusiness ideology, 8
Apartheid, 127
Arbatov, Gyorgy, 185
Arbenz, Jacobo, 84
Arendt, Hannah, 27, 295
Armaments, 98
Armed services, reorganization of, 10
Arms control. *See also* Disarmament
  disarmament vs., 105
  and military and defense contract bribery, 107
  regional arrangements for, 137
Arms Control and Disarmament Agency (ACDA), 128, 208
Arms race. *See also* Disarmament; Nuclear weapons
  cause of, 207

Arms race *(continued)*
  dangers of, xiii, 32–33, 191, 204
  effect on Third World of, 131
  and issue of convergence, 190–93
  during Kennedy administration, 53–59
  national security and, 90–92
  proposals for controlling, 33–35
  public opinion regarding, 96
  Soviet-U.S., 75–78, 186, 192
  as white-race phenomenon, 125
Arms Race and Nuclear Weapons Project, 284
Arms sales, foreign policy control through, 83–84
Asian War Crimes Trials, 32
Atomic bomb, possession of, 31
Austria, 74, 153

Barnet, Richard, 22
Berle, A. A., 8
Berlin crisis of 1961, 56, 115
Biddle, Francis, 146
Bill of Rights, 294, 297, 300. *See also* Constitution, U.S.
Bipolarism, 138
Black Americans
  segregation of, 80, 189
  Vietnam War and, 142
Blackett, P. M. S., 110
Bohr, Niels, 31
Bolshevik Revolution, 181, 295, 303, 309
Bonhoeffer, Dietrich, 168
Bonner, Yelena, 182

311

312   INDEX

Borah, William, 144
Boston Five, 167
Brandeis, Louis, 21
Brandt, Willy, 213–14
Brazil, 87
Brezhnev, Leonid Ilich, 203
Brodie, Bernard, 63
Browder, Earl, 7
Brushfire war, 91
Brzezinski, Zbigniew, 198
Bulganin, Nicolai, 75
Bundy, McGeorge, 15, 60, 61, 71
  career of, 101–2
  national security views of, 104–9
  role in building up war-making capacity, 102–3
  views on presidency, 113–14
  views regarding nuclear weapons, 108–17
Burnham, James, 12
Bush, George, xiii
  defense policy of, 93
  economic policy of, 90
Bush administration
  and dismantling of national security apparatus, 212
  and NATO, 215
  position on nonproliferation treaty, 206

Capitalist system
  national security state and, 35
  post–Second World War, 7, 8
Carter, Jimmy
  foreign policy of, 82
  and SALT II, 107
  signing of Covenants on Economic and Social Rights, 127
Castro, Fidel, 20, 108
CBUs (cluster bomb units), 282
Central Intelligence Agency (CIA).
  See also Covert operations
  activities, 16, 17, 25
  charter for, 135
  court cases involving, 22
  creation of, 9–10
  during Eisenhower administration, 64–66
  power of, 14–15

Cheney, Richard, 93, 94
Chile, 17, 21, 25, 86–87
China, 28–29, 83, 218
Churchill, Winston, 7, 31
CIA. *See* Central Intelligence Agency
Citizen inspection, 247, 278
Citizenship
  definition of, xiii-xiv
  principles of, 35–36
  Sartre and concept of, 167
City, contradiction between national security state and, 28
Civil defense policy, during Kennedy administration, 59–62
Civil rights movement, 25, 189
Clark, Mark, 153
Class conflict, national security state and, 80
Climate modification, 282
Cluster bomb units (CBUs), 282
Coalitions, problems in bringing together, 4–5
COINTELPRO program, 16
Colby, William, 20
Cold War period
  assessment of, 218, 307–10
  cost of, 202
  development of national security state during, 5, 308
  and Eisenhower, 46–47
  hope following end of, 211–12
  labor unrest during, 10–12
  logic and dynamics of, 190–91
  military buildup during, 69–71, 280
  need for history of, 223
  policies of, xi, xiii-xv, 73–76, 90, 307
  and racial equality issues in U.S., 80
  U.S.-Soviet relations during, 201–5
Comity rule, 134
Committee on the Present Danger, 107
Communism
  McNamara's views on, 49
  and Reagan administration foreign policy, 84
Communist party (Soviet), 182
Communist party (U.S.), 7, 16
Comprehensive Test Ban (CTB), 265, 268
Comstock, Craig, 32

Congress, U.S.
  justification of covert operations by, 135
  Kennedy's relationship with, 47
  and office of presidency, 13
  and power to make war, 162, 303
  role in defense budget, 92
  role in foreign policy, 88–89
Constitution, U.S.
  amendment on common defense, 130
  Declaration of the Rights of Man vs., 299–303
  Ninth Amendment rights, 25
  preamble to, 297
Convergence, 190–93
Counterforce strategy, 56–59, 91
Covenants on Economic and Social Rights, 127
Covert operations. *See also* Central Intelligence Agency
  and foreign policy issues, 133–34
  as indirect military engagement, 86–88
  legislation justifying, 135
Cox, Arthur Macy, 10
CREEP, 16
Criminality, and national security state, 19
CTB. *See* Comprehensive Test Ban
Cuba, 20, 29
  invasion of, 46
  involvement in Africa of, 134
Cuban missile crisis, 58, 108, 177
Currency system, 89–90
Czechoslovakia, 74, 75, 307

Danger and Survival, Choices about the Bomb in the First Fifty Years (Bundy), 103–6, 112, 115–17
Decapitation strategies, 115
Declaration of Independence, 294
Declaration of the Rights of Man
  concept of human rights and, 293
  preamble to, 293
  relevance and meaning of, 296–306
  U.S. Constitution vs., 299–303
Defense contract system, and unemployment, 11
Defense Department, U.S.
  budget for, 34–35, 68, 92

Defense Department, U.S. *(continued)*
  and doctrine of deterrence and counterforce, 91
  during Eisenhower administration, 55, 57–58
  during Kennedy administration, 50, 54, 57–58, 60–62, 84
Defoliants, 281
Demilitarist principles
  toward Germany, 147–53
  toward Japan, 148, 153–58
Democracy
  choice of, 299
  fear of concept of, 295
  and national security state, 188–89
  new world view of, xi
  purpose of, 119
  U.S. tradition of, 122–23, 222–23
Democrats, administration of Republicans vs., 45
Denazification process, 152–53
Détente, 203–5, 217
Dewey, John, 144, 162, 294, 296
Dirksen, Everett, 86
Disarmament. *See also* Arms control
  initiation of, 266
  during Kennedy administration, 47–48, 112
  need for, xv, 76, 96–97, 109, 206–8
  period of transition to, 98–99
  proposals for, 128–32. *See also* Treaty on Common Security and General Disarmament
  requirements for, 229
  Soviet need for, 185–86
  Soviet-U.S. efforts to achieve, 58, 97, 105, 112, 268–70
  United Nations Security Council and, 34, 97–98, 233, 234, 264–65
  value of negotiations for, 91
Donovan, William, 65
Douglas, William O., 122
Dual State, national security state and, 18–22
Dulles, John Foster
  defense policy of, 47, 53, 63, 74
  role in U.S.-Soviet disarmament negotiations, 106

314   INDEX

East Germany, 85. *See also* Germany
Eastern Europe. *See also* Warsaw Pact
   during Cold War period, 73–74
   and need for NATO, 120
Economic aid, proposed rules for, 136
Economic policy
   and protection of power of U.S.
      dollar, 89–90
   and U.S. need for dominance, 81–83
Eden, Anthony, 74–75
Egalitarian interdependence, 296, 306
Eisenhower, Dwight D., 46–47
Eisenhower administration
   defense budget during, 92–93
   defense policies of, 53–55, 59,
      62–69, 93
   economic decision making in, 82
   foreign policy of, 86
   navy during, 69–70
Electromagnetic pulse (EMP)
   weapons, 282
Employment Act of 1946, purpose of,
   10
Enhanced radiation (ER) weapons, 282
Estonia, 202
Europe. *See also* Eastern Europe
   effect of disarmament on, 138,
      215–16
   effect of U.S. military personnel on,
      217
   post–Second World War dependence
      on U.S., 7
Excise profits tax, on defense and
   national security contracting, 98
Executive Order 9835, 15
Existentialism, 169, 170

Fair Deal policies, xi
FBI. *See* Federal Bureau of
   Investigation
Federal Bureau of Investigation (FBI)
   activities of, 7–18, 23–25
   charter for, 135
   files on citizens kept by, 5
   and Martin Luther King, 16
   power of, 14–16
Fermi, Enrico, 106
Fleming, D. F., 203
Flood, Dan, 67

Ford, Gerald, 22, 57, 69
Ford administration, 90
Foreign policy
   overseas attachments as American, 96
   principles for U.S., 133–38
   U.S. popular opinion regarding, 216
Forrestal, James, 48
40 Committee, 16, 19, 21, 23
France, 215
Free world, 96
Freedom, 295
French Revolution, 293–95, 303
Friedman, Milton, 83
Fulbright, J. William, 122

Galanskov, Yuri, 180
Garces, Joan, 213
Gatto incident, 23
Gehlen, Gerhard, 10
General Assembly (United Nations).
   See also United Nations
   resolutions of, 30, 95, 127, 136
   role in disarmament, 137
Geneva Protocol of 1925, 268, 270
Genscher, Hans-Dietrich, 213–14
Germany. *See also* East Germany;
   West Germany
   attempt to destroy militarism in,
      147–53, 161–62
   Berlin crisis of 1961 and state of, 56,
      115
   concerns of Soviets regarding, 85,
      137, 185, 205, 213
   defense spending in, 80
   invasion of Soviet Union by, 200–201
   punishment for war crimes of, 147–48
   unification of, 76, 85–86, 137
   Western control over, 213, 219
Gilligan, Carol, 305
Globalism, 221, 222
Goodman, Paul, xiv
Goodpaster, Andrew, 217
Gorbachev, Mikhail, xi, 307, 310
   and arms race, 76, 117
   impact of, 195–96, 218
   national dissolution as problem for,
      115
   rise to power of, 201
   style of, 196, 203

Great Britain
 and disarmament, 215
 imperialism of, 134
Great Depression, 8
Great Society policies, xi
Greece, 9
Gromyko, Andrei, 213, 265
Guatemala, 84

Haig, Alexander, 78–79
Herbicides, 281
Herzen, Alexander, 310
Hitch, Charles, 56
Ho Chi Minh, 7
Hoover, J. Edgar, 5, 15
Hughes, Emmet John, 46–47
Human rights
 Anglo-American concept of, 293
 and political right, 225
 at time of drafting of Constitution, 297
Humphrey, George, 54, 63
Humphrey, Hubert, 224
Hungarian uprising of 1956, 74, 171, 307
Hussein, Saddam, 85
Hydrogen bomb, 106, 168

IAEA. *See* International Atomic Energy Agency
Ichiro, Hatoyama, 155
ICJ. *See* International Court of Justice
IDO. *See* International Disarmament Organization
Imperialism
 as instrument of domestic policy, 25–35
 post–Second World War period and, 145–46
 results of, 30, 134
India-Pakistan dispute of 1973, 84
Indochina War. *See* Vietnam War
Industry, benefits of national security system to, 79, 80
Institute for Policy Studies, during 1960s, 4
Institute for Strategic Studies (England), 284
International Atomic Energy Agency (IAEA), 239, 272, 279, 287

International Court of Justice (ICJ), 259, 272, 289
International Disarmament Organization (IDO), 233–34, 237–51, 253–62, 266–68, 270–76, 278–81, 285–90
International law
 basic premises of, 126, 127
 defense and disarmament conducted under framework of, 96, 99
 and principles of nonintervention, 134
 principles recognized by Nuremberg Charter, 146
 and purpose of war, 145
International Peace Research Institute (Norway), 284
International satellite-monitoring agency (ISMA), 286
Internationalism, 26, 127
Iran, 84, 88, 219
Iraq, 219, 274
ISMA. *See* International satellite-monitoring agency
Israel, 217
Italy, 17

Jackson, Robert, 146, 148
Japan
 attempt to destroy militarism in, 148, 153–58
 bombing of, 110, 111
 defense spending in, 80
 economic progress of, 218–19
 future outlook for, 76
 punishment for war crimes of, 147
 and Second World War, 110–11
Johnson, Louis, 48
Johnson, Lyndon B.
 defense policy of, 106
 support for, 14
 and Vietnam War, 29, 123, 142
Joint accountability system, 135
Joint Chiefs of Staff system, 10
Joint Statement of Agreed Principles for Disarmament Negotiations (McCoy-Zorin Agreement), 229, 266

Kahn, Herman, 55, 186
Kastenmeier, Robert, 32
Kaufman, William, 56
Kaysen, Carl, 60, 102
Keenan, Joseph B., 143
Keeny, Spurgeon, 57
Kellogg, Frank, 145
Kellogg-Briand Pact (Pact of Paris of 1928), 144–45
Kennan, George, 75, 103, 205
Kennedy, John F., 4–5
  background of, 47
  debates with Nixon, 46
  disarmament interests of, 112
  relationship with Bundy, 102
  and Vietnam War, 111, 142
Kennedy, Robert, 4–5, 66
Kennedy administration
  civil defense during, 59–62
  defense policy of, 50–59, 66–68, 84, 93, 106–7
  economic decision making in, 82
  navy buildup during, 69–71
  and nuclear weapons, 53–54, 105–9
Keynes, John Maynard, 11
Khrushchev, Nikita, 56, 58, 177, 186, 190
King, Martin Luther, Jr., 4–5, 16
Kirkpatrick, Jeane, 224–25
Kissinger, Henry, 21, 29, 59
  foreign policy of, 83, 203
  relationship with Bundy, 102
Kolko, Gabriel, 167
Korean War, 64, 65
  indirect involvement and, 86
  losses in, 29
Korry, Edward, 88
Kristol, Irving, 8
Kropotkin, Piotr Alekseyevich, 180

Labor
  organized, during Cold War period, 10–12
  post–Second World War situation, 9
Labor strikes, post–Second World War, 9
Labor unions
  for armed forces, 132
  no-strike pledges by, 9

Laird, Melvin, 69, 144
Latin America, 219–20
Law. *See* Rule of law
Law of the Sea Treaty, 82
LeMay, Curtis, 5
Lenin, Vladimir Ilyich, 180, 181, 186
Liberalism, and national security state, 36
Liddel-Hart, B. H., 63
Linkages, in politics, 4
Lovett, Robert, 48
Lowenstein, Allard, 225
Lucey, Pat, 144
Lukács, George, 178
Lumumba, Patrice, 16

MacBride, Sean, 34
MacDonald, Dwight, xi-xii
Malcolm X, 4–5
Malraux, André, 170–71
Mansfield, Mike, 88
Marbury v. Madison, 21, 23
Marshall Plan, 207
McCain, John, 70, 71
McCarthy, Eugene, 225
McCarthy, Joseph, 15
McCloy, John, 45, 208
McCloy-Zorin Agreement of 1961, 97, 112, 229, 266
McGovern, George, xii, 92
McNamara, Robert
  background of, 48
  role in building up war-making capacity, 102–3
  as secretary of defense, 48, 53, 57–58, 93, 217
  view of Vietnam War, 142
  views on communism, 49
Media Papers, 25
Medvedev, Roy, 174, 181–82
Mexico, 220
Middle East, military bases in, 84
Militarists, 152
Military academies, 261–62, 290
Military dominance, U.S. need for, 81–83
Military engagement
  and alliance structure, 88–89
  direct, 85–86

Military engagement *(continued)*
  indirect, 86–87
  and U.S. control, 83–85
Military officer class, 78–79
Military Staff Committee (MSC), 264–65, 274, 275
Montgomery, John, 149, 152–53
Moynihan, Daniel, 142
MSC. *See* Military Staff Committee
Multinational corporations, 29
Murdock, Iris, 170
Muslim fundamentalism, 219

National Security Act of 1947, 9–10, 162, 223
National security advisers, 102
National Security Agency (NSA), 22
National Security Council (NSC)
  authorizaton of covert operations by, 21
  creation and purpose of, 9, 10
  policies of, 3
National Security Defense Memorandum 40 of 1970, 19
National security state
  as American version of Dual State, 19
  and American world supremacy, 6–10
  arbitrary power and, 16–18
  contradiction between city and, 28
  democracy and, 187–88
  emergence of, 4, 6, 35, 123–24
  explanation and impact of, 9, 35–37, 119
  imperialism as instrument of domestic policy in, 25–35
  need to dismantle, 120–21
  role in Cold War of, 308
  role of organized labor in, 10–12
  and rule of law, 14–25
  views regarding continuation of, 119–20
National security system
  arms race and, 90–92
  benefits derived from, 78–79
  and dismantling of national security state, 135
  economic and military dominance and, 81–83

National security system *(continued)*
  non-nuclear military engagement and, 83–89
  as problem for U.S. citizens, 77–78
  protection of U.S. dollar and, 89–90
NATO. *See* North Atlantic Treaty Organization
Natural Resources Defense Council (NRDC), 289
Naval ships, 250, 280
Navy, U.S., buildup of, 69–71
Nazis, 3
Nazism, attempt to destroy, 148, 149, 152–53
Negative convergence, 190–92
New Deal, 4, 7–8
New Frontier policies, xi
New Look, 62
New Realism, 199
Nicaragua, 87
Niebuhr, Reinhold, 10, 104
Nixon, Richard M., xii, 189
  actions during presidency, 16, 21
  debates with Kennedy, 46
  foreign policy of, 83, 203
  support for, 14
  Watergate and, 78–79, 114
Nizan, Paul, 167
Non-Proliferation Treaty (NPT), 268–70, 287
Noninterference principles, 133
Nonproliferation treaty, 206
Noriega, Manuel, 84
North Atlantic Treaty Organization (NATO), 205, 206
  alliance disagreement within, 88–89, 137
  and arms race, 122
  planning strategies for, 212–13
  reason for existence of, 120
  role in disarmament, 94, 233, 266
  shifting views regarding, 215–16
  and Soviet Union, 75, 109
  U.S. involvement in, 214
NPT. *See* Non-Proliferation Treaty
NRDC (National Resources Defense Council), 289
NSA. *See* National Security Agency
NSC. *See* National Security Council

Nuclear arms race. *See* Arms race
Nuclear energy ban, 279
Nuclear free zone concept, 34
Nuclear military waste, 114–15
Nuclear test ban agreement, 106
Nuclear weapons. *See also* Disarmament; Treaty on Common Security and General Disarmament
  aftereffects of testing, 115
  and doctrine of deterrence and counterforce, 91–92
  first-use issues of, 265
  genocidal power and, 305
  and Kennedy administration, 53–54, 105–9
  as ordinary weapons, 96
  president's war-making power, 114
  Soviet position regarding use of, 186–87
  U.S. position regarding, 31–32, 187
  used for political bargaining, 55–59
Nuremberg Tribunal, 32, 245
  charter and principles resulting from, 128, 129, 139–40, 146
  extracts from Charter of, 276–77
  and Kellogg-Briand Pact, 144–45

Operation Carte Blanche, 59
Operation Hoodwink, 16
Operations Coordination Board, 102
Oppenheimer, Robert, 7, 31, 106
Organized labor, 10–12. *See also* Labor unions

Pact of Paris of 1928 (Kellogg-Briand Pact), 144–45
Panama, 84
Pentagon Watchers (Rodberg and Shearer), 45
Persecution, xii
Philippines, 219, 226
Phoenix program, 20
Pipes, Richard, 197–98
Pittman, Steuart, 61
Plausible denial doctrine, 22, 23
Poland, 74–75, 205
Political dominance, U.S. need for, 81–83

Politics, violence in, 4–5
Population evacuation, 60
Populism, 8
Portugal, 29
Positive convergence, 192–93
Power
  arbitrary, 16–18
  of government, 298
Presidency
  Bundy's views on, 113–14
  shifting power and support for, 12–14
Pressure Strategy, 197–98
Prohibition of the Development, Production and Stockpiling of Bacteriological (Biological) and Toxic Weapons (1975), 281
Protocol for the Protection of Non-Combatants (1977), 281
Puerto Rico, 29

Quayle, Dan, 219

Rabi, Isidore, 106
Race conflict, national security state and, 80
Radford, Arthur, 68
Rapacki Plan, 205
Ravenal, Earl, 129
Reagan administration
  foreign policy of, 82–83
  national security policy of, 76–77, 80, 132
  and protection of power of U.S. dollar, 90
Reconstructive convergence, 192–93
Repression, 159
Republic, U.S. as, 121–22
Republicans, administration of Democrats vs., 45
Robespierre, Maximilien, 295, 297
Rockefeller, David, 59, 102
Rockefeller, Nelson, 21, 54–55, 59, 60, 102
Rodberg, Leonard, 45
Roosevelt, Franklin D., 3–4, 7
  end to spheres of influence and decolonization by, 221
  office of presidency during, 12

Roosevelt, Franklin D. *(continued)*
    and success of New Deal, 7–8
    wartime addresses of, 148–49
Rosenberg case, 31
Rostow, Eugene, 142
Rostow, Walt, 14, 67, 101
Rowen, Henry, 56
Rule of comity, 134
Rule of law
    arbitrary power and, 16–18
    national security state undermining, 14–16
    and principles superior to state, 24–25
Rusk, Dean, 26, 85, 86
    view on Vietnam War, 141

Sakharov, Andrei, 168–69, 174, 181–83
Salaries, in defense corporations and federal government, 98
Sartre, Jean Paul, 167–73
Satellites, 248, 279
Schelling, Thomas, 55
Schlesinger, Arthur, Jr., 27, 91–94, 102
Schwartz, Bernard, 15–16
SDI. *See* Strategic Defense Initiative
Second World War
    bombing of Japan during, 110
    and Cold War, 309
    and ethics of war, 145
    losses resulting from, 188
    Soviet Union and, 110–11
    status of U.S. after, 6–10, 162, 214, 221
Secrecy, Soviet obsession with, 78
Secret Army Organization, 18
Security Council (United Nations). *See also* United Nations
    authority of, 133, 224
    new framework and expanded membership in, 95
    resolutions of, 136
    role in disarmament, 34, 97–98, 137, 233, 234, 264–65
SFRY. *See* Socialist Federal Republic of Yugoslavia
Shearer, Derek, 45

Sherwin, Martin, 31
Shultz, George, 82, 197
Smith, Adam, 186
Smith, Margaret Chase, 57
Smith, Walter Bedell, 65
Social reconstruction, xiv-xv, 225
Socialist Federal Republic of Yugoslavia (SFRY), 277
Socialist Workers Party, 16
Sohn, Louis, 128
Solzhenitsyn, Alexander, 168, 173–81
Sorenson, Theodore, 60
South Africa, 82
Soviet Union
    and arms race, 75–78, 186, 192
    and atomic energy planning, 31
    and Cold War, 197, 201–5, 308–10
    and concerns regarding Germany, 85, 137, 185, 205, 213
    development of intelligence network on, 10
    disarmament efforts with U.S., 58, 97, 105, 112, 268–70
    disarmament issues and, 207–8, 265, 266, 274, 275, 277
    and Eastern Europe, 73–76
    examination by Solzhenitsyn of, 174
    fourteen-point program for, 181–82
    Hitler's invasion of, 200–201
    Nixon administration's view of, 83
    relationship with Kennedy administration, 52, 56–61, 68–70
    role in Second World War, 110–11, 168
    shifts in relationships to and within, 199–201, 218
    trade with, 29
    U.S. military strategies concerning, 91, 93, 115
    use of navy by, 280
    views of, 120, 197–98
Special Group (National Security Council), 19, 20
Stahr, Elvis, 67–68
Stalin, Joseph, 168, 174, 181, 308, 309
Stassen, Harold, 74, 222
State Department, U.S., and Central Intelligence Agency, 88

Stennis, John S., Jr., 70
Strategic Defense Initiative (SDI), 285
Surveillance technology, 285
Suzuki, Yoshio, 157
Symington, Stuart, 54, 57
Szilard, Leo, 110

Taft, Robert, 45, 121–22
Taft-Hartley Act, purpose of, 11–12
Tax, excise profits, 98
Taylor, Maxwell, 15, 62–64, 66–67
Taylor, Telford, 147
Teller, Edward, 282
Thee, Marek, 107
Third World
 effect of arms race on, 131
 Soviet relations with, 205
 wars in, 219–20
Thomas, Albert, 62
Tokyo Tribunal, 245
Totalitarianism, 17
Trade
 benefits of arms, 79–80
 national security state as hindrance to, 120
Trade Act, amendment to, 29
Treaty on Common Security and General Disarmament
 basic commitments of, 232, 263–65
 common security and international organizations in, 242–44, 274–75
 explanation of, 227–28
 general principles of, 232–35, 265–68
 industrial plants and economic conversion issues in, 260–62, 289–91
 initial declarations of, 235–38, 268–71
 international disarmament organization in, 238–42, 271–74
 purpose of, 229
 ratification and conflict between other treaties and, 262–63, 291
 stages of disarmament in, 244–52, 276–83
 verification, inspection, and assurance issues in, 254–60, 284–89

Treaty on Common Security and General Disarmament *(continued)*
 weapons, forces, and industrial capacities to be retained at end of disarmament process, 252–54, 283–84
Trinidad, 29
Trofimenko, Henry, 200–201
Truman, Harry
 foreign policy of, 73
 labor dealings of, 9
 view of Soviet Union, 111
Truman administration, 82
Truman Doctrine, 207
Turchin, V. F., 181–82
Turkey
 aid for, 86
 removal of missiles from, 113
 U.S. intervention in, 9

Ultranationalism, post–Second World War attempt to destroy, 147, 153–55, 157, 158, 160–61
U.N.. *See* United Nations
U.N. Charter of Security, 129
U.N. Conference on Disarmament, 265
U.N. University (UNU), 272
Unemployment rate
 in 1930s and 1940s, 7–8
 and protection of U.S. dollar, 90
 war preparations and war and, 11
United Nations Relief and Rehabilitation Agency, 207
United Nations (U.N.). *See also* Treaty on Common Security and General Disarmament
 benefits and problems of, 94–95
 charter of, 133, 136, 188, 199, 221, 232, 263–65, 272–73, 283
 differing views of, 122
 and General Assembly resolutions, 30, 95, 127, 136
 need for revitalized, 125
 principles used by Soviet activists, 182
 role in disarmament, 128, 136–38
 role of, 223–25
 Security Council of, 34, 133, 136, 233, 234, 264–65

United Nations *(continued)*
  university of, 136
  U.S. voting history for trade and development resolutions, 82
United States
  Cold War policy of, 201–3
  forms of government in, 121–28
  as loser in Cold War, 197
  mission of, 224
  post–Second World War status of, 6–10, 162, 214, 221
  use of navy by, 280
Universal Declaration of Human Rights, 182
UNU (U.N. University), 272
U.S. v. Nicaragua, 188

Vance, Cyrus, 82, 265
Veblen, Thorstein, 295
Versailles Treaty (1919), 68
Videl, Gore, xii
Vietnam War
  conditions for successful ending of, 159
  and democratic view, 122–23
  as example of limited-war strategy, 101
  foreign relations and, 29–30
  indirect involvement in, 86
  justification for, 142–43
  Kennedy and, 111
  losses and consequences of, xiii, 29, 224
  responsibility for, 140–41
  U.S. activity in, 64, 85, 88, 190
  and U.S. economic interests, 82
  and Vietnam refugees in U.S., 151
  weapons used in, 111, 281, 282
Violence, in politics, 4–5
Viral bacteriological poisoning, 282–83

Wallace, George, 5
Wallace, Henry, 96

War
  position at Nuremburg regarding, 145
  power of Congress to make, 162
  punishment of elites for, 159–60
  responsibility for, 144–46
War crimes
  imposition of standards of punishment for, 148
  post–Second World War punishment for, 147
  view of, 145
War Powers Act, 224, 303
Warsaw Pact, 205, 206. *See also* Eastern Europe
  disagreement within, 89
  disarmament arrangements with, 94, 137, 233, 266
  as drain on Soviet Union, 75
Washington Naval Conference, 280
Watergate affair, 114
Weapons. *See* Nuclear weapons
Weapons costs, 98. *See also* Nuclear weapons
Weather modification, 282
Weinberger, Caspar, 91, 93
West Germany, 56, 75. *See also* Germany
Whistle Blower's Act, 303
Wiesner, Jerome, 57
Wilson, Charles, 54, 62
World Security Agreement (WSA), 242–44, 275
World War II. *See* Second World War
Wright, Quincy, 30
WSA. *See* World Security Agreement

Yanov, Alexander, 198
Yarmolinsky, Adam, 61
York, Herbert, 75, 78
Yugoslavia, 130

Zhadanov, Andrei, 176
Zonal disarmament, 246, 278
Zorin, Valerian, 74, 208, 222
Zuckerman, Solly, 59, 204